The Vegetarian Passport Cookbook

The Vegetarian Passport Cookbook

Simple Vegetarian Dishes from Around the World

Linda Woolven

The Vegetarian Passport Cookbook
Copyright © 2005 Linda Woolven

Fitzhenry and Whiteside Limited
195 Allstate Parkway
Markham, Ontario L3R 4T8

In the United States:
121 Harvard Avenue, Suite 2
Allston, Massachusetts 02134

www.fitzhenry.ca godwit@fitzhenry.ca

Fitzhenry & Whiteside acknowledges with thanks the Canada Council for the Arts, and the Ontario Arts Council for their support of our publishing program. We acknowledge the financial support of the Government of Canada through the Book Publishing Industry Development Program (BPIDP) for our publishing activities.

National Library of Canada Cataloguing in Publication
Woolven, Linda
The vegetarian passport cookbook: simple vegetarian dishes from around the
world / Linda Woolven
ISBN 1-55041-331-7
1. Vegetarian cookery. I. Title.
TX837.W66 2005   641.5'636   C2005-900463-8

US Publisher Cataloging-in-Publication Data
Woolven, Linda.
The vegetarian passport cookbook: simple vegetarian dishes from around the world / Linda Woolven. −1st ed.
[240] p. : ill. ; cm.
Includes index.
Summary: Over 350 vegetarian recipes from around the world.
ISBN 1-55041-331-7 (pbk.)
1. Vegetarian cookery. I. Title.
641.5636 dc22   TX837.W66   2005

Designed by Karen Petherick, Intuitive Design International Ltd.
Cover images: ©Lifestock Photos
Illustrations: Michael Petherick
Printed and bound in Canada

1 3 5 7 9 10 8 6 4 2

CONTENTS

Introduction

Welcome to the world of international cuisine and the beginning of a wonderful journey overflowing with exciting new tastes and textures. This easy-to-use cookbook serves up original all-vegetarian recipes from across the globe that are at once tasty, yet simple to follow and incorporate ingredients that are commonly found in your grocery store and local markets. The results will tantalize the nose and palate, rekindle memories of adventures past, and inspire a new love for the incredible foods that the world has to offer. There is no better way to discover a country than through its tastes and traditions—so dig right in. *The Vegetarian Passport* offers a world of both.

You will find information in this cookbook about how food is eaten in different regions all over the world, and the various cultures that have hosted me over my many years of travel. There is information on how to eat a healthy diet and also, what to eat and what to avoid, from choosing between healthy and bad fats, to knowing the amounts and types of food to eat each day that will help you achieve optimal health. Basic cooking terms are explained in simple, straightforward language. And a foolproof cooking chart for grains and beans is also included for quick and easy reference.

And, of course, there are the recipes. A lot of them—each with a little introductory story as an apéritif, or information on how to eat the dish, or what to eat it with, or what the dish tastes like. There are daring originals, plus new versions of well-loved vegetarian favourites like lasagna, hummus and Greek salad. There are sections on snacks, dips, spreads and sauces, salads and dressings, soups and stews, main dishes and accompaniments, pasta, rice and grain dishes, beans and lentil dishes, desserts and drinks, and vegetarian barbecue—all with an international theme. Not every dish can necessarily be found in the country where I have listed it. Many of the dishes were quite simply inspired by the foods and spices of the country or region of origin. Other times, I have adapted a recipe to a region by substituting certain local ingredients.

I first became a vegetarian on my honeymoon in Greece. I was sitting on a gorgeous beach and it dawned on me that I didn't have to eat animals to survive—that I could actually be healthier without eating meat. Also, for the first time, I was moving into my own place and could cook what I wanted, how I wanted. The question was: what to prepare? I've always loved new and exciting things— especially when it came to food. So I immediately looked to different countries and regions from all over the world for culinary inspiration. I quickly discovered that each country had unique and delicious dishes that I could incorporate into my daily diet. I also love to travel and found that everywhere I went I picked up ideas for new dishes. Every time I left home I couldn't wait to get back again to experiment with all these amazing new foods and tastes. Dinner in our house takes us to a new destination with an exciting new taste experience each night: all inspired from the international scene.

This book grew out of an ever-evolving stack of my own handwritten recipes that kept getting higher with each successfully yummy dish that I perfected. It was also created for the many people who tried my dishes and wanted me to share my recipes. It took years of travel (and eating) to gather enough great dishes and stories to complete this cookbook. And it is my hope that through these recipes you are welcomed into the world of my family and the many friends I have met around the globe.

The Vegetarian Passport Cookbook

Simple Vegetarian Dishes from Around the World

The Mediterranean Region

The countries in this incredibly scenic region share a lot of similarities. Dinner is usually a late affair, starting around 8 or 9 pm and lasting for as long as you do. It's also a social time, when friends and family gather and talk about everything from the day's events to world issues and sports. And, of course, guests are always made to feel as welcome as a dear friend or a cherished family member.

GREECE Greeks love to sit and talk over food and drink, and they often gather outside in a garden or under a canopy of grape vines to do so. The food is always prepared with the freshest ingredients, including plenty of olive oil, lemon juice, fresh herbs, fruits and vegetables and, of course, good, hearty bread. Herbs, like oregano, grow wild and well in Greece because the soil is so rocky and the air so hot. The sun seems always to be shining and the sky is clear and blue.

Don't be surprised to find that dinner can continue well past midnight, with perhaps some bouzouki music, Greek coffee, retsina (a traditional wine that has a small amount of pine resin added to it) or Metaxa (a Greek brandy)— and, always, conversation, often about politics or soccer. The people are friendly and warm and they love to eat. The food is often fresh from the host's garden, or from a truckload of food brought fresh from the nearest farmer's garden, or from food sold in the street markets in the early morning. Shopping usually turns into a social event with friends and neighbours. First there's a visit to the bakery, then the farmers' fresh fruit and vegetable stalls, the cheese store, and perhaps the local corner store, with greetings exchanged at each stop.

As a traveller in Greece, I was taken into many homes where I was always made to feel welcome and never allowed to leave until I had eaten and drunk plenty—and talked too, in a little Greek, a little English, a little French or German, and a lot of gestures and pantomime.

To me there is little better than a fresh Greek salad, good bread and olives, some spanakopita or yemista or moussaka, a glass of retsina, and Greek coffee, shared with friends who want to sit and talk and enjoy.

Yamas!

FORMER YUGOSLAVIA

I was only in two regions of what, at the time, was called Yugoslavia. And even then, in 1989, I noticed how vastly different the two regions were from each other. In Macedonia there was a definite Greek and Turkish influence, both in the buildings and among the people. Food also had a mixture of influences. I had a meal of bean soup, stuffed pepper/eggplant and Turkish, or Greek, coffee. The Macedonian people were friendly, and one woman I stayed with insisted on cooking for me, driving me around in her car, and showing me the cheapest place in town to eat—a cafeteria where you could get a full meal, cheap! Apparently fast, too. Once we watched a man eat a complete dinner in sixty seconds flat! We actually timed him.

I often saw freshly made pastas laid out to dry on white sheets on the grass. Everything that I ate was fresh, usually purchased at the gorgeous and cheap outdoor markets. It was there I discovered what a real tomato tastes like, and, believe me, ours don't even come close. I also discovered the most wonderful mango ice cream that almost convinced me to move there. Yum!

In Dubrovnik, I noticed Hungarian, Austrian and Italian influences. I could get burek, a flaky cheese pie, Greek delicacies, Hungarian cuisine, and lots of delicious pizzas and pastas with a Dubrovnik influence. The Dubrovnikites tended to eat later than the Macedonians, often outside on cobblestone streets or in the squares. The food, like its people, was friendly and warm and inviting!

Ziveli!

ITALY

Greeks and the Italians share some wonderful similarities. The people love to socialize over food and make an evening out of it. They often gather in squares or on front doorsteps to spend time with friends and family and watch other people. I was invited into many people's houses—people I didn't even know—to share a meal with them or have a drink. And, of course, every-thing was washed down with lots of delicious wine, often made locally and served in terra cotta pitchers.

The Italians love to eat. And they know how, too. The meal usually starts with an antipasto, and then a salad, sometimes soup, followed by pasta, and the main course, ending with dessert and espresso or cappuccino, and always accompanied by plenty of wine and often Amaro (a bitter-tasting liqueur). I was amazed to see slender people eat all the courses. I had no idea where they were putting it all.

One thing that I found very surprising was that meat is used in a lot more dishes than I thought. People would often say to me, "There's no meat in this, just a little in the sauce."

The food becomes spicier the further south you go, the south being famous for its red pepper cheese. Yum! And, of course, the Italians are famous for their pizza. The crust is thin and crispy and delicious—baked in wood-burning pizza ovens. No one makes it as good!

One particular restaurant I visited captured the spirit of Italy for me. The owner's name was Luciano. Every night we sat outside among the potted geraniums, with the mountains behind us, the sea in front. Luciano would proudly bring us a completely different and wonderful pasta dish every night, while his young daughter sat and drew pictures of us. People would join us for some wine, and we'd talk in the usual mixture of English, Italian and pantomime. Everything tasted better eaten outside, surrounded by lemon trees, flowers, mountains and the sea. The food was always fresh and prepared with plenty of olive oil and fresh basil.

I often shopped in the street market and purchased the freshest fruits, vegetables and cheeses. I cooked outside on the terrace under a vine-covered roof. I discovered that if you don't prepare your pasta just right, the Italians will take over and show you how to do it the Italian way, adding fresh pasta, cheeses, herbs and vegetables from their own gardens.

Salute!

FRANCE

French cooking offers a number of good, if somewhat rich, choices for the vegetarian. There are quiches, soufflés, tians, salads, galettes and crêpes. Many of these contain a fair amount of eggs, cheese and milk, but I have found that in some cases you can lower or completely eliminate the fat by replacing the dairy milk and cheese with soy milk and soy cheese.

French food, and its many sauces, is well complemented by wine, fresh fruit and cheese. Often the salad is served at the end of the meal, just at the point when you couldn't possibly eat another rich dish. But then … there's always dessert.

Bon appétit!

SPAIN

The Spanish generally eat their main meal at midday, and it's usually a lengthy affair where shops and businesses close down for a proper hot lunch. Sometimes they eat outside in squares, beside churches and rose bushes, and sometimes inside, under hanging guitars and pottery—often accompanied by Flamenco music and dancers.

The food is fresh and flavoured with olive oil, lemon juice and olives. Saffron and other herbs and spices perk up many dishes, like paella, the national dish. Artichokes are often served as appetizers, and everything is washed down with wine—and Spain has some fabulous wines, including its famous Sangria and sherry port. I didn't find a lot of vegetarian food in Spain other than gazpacho, which in itself is well worth going to Spain for—potato omelettes, and lots of artichokes. In the village of Cathorla, however, we asked for vegetarian food, and the owner provided a feast—one magnificent dish after another.

For me, Spain is colour, heat and friendly people.

Salud!

PORTUGAL

Portugal has a few very good dishes to offer the vegetarian, and one of them—potato soup with either green beans or cabbage—is both filling and delicious and can be found in just about every restaurant in one form or another.

Like other Mediterranean countries, the people in the coastal region of Portugal use lots of lemon, olive oil, garlic and very fresh ingredients in their cooking. Meals are eaten either inside or out, depending on the weather, with dinner usually around 7 or 7:30 in the evening.

And no matter what you eat, you must try the wines. Portugal has some wonderful wines, my favourite being the vino verdes, or young green wines that taste of green apples. They go well in the heat and with the colour and taste of much of Portuguese food. Portugal also produces delicious port wine and some lovely sharp cheeses, as well as lots of olives, bread, fruits and vegetables. Perfect for picnics among the jutting rocks on the colourful coastline or the hilly interior.

Meals are usually not as lengthy an affair although in the evenings, many would gather in the mosaic streets of Lisbon or in bars watching soccer or American sitcoms, while having a drink with friends.

Being close to North Africa, Portugal has absorbed some of its influences—spices, like cumin and an abundance of fruit from Morocco. I wonder who eats all the lemons we saw in people's gardens? I guess the lucky homeowners themselves, and perhaps the occasional traveller.

A Sua Saude!

BRITISH ISLES Vegetarianism has really caught on in England, especially in London. Traditionally, there have been a few good vegetarian dishes in the British Isles, such as oatcakes, scones, potatoes with kale or chard, and of course, Welsh rarebit. The story goes that when a hunter came home empty handed, there would be Welsh "rabbit" for supper–bread with a cheese sauce over it.

There is little better than oatcakes smothered in honey with proper British tea and perhaps some cucumber and watercress sandwiches, scones, strawberries and cream. Yum! Or, for those who aren't into tea, check out the pubs with their stouts, ales and meads.

Cheers!

EASTERN EUROPE My experience with Eastern European cooking comes mostly from relatives and people I have met from the region. The food tends to be heavy, hearty and filling. Usually soup is included in the meal. Very often a large lunch is followed by a large supper. Salads are made with very few vegetables, and they're often puréed or shredded instead of cut in chunks.

Some traditionally made dishes are bean and pea soups, latkas and cabbage rolls. Certain herbs and spices are predominant in certain countries; for example, in Hungry paprika is used a lot.

You can't rush an Eastern European meal. You must take time out to sit down and enjoy the food, and when you're too full to move, you sit and talk with family and friends about politics or other matters. And no one leaves the table hungry; there's always someone encouraging you to eat more because you're too thin!

RUSSIA Russian food has many vegetarian options, especially for the poor man. Russians eat a healthy diet consisting of whole grains and vegetables such as beets, potatoes, parsnips, cabbage, beans, millet, kasha, other grains and good, hearty dark rye bread.

Some typical dishes are borscht, perogis, a kind of caviar made from eggplant, and potato or cabbage soup. They also produce a few cheeses and plenty of vodka to wash it all down with.

Meals in Russia can be a lengthy social affair, full of talk and drink, beginning with a sampling of hors d'oeuvres to whet the appetite of the hungry traveller. Any meal in Russia is bound to include lots of bread and potatoes.

A Taste of Africa

MOROCCO

Morocco is a country of many influences, made up of many people, including the Berbers, the Arabs, the French, and the Africans. It's a country of mountains, deserts and the sea. And its food reflects all of these things.

Moroccan cuisine features fruit, fresh and dried, vegetables, grains, honey, nuts, seeds, herbs and spices. Drinks are often made from fresh fruit or nuts and are consumed much more than alcohol.

Eating in Morocco can be a lengthy affair with guests reclining on couches around a low table. The hands are washed at the table and courses are brought in one at a time, ending with the traditional mint tea. It's polite to drink three cups and then it's time to go. Food is eaten with the right hand only, and then only the first three fingers are used. Bread is an important "utensil" since no cutlery is used. While you eat, you may be entertained by belly dancers and plenty of conversation and music during the evening.

The Moroccan national dish is couscous, and it's very easy to make a delicious vegetarian couscous. Dishes such as chilled cucumber soup, salads of fruits and grains, and grilled or fried eggplant offer some choices for the vegetarian.

ETHIOPIA

In Ethiopia, no matter what you eat, it's traditionally served with a flat, pancake-like bread called injera that also serves as a utensil. And, incidentally, the bread is also delicious and gluten free. It is said in Ethiopia that if you share food from the same plate, you will always be friends, and so a typical feast is served on a huge platter covered with injera, topped with many portions of various wats, or stews, and/or salads. Typically, a unique flavouring is used to create many Ethiopian dishes—a combination of spices, butter, herbs, and red chilli pepper that make a dish quite fiery.

Ethiopia offers a number of good vegetarian dishes made from split peas, chickpeas, lentils, salads, greens, cabbage, tomatoes, and potatoes.

Eating is a social affair, where everyone sits around the central platter eating carefully with a piece of injera, making sure not to touch either the food or the mouth with the hands.

NORTH AFRICA AND THE MIDDLE EAST The area offers a fair number of dishes for the vegetarian. There is baba ghanouj, rice with lentils, hummus, falafel, pita bread, tabbouleh, cucumber salad and baklava. A typical Middle Eastern meal might include portions of each, using pita bread both as a wrap and a utensil. And, if you can handle it, there is also very strong, thick coffee to follow.

Typical spices and herbs include cumin, cayenne, garlic, parsley, oregano and sea salt.

A Taste of Asia

Asian people have mastered the art of cooking vegetables. The vegetables are always beautifully cut, combined and cooked just right—never mushy. Cooking them quickly in a wok over high heat leaves the vegetables crisp, yet hot and steamy at the same time.

There are many meatless dishes in Asia. Stir-fries, soups, rice and noodle dishes offer many good choices for the vegetarian. Rice, rice noodles, tofu, bamboo, bok choy, bean sprouts, snow peas, mushrooms, water chestnuts and many other vegetables and sauces are found in Asian cuisine.

The meal is usually, but not always, served all at once, or preceded by a soup. Sweets are sometimes served after a meal. In many countries chopsticks are used to eat almost everything, including soup, where you just drink what you can't pick up.

Each region has its own speciality dishes, and the sauces vary greatly, from sweet and sour, to Szechwan, to miso or tamari flavouring.

Asians tend to eat less meat and thus pass on a great tradition from which the vegetarian can learn much.

INDIA India offers the vegetarian a wealth of dishes, since a large part of the country is vegetarian. A typical Indian feast consists of many dishes, such as cheese curry, vegetable curry, dal, curried cauliflower and peas, raitas, chutnies, rice and chapattis, served all at once along with lots of small bowls containing a variety of condiments, such pickles, sauces, dried fruit, nuts, seeds and vegetables. The food varies from mild to quite spicy and takes on its distinctive flavour from the combination of spices. Combining spices in India is an essential component of cooking that has been fine-tuned over centuries. A typical curry mixture may contain more than fifty-three different spices. Each chef puts her signature on a dish by the specific amount and combination of spices.

Because India is a hot country, meals are usually accompanied by mango juice or other fruit drinks, coconut milk, ginger beer and spiced tea.

THAILAND AND INDONESIA

This is a very varied part of the world, and I am most familiar with Thailand's cuisine. As a tourist in Thailand, it was easy to find vegetarian options. Thailand offers veggie soups that are whole meals, curries that are rich in coconut milk and nicely spiced, rice dishes, pad Thai and lots of delicious mango salads. There are even completely vegetarian restaurants. In Thailand the food is not only delicious but it is presented well and often served with an edible flower on the plate. Interestingly Thai portions are usually a little smaller than what I have seen in other countries, but I think this is just another reason to keep you coming back for more. Thai food is colourful, like the country itself.

The cuisine in Indonesia, on the other hand, makes liberal use of tofu and tempeh to substitute for meat dishes, and spices, vegetables and coconut milk can be found in a multitude of dishes. And, like Thailand, the food is bright and colourful. Indonesians are also famous for a style of eating known as the rijsttafel, which means the rice table, where a large number of dishes are placed on a large buffet table. Luckily, many of the dishes are vegetarian.

The Vegetarian Passport Cookbook

A Taste of the Americas

**CARIBBEAN
(JAMAICA)**

As a tourist in Jamaica I remember luscious buffets full of vegetarian choices, no doubt the influence of the Rastafarian culture.

    The food is colourful, some sweet and some spicy. Dishes such as pumpkin soup, rice with beans, stuffed squash, black bean soup and many salads are popular in the Caribbean. There are also many African influences, especially in the use of spices. A typical Caribbean meal is a warm affair of colourful dishes made with food from people's gardens, all served up at once to delight the guest. You will not leave the table hungry.

MEXICO

The food of Mexico, like its people, is warm and colourful. And for the vegetarian there is plenty of choice, varying from spicy to mild. Tomatoes, beans, corn, and avocado figure highly in this cuisine as do hot chilli and jalapeno peppers. Typical dishes include bean or vegetable burritos, tacos, enchiladas, salads, corn-husk lasagna, corn husks stuffed with beans, refrittos, salsas and nachos. For a Mexican feast, serve many different dishes buffet style, making sure to include plenty of variety, as well as salads and fruit. Serve the meal around midday, and then take your siesta in the heat of the afternoon.

**NORTH
AMERICA**

Almost anything goes in North American cuisine. Everyone else's dishes are prepared and eaten in just about any manner, from the cookout or barbecue, to the nine-course meal in a fancy dining room, and, of course, TV trays in front of the television, indicating that one thing we've clearly lost is the art of eating and socializing. There's no end of convenience foods that could kill us, but they save us time! Even our own cheese, the orange cheddar, is dyed to look appealing.

    The one thing we do seem to like is our salads. We eat all kinds of them in every possible combination. We also have versions of everybody else's cuisine—Chinese food, pizza, pasta, Indian food, Greek, Ethiopian, Middle Eastern, Mexican … the list goes on. Fortunately, it means there are plenty of vegetarian choices, and for the imaginative cook the possibilities are limitless.

    So eat whenever you want, however you want, whatever you want, and wash it down with just about anything, and you'll be doing it the North American way.

SOUTH AMERICA

Peru is a country of soaring mountains and colourful people with colourful cooking to match. And, like the indigenous people that live there, the food is hearty. As a tourist in Peru, I was told that there are over one-thousand varieties of potatoes: some are the size of peanuts and some exceedingly large. Pumpkins and potatoes show up in many dishes, as do green beans, corn and peppers. Two of the gluten free grains/seeds are also used in Peru: quinoa and amaranth. You can find these in local health food stores. Travelling in Peru was easy, since there is plenty of food for vegetarians. So enjoy! When you make their soups don't be shy about it: when it says to throw in the cob of corn, cut it up and toss it in—same goes for the pumpkin. In much of the rest of South America you will find potatoes, grains like quinoa and amaranth, beans and corn as well.

ENJOY!

Helpful Hints

Reaching and Maintaining Optimal Health

To reach and maintain good health, try to eat at least four servings of whole grains a day, from a wide variety of grains. A serving is, for example, 1 slice of bread or 1/2 cup of cooked grain. If you are wheat and gluten sensitive, try rice, quinoa, millet, teff, buckwheat and amaranth. Many of the grains in the following recipes can be substituted for other grains if need be or if desired. Also include at least four to eight servings of vegetables a day, including one from the dark leafy family, like broccoli, bok choy, Brussels sprouts, chard, collard greens, beet greens, mustard green, etc. A serving is, for example, 3/4 to 1 cup of cooked green vegetables or 1 raw carrot. Prepare them simply, for example in a salad or steamed, drizzled with a little flax seed oil—a rich source of essential fatty acids that are crucial to good health—or tamari, or use them in more elaborate dishes.

Strive for balance. If you eat something rich or full of sugar, balance out the day with something lighter. We rarely eat dessert in our house, and when we do, we tend to eat fruit, usually some time after the meal. Try to eat at least 2 to 4 servings of fruit a day. A serving is, for example, 1 medium-sized apple. The key to good health is a well-balanced diet that has variety, is low in saturated fats and high in fibre. Be sure to always use whole grains. Avoid hydrogenated fats and trans-fats. Instead choose non-hydrogenated fats and other healthy oils like olive oil and flax seed oil (see "About Fats" below for more information). But don't cook flax seed oil as it damages the oil.

Round out your diet with seeds, nuts, 1 to 3 servings of legumes (1/2 cup cooked legumes equals a serving), and dairy, if you aren't a vegan. You don't need dairy to be healthy, but if you are worried about getting enough vitamin B12, eat alfalfa, spirulina, sea vegetables, miso or other sources of B12. Try to include some sea vegetables in your diet. They are full of vitamins and minerals, including iron, B12, calcium and many more. And for soup stock, try using miso. It's full of vitamins, minerals, protein and friendly flora, which aid digestion.

About Fats

The word that has led to the greatest confusion in health and dieting is "fat." Contrary to what is often said, not all fats are bad. Some are actually good for you and will not cause weight gain but will help you lose weight. They can also help fight illness.

Fats have long chains of carbon molecules. When every one of those carbon molecules has had a hydrogen molecule bound to it or, in other words, has been saturated with hydrogen, it is called a saturated fat. Saturated fats are bad for you. They damage your body's cell membranes, preventing your cells from functioning properly. They also cause inflammation in the body and are linked to many of today's major diseases, such as arthritis. Meat and dairy are very high in saturated fat. When some of the carbon molecules are not bound to hydrogen, the fat has not been saturated with hydrogen and is called an unsaturated fat. It can be either a monounsaturated fat or a polyunsaturated fat, depending on how many carbon molecules are free of hydrogen. These are the healthy fats that are found largely in plant foods. Olive oil is an example of a monounsaturated fat, and it is the healthiest oil to cook with. Flax seed oil is an example of a polyunsaturated fat, and it is the healthiest oil to use uncooked. A healthy vegetarian diet is better for you because it reduces saturated fats and is high in unsaturated vegetable oils.

But be careful of margarine! When an unsaturated vegetable oil, like that found in margarine, has hydrogen molecules added to it, it has been hydrogenated or partially hydrogenated. These fats are the nasty trans-fats so much in the news lately. Because they have been turned into saturated fats, trans-fats have all of the dangers of saturated animal fat. If you like the taste of cooking with margarine, be sure to find one that is "non-hydrogenated." And watch out because these unhealthy trans-fats are hidden everywhere, especially in pre-packaged foods.

About Herbs

Throughout the book I have given measurements for both fresh and dried herbs when either can be used without sacrificing taste. If you don't have the fresh herb, use dried. The general rule is 1 tbsp (15ml) fresh = 1 tsp (5ml) dried. Add fresh herbs near the end of the cooking time, in the last few minutes, so that they retain their flavour. Fresh herbs are used in salads, but if you are in a hurry and don't have fresh, you can use dried. In cooked dishes, dried herbs are usually used when the fresh herbs can't be added near the end of cooking time. I dry my own herbs from my garden and use them fairly quickly so they still retain their flavour. In the case of basil, cilantro, coriander leaves and parsley, I prefer fresh because they tend to be tasteless when dried.

Herbs aren't just great tasting, but also promote good health. They are very rich in antioxidants, powerful nutrients that help to fight off free radicals that cause disease. So use them freely, and adjust amounts to your own taste.

Grain and Bean Chart

Bring water to a boil and add the grain or legume and allow to boil for a few minutes, then turn down to a very low boil or simmer. Keep covered, at least part way, and stir if needed. Check water level occasionally as different stoves produce different heat levels, so you may need to add more water. For instance, our stove was manufactured in 1959 and seems to get hotter than most stoves. Also, cooking time can vary depending on the length of time foods have been stored and the heat of the stove, so always taste everything before you assume it is done. Nothing tastes worse than under-cooked legumes.

Caution: Cook red kidney beans at a high boil for at least 10 minutes to prevent the possibility of hemagglutinin forming. It can cause food poisoning.

*When cooking bulgur, put the bulgur in a bowl and pour the boiling water over it, cover and allow to stand for 20 minutes. Then fluff with a fork and it's ready to eat. When cooking couscous, put the grain in a bowl and add a little salt. Then pour boiling water over it, let it cool a little, and rub the grains with your fingers and allow to stand for 10 minutes. You may need to repeat this process if the grain hasn't fully expanded. Then put the grain on cheesecloth and set it in a steamer, cover, and steam for 15 minutes. Fluff with a fork and serve.

1 cup (Dry) (250ml)	Water	Cooking Time	Yield
Grains:			
barley	3 1/2 c (875ml)	80 mins	3–3 1/2 c (875ml)
brown rice	3 1/4 c (800ml)	40 mins	3 c (750ml)
*bulgur	3 c (750ml)	15–20 mins	2 1/2 c (625ml)
millet	3 1/2 c (875ml)	40–50 mins	3 1/2 c (875ml)
cornmeal	4 c (1 litre)	20 mins	3 c (750ml)
quinoa	2 1/4 c (560ml)	15 mins	2 1/2 c (625ml)
wild rice	4 1/2–6 c (1125–1500ml)	65–70 mins	2 1/2 c (625ml)
*couscous	4 c (1 litre)	15 mins	1 1/2 c (375ml)

1 cup (Dry) (250ml)	Water	Cooking Time	Yield
Beans:			
adzuki	3 1/2 c (875ml)	45 mins	2 c (500ml)
black beans	4 1/2–5 c (1125–1250ml)	2 1/2 hrs	2 1/2 c (625ml)
black eyed peas	3 1/4 c (800ml)	1 hr	2 c (500ml)
chickpeas	4 1/2 c (1125ml)	3 1/4 hrs	2 c (500ml)
kidney beans	3 1/2 c (875ml)	1 1/4–1 3/4 hrs	2 1/4 c (560ml)
green lentils	3 c (750ml)	45 mins–1 hr	2 c (500ml)
red lentils	2 c (500ml)	20 mins	1 1/2–1 3/4 c (375–430ml)
split peas, green and yellow	3 c (750ml)	45 mins–1 hr	2 1/4 c (560ml)
lima beans	4 c (1 litre)	2 1/2 hrs	2 c (500ml)
pinto beans	4 c (1 litre)	2 1/2–3 hr	2 1/2 c (625ml)
mung beans	3 c (750ml)	1 hr	2 c (500ml)
navy beans	4 1/2 c (1125ml)	3 1/2 hr	2 1/4 c (560ml)
soy beans	3 1/2 c (875ml)	2 1/2–3 hrs	2 1/4 c (560ml)

Substitutes

Many of the recipes in this book can be made by substituting soy milk and soy cheese for dairy milk and cheese. Eggs can be replaced with an egg substitute, but if you're using eggs, try to use free-range eggs: they are healthier and the chickens are raised in a healthier environment. Also, if you're trying to cut down on fats, try sautéing with vegetable broth instead of oil.

Terminology

Blend: Put the ingredients in a blender or food processor and blend until smooth. If you blend soup in a blender, be sure to wait until it's cool before blending to avoid cracking the glass. Only half fill the blender each time.

Purée: To reduce food to a smooth, thick liquid. This can be done with a hand-held blender that goes directly into the soup pot—be careful not to splatter the hot liquid on yourself—or it can be done in a blender or food processor as described above.

Sauté: To cook something gently in a little fat or oil while stirring. Often used for cooking onions and other vegetables. Onions tend to cook slowly and sometimes require a little more fat or, if you like, water or stock to prevent them from browning. When you add water, it's called "candying" and creates a sweeter flavour. I often do this to cut down on the fat.

Knead: To push and turn dough to make it stretchy and to help the loaf rise. Kneading takes about 10 minutes for two loaves in order to get the right consistency. Lightly flour the surface you are using to keep the dough from sticking. To knead, keep working the dough around into a ball shape. Press down on the dough with the heel and palm of your hands, lift and turn the dough and repeat. If the dough becomes stiff, add a little water to your hands. If it is sticky, add a little more flour.

Abbreviations

I have used abbreviations for some words:

Measurements

c   = cup(s)
cm   = centimetres
g   = grams
ml   = millilitres
tbsp = tablespoon
tsp = teaspoon

Notes

The Vegetarian Passport Cookbook

The Vegetarian
Passport Cookbook

Snacks and Breads

Energy Balls (Peru)

For long fall hikes through the woods, try these balls for quick energy. I picked them up in Peru where a child of nine was selling them, and his story was right out of *Oliver Twist*.

1/2 c	puffed cereal, like quinoa or amaranth	125ml
1 c	dried dates	250ml
1/2 c	sweetened coconut	125ml
1/4 c	almonds or cashews	60ml
1/4 c	brown sesame seeds	60ml
1/4	raisins	60ml
1-2 tbsp	honey, enough to form balls	15-30ml

☛ Put in a food processor and blend well. Form into little balls and allow to harden a little in the fridge. Serve.

Cheese Balls (North America)

Bite size little appetizers that go well any time.

1 c	whole wheat flour	250ml
1 tsp	baking soda	5ml
	enough milk to make a dough	
	cheddar cheese cut in 1/2-inch (1cm) cubes	
	freshly grated Parmesan cheese	

☛ Mix together the flour and the baking soda. Add the milk, slowly, stirring to get the consistency of moist dough. Roll the dough out flat to a thickness of 1/4" (1/2cm). Cut out small circles, about 3" (7.5cm) in diameter, using a circular cookie cutter. Wrap each circle of dough around a piece of cheddar and then roll in the Parmesan cheese. Bake at 350F (180C) for about 20 minutes or until slightly golden. Eat hot.

Whole Wheat Bread (North America)

Excellent whole grain bread that feels, tastes and smells the way bread should.

1 tbsp	brown sugar or honey	15ml
1 tbsp	active dry yeast	15ml
	pinch of vitamin C powder	
3/4 c	hot water, approx. 110F (45C)	185ml
1 c	water	250ml
1/4 c	milk or water	60ml
3 tbsp	butter	45ml
1 tsp	sea salt	5ml
4 1/2 c	whole wheat flour	1125ml
1	egg, beaten (optional)	1

☛ Mix together the sugar, yeast, vitamin C and hot water and leave for 10 minutes, until frothy. Meanwhile, in a large bowl mix together the rest of the ingredients. Add the yeast mixture and mix well. Turn out onto floured surface and knead for 10 minutes. Divide dough in half and put each half into a greased, warmed loaf pan. Shape to fit pan. Cover with plastic bags and allow to rise for 30 minutes. Remove the bags and place loaves in a preheated oven, at 450F (230C), and bake for 40 to 55 minutes, removing when a toothpick comes out cleanly. Makes 2 loaves.

Or, you can braid the dough. Divide into three equal pieces, roll into thick strands, the length and width of which will depend on how wide and long you want the loaf to be. Place the strands on a greased cookie sheet and braid by overlapping the strands. Pinch the ends together and bake according to the instructions above. Different shaped loaves will have different cooking times. Remove your loaf when a toothpick comes out cleanly.

Or, make various shaped rolls and buns and place on a greased cookie sheet and bake at 450F (230C). The baking time will again depend on the size and shape of the loaf. It is best to start checking early—for small rolls and buns, 10 to 15 minutes; longer for larger ones. Your loaf is done when a toothpick comes out cleanly. You can also sprinkle the top of the dough with sesame seeds or poppy seeds before baking.

Stuffed Eggs (Eastern Europe)

Great for picnics and parties.

4	hard-boiled eggs, shelled and sliced in half lengthwise	4
1	very small onion, finely chopped and sautéed in 1 tsp (5ml) of oil until very tender (optional)	1
1 tsp	paprika powder	5ml
2 tbsp	mayonnaise	30ml
1–1 1/2 tbsp	lemon juice	15–22ml
	salt and pepper to taste	

☛ Gently remove the egg yolks and place them in a bowl. Mash well and add the remaining ingredients. Mix well and stuff each egg white with the flavoured yolks. Serve chilled.

Tamari Almonds (Asia)

A big hit at parties. I have sold these through health food stores and they're favourites.

2 c	raw almonds	500ml
1 tbsp	sesame oil	15ml
1/4 tsp	cayenne powder	1ml
2 tbsp	tamari soy sauce	30ml
	a little salt (optional)	

☛ Heat the almonds in a frying pan on low to medium heat and add the other ingredients. Mix well and cook for 3 to 4 minutes, tossing to prevent burning. Serve hot or cold.

Chapattis (India)

Delicious with any Indian meal or to use as a wrap.

2 c	whole wheat flour	500ml
1/2 tsp	salt	2ml
	water	

☛ Mix together the flour and salt. Slowly add enough water to make a slightly dry dough. Mix well and knead on a well-floured surface. Then pinch off 1" (2.5cm) balls and roll each one into a very thin round—as thin as possible without being so thin that it breaks when you transfer it to the pan—6–8 inches (15–20cm) in diameter. Cook individually in a lightly oiled frying pan on medium high heat, pressing down with a kitchen towel to form air pockets. Bread should puff up. Cook both sides and remove from heat as soon as done, about 3 to 4 minutes. Avoid burning. Serve with Indian food or as a burrito wrap.

Corn Bread (North America)

Excellent with black-eyed peas, steamed greens or Mexican food. Try the variations—they're all good. If you like it spicier, add more chilli powder.

2 1/2 c	cornmeal	625ml
1c	whole wheat flour	250ml
2 tsp	wheat germ	10ml
1/2 tsp	salt	2ml
1 tsp	baking powder	5ml
1/2 tsp	baking soda	2ml
1/4 tsp	chilli powder	1ml
	grinding of black pepper	
3 tbsp	dark brown sugar	45ml
2	eggs, beaten	2
4 tbsp	melted butter	60ml
1 1/2 c	milk or soy milk, or water	375ml
1–2	cobs fresh corn, grated (optional)	1–2
1 c	grated cheddar cheese (optional)	250ml

☛ Mix together the dry ingredients first and then add the liquid ingredients. Add the corn and/or cheddar cheese, if you're using them. Mix well. Pour into a greased, 8" x 8" (20cm x 20cm) square baking pan. Bake at 400F (200C) for 40 to 50 minutes, or until a toothpick comes out cleanly. Serve hot with butter.

Samosas (India)

You'll find these spicy little snacks all over India and in Indian restaurants. They're very popular at vegetarian food fairs, too.

1 c	whole wheat flour	250ml
1/4 tsp	salt	1ml
1/4 tsp	coriander powder	1ml
1 tsp	baking powder	5ml
1 tbsp	olive oil	15ml
1/4–1/2 c	milk or soy milk	60–125ml

☛ Mix together the flour, salt, coriander, baking powder, 1 tbsp (15ml) of olive oil and milk and knead into a soft dough. If the dough is sticky, add more flour. Separate into little balls, about 1 1/2" (4cm), and roll each one out into a circle about 1/4" (1/2 cm) thick and 4–4 1/2" (10–11cm) in diameter. Cover with a tea towel while you make the filling.

FILLING ... 1 tbsp	olive oil	15ml
2	medium onions, chopped	2
2	cloves garlic, minced	2
1	potato, cut into small cubes	1
1/4	yam, diced	1/4
1 tbsp	black mustard seed	15ml
1 tsp	cumin powder	5ml
1 1/2 tsp	coriander powder	7ml
1/4 tsp	turmeric powder	1ml
1/4 tsp	cayenne powder, or more	1ml
1	dried bay leaf	1
	pepper and salt to taste	
3/4 c	water	185ml
1/2 c	frozen peas	125ml
1 inch	carrot, cut into matchsticks	2.5cm
	olive oil	

☛ Sauté the onions in the oil on low heat until soft. Add the garlic, potato, yam, and spices and sauté for 3 to 4 minutes. Add the water, cover and cook until the potato is soft, stirring frequently and adding water to prevent sticking. Add the remaining ingredients and cook for 2 minutes, uncovered, allowing any water to evaporate. Remove the bay leaf. Place some filling on each circle of dough and fold in half. Pinch the edges to seal and brush with a little oil. Fry in hot oil until golden, or bake on a cookie sheet at 375F (190C) until golden.

French Toast (Eastern Europe)

An excellent version of a classic.

2	eggs, beaten	2
3/4 c	milk	185ml
	salt and pepper to taste	
	drop of vanilla extract	
	a little cinnamon powder (optional)	
4	large slices of pre-sliced challah bread	4
	butter for cooking	
	maple syrup (optional)	

☛ Beat together the eggs, milk, salt, pepper, vanilla and cinnamon, if you're using it. Drop each slice of bread in the batter and coat well. Melt 1–2 tsp (5–10ml) of butter at a time in a frying pan and cook each piece of bread on both sides until golden, adding more butter if necessary. Serve hot with syrup, if desired, or jam.

Oatcakes (Scotland)

Excellent for breakfast or teatime or just plain snack time. I don't even like honey, but it tastes delicious on these. Do toast the oats first, it makes a huge difference in taste.

2 c	rolled oats	500ml
1/2 tsp	salt	2ml
1 tsp	baking powder	5ml
2	eggs, beaten	2
1/2 c	soft butter	125g
2 tsp	whole wheat flour	10ml
	honey	

☛ Place the oats on a cookie sheet and put them in the oven at 375F (190C). Toast, stirring from time to time, until they begin to brown. Watch them closely so they don't burn. Mix together the remaining ingredients and add the toasted oats. Mix well and form into small cakes, about 2" (5cm) in diameter. Place on a greased cookie sheet and bake at 375F (190C) for 15 to 20 minutes, or until cooked through: they should be slightly golden but not burnt. Serve hot with honey.

Porridge (North America)

These are just a couple of possibilities. It's easy to make up your own version for a healthy start to your day: even if you hate breakfast, there may be days when you need a good one.

VERSION 1

6 tbsp	white rice	90ml
6 tbsp	cornmeal	90ml
1 1/2 tbsp	couscous	22ml
4 tbsp	bulgur	60ml
3 c	water	750ml
1 tsp	brown sugar	5ml
1	mashed banana (optional)	1
1 tbsp	nuts (optional)	15ml
1 tbsp	seeds (optional)	15ml
1 tbsp	raisins or chopped dates (optional)	15ml

☛ Mix together the grains and the water and cook in a double boiler for about 20 minutes, stirring and checking the water level. When the grains are tender, add the remaining ingredients and stir well. Serve hot.

VERSION 2

1/4 c	bulgur	60ml
4 tbsp	cornmeal	60ml
4 tbsp	oats	60ml
4 tbsp	millet	60ml
2–3 c	water	500–750ml
1 tsp	brown sugar (optional)	5ml
	fruit, nuts or seeds (optional)	

☛ Prepare in a double boiler as above.

Garlicky Mushrooms (Mediterranean)

Great for buffets or as an appetizer. They're garlicky and delicious.

1/4 c	olive oil	60ml
2 tbsp	lemon juice	30ml
2 tbsp	red wine	30ml
1/8 tsp	Dijon mustard (optional)	1/2ml
3	cloves garlic, minced	3
1/8 tsp	salt	1/2ml
	pepper to taste	
1 tbsp	fresh or 1 tsp dried oregano or basil	15ml
2 c	small button mushrooms	500ml

☛ Whisk everything together, except the mushrooms. Pour over the mushrooms and marinate for 6 hours, tossing gently from time to time to coat all the mushrooms. I like to marinate them in the fridge and then bring them to room temperature 1 hour before serving. If you like, you can add a little chopped feta cheese.

Stuffed Mushrooms (France)

This is an all-time favourite of mine, and everyone else who tries them, too. It's a perfect appetizer or great for parties or just a late-night snack. We always have these when we want something special for a few guests. Use extra old cheddar—it adds a nice sharp flavour.

12	button mushrooms, stems removed and finely chopped	12
1 tbsp	butter	15ml
1/2	small onion, finely chopped	1/2
1	garlic clove, minced	1
3/4–1 c	bread crumbs made from whole wheat bread	185–250ml
2 tsp	vegetarian Worcestershire sauce	10ml
1/4–1/2 c	grated extra old cheddar cheese	60–125ml
	pepper to taste	
1/2 tsp	dried thyme	2ml
	water/wine	

☞ Sauté the onion in the butter on low heat until tender. Add the garlic and sauté for 1 minute. Add the finely chopped stems of the mushrooms and sauté for 4 minutes. Add the remaining ingredients, except the water/wine, and heat through. Mix well and stuff some of the filling into each mushroom cap. Place in a casserole dish, adding 2 tbsp (30ml) of water or wine to the bottom of the dish, and bake, covered, at 375F (190C) for 20 to 25 minutes. Serve hot.

Cheesy Mushroom Appetizer (North America)

Simple and good. A well-spiced herb bread, with or without the cheese.

4	slices whole wheat bread	4
	olive oil	
1 tsp	butter	5ml
2 c	finely chopped mushrooms	500ml
1/4 tsp	garlic salt	1ml
1/4 tsp	dried thyme (optional)	1ml
1	clove garlic, minced	1
	pepper to taste	
1 tbsp	red wine (optional)	15ml
	a little grated cheddar cheese or soy cheese (optional)	

☞ With a small, round cookie cutter, cut out 4 rounds from each slice of bread. Brush the rounds with olive oil and place them on a cookie sheet. Meanwhile, in a frying pan, melt the butter and sauté the rest of the ingredients, except the cheese, until the mushrooms are browned. Remove with a slotted spoon and press a little of the mixture onto each round. Top with cheese, if you're using it. Bake at 350F (180C) for 3 to 7 minutes or until toasted and the cheese is melted. Serve hot.

Egg Rolls (Asia)

For buffets, party finger food, or as an appetizer. Serve with plum sauce and hot honey mustard sauce.

1 tbsp	olive oil	15ml
1	medium onion, chopped	1
1 c	finely sliced mushrooms	250ml
1 c	finely shredded green cabbage	250ml
4	scallions, chopped	4
1 c	mung bean sprouts	250ml
1/4–1/2 c	carrot matchsticks	60–125ml
2 oz	bamboo shoots (optional)	60g
1 tbsp	sherry (optional)	15ml
3 tbsp	soy sauce	45ml
	pepper to taste	
1 tsp	cornstarch	5ml
1/8 tsp	ginger powder	1/2ml
	pinch of cayenne powder	
	egg roll wrappers (available in most supermarkets or Asian stores)	
	oil for deep frying or baking	

☛ Sauté the onion in the olive oil on low heat until tender. Add the mushrooms, cabbage and scallions and sauté for about 5 minutes. Add the remaining ingredients and cook for 3 to 4 minutes. Allow liquid to thicken. Place a little filling in the middle of each wrapper. Fold in three sides like a packet, then fold over the top half and roll into the shape of an egg roll to close. If necessary, seal with a little water. You can either deep fry them at this point until they are golden or brush them with oil and bake on a cookie sheet at 350F (180C) for about 15 to 25 minutes, or until golden. Serve hot with plum sauce or hot honey mustard sauce for dipping.

Cheese Scones (British Isles)

Delicious with any soup or stew—or for a proper tea.

1 1/8 c	whole wheat flour	280ml
2 1/4 tsp	baking powder	11ml
1 1/4 tsp	mustard powder	6ml
1/4 tsp	sea salt	1ml
1/4 c	soft butter	60ml
2/3 c	cheddar cheese, grated	160ml
3 fl oz	milk or soy milk	95ml

☛ Mix together the dry ingredients and then add the butter, cheese and milk. Mix well and knead on a floured board for 3 to 4 minutes. The dough should be of medium consistency. Roll out the dough to about 3/4" (2cm) thick and cut into 3" (7.5cm) circles using a circular pastry cutter or a drinking glass. Place dough on a non-stick cookie sheet and bake at 400F (200C) for 10 to 15 minutes, or until golden. Serve hot.

Spicy Indian Nuts (Version 1) (India)

These well-spiced nuts are great for parties.

1 c	raw sunflower seeds	250ml	
1 c	raw peanuts	250ml	
1/2 c	sliced almonds	125ml	
1/4 c	brown sesame seeds	60ml	
	a few pecans and cashews		
1 tsp	olive oil	5ml	
3/4 tsp	chilli powder	3ml	
	dash of cayenne powder		
1 tsp	powdered tandoori barbecue masala	5ml	
	pinch of sea salt		

☛ Heat the nuts in a frying pan on medium heat until they begin to crackle. Add the oil and the spices and mix to coat well. Serve.

Spicy Indian Nuts (Version 2) (India)

This version has a spicy barbecue flavour.

1 c	raw peanuts	250ml
1/2 tsp	olive oil	2ml
1/2 tsp	powdered tandoori barbecue masala	2ml
1/8 tsp	chilli powder, or more	1/2ml
	dash of cayenne powder	

☛ Roast the nuts in a frying pan on medium heat and add the other ingredients. Mix to coat well. Serve.

Roasted Asian Nuts (Asia)

These nuts have a distinct Asian flavour, and they make a healthy snack too.

1 c	raw peanuts	250ml
1/2 c	brown sesame seeds	125ml
1/2 c	slivered almonds	125ml
1/2 c	sunflower seeds	125ml
2–3 tbsp	tamari sauce, or soy sauce	30–45ml
1	tbsp sesame oil	15ml
1/2 tsp	ginger powder	2ml
1/4 tsp	honey	1ml
1/8 tsp	garlic powder	1/2ml
1/8–1/4 tsp	cayenne powder	1/2–1ml

☛ Heat the nuts in a frying pan on medium heat. When they are hot, add the remaining ingredients, cook for a few minutes, and mix well to coat. Serve hot or cold.

Notes

Dips, Spreads and Sauces

Avocado Spread (Mexico)

I love the tangy flavour of this spread, but I'm an onion, garlic and lemon lover, so this one is perfect for me. You can adjust the amount of garlic and lemon juice to suit your taste. It makes a nice first course if you're having chilli or another Mexican dish as the main course. This one's a party favourite, too.

1	avocado, peeled, pitted and cubed	1
2 tbsp	lemon juice	30ml
	pepper and salt to taste	
1	large garlic clove, minced	1
	dash of cayenne pepper	
1–2	scallions, chopped (optional)	1–2

☛ Place ingredients in a blender or food processor and blend well. Serve chilled on crackers, with tortilla chips, as a stuffing for Mexican food or as a sandwich spread (add lettuce, tomato, and sprouts).

Eggplant Dip (Russia)

A version of this dish is served in a dairy restaurant in Toronto as "vegetarian chopped liver." They add cheese and leave out the beet. The pretty colour of this dip makes it unusual, and a good choice if you're looking for contrast. The horseradish adds a bit of zip, but is optional. Nice on black bread.

1	eggplant	1
2	medium onions, chopped and sautéed in oil until soft	2
2	cloves garlic, minced	2
1	small beet, peeled and chopped	1
	pepper and salt to taste	
2 tbsp	lemon juice	30ml
2 tbsp	olive oil	30ml
1	scallion, finely chopped	1
1/2 tsp	horseradish (optional)	2ml

☛ Preheat the oven to 375F (190C). Pierce the eggplant several times with a fork and bake in the oven on a cookie sheet until soft, about 1 hour. Peel and scoop out the insides and discard the skin. Chop the eggplant finely. Place all the ingredients in a food processor or blender and blend until smooth. Serve chilled as a dip or spread.

Bean Pâté Spread (Middle East)

This is a well-flavoured Middle Eastern spread that's delicious on whole grain crackers with some olives on the side. In the Middle East it's often served as a snack with dried fruit and tea.

In a blender or food processor place:

1 c	green lentils, cooked	250ml
1	medium onion, chopped and sautéed in oil until translucent	1
1–2	cloves garlic, minced	1–2
1 tbsp	fresh parsley	15ml
3 tbsp	lemon juice	45ml
1 tsp	olive oil	5ml
1 tsp	sesame oil	5ml
	pepper and salt to taste	
1/2 tsp	cumin powder	2ml
1 1/2 tbsp	tahini paste	22ml
4 tbsp	chopped olives, green or black	60ml
	dash of cayenne pepper	
1/2 tsp	dried sumac	2ml

☞ Blend until smooth. Use as a dip or with crackers or as a sandwich filling.

Herbed Feta Spread (Eastern Europe)

Tangy and delicious. Excellent served on crackers or small breads with a cool glass of retsina. Try a few olives with it too.

In a food processor or blender place:

4–5 oz	feta cheese	120–150g
1 1/2 tsp	dried oregano	7ml
4–5 tbsp	olive oil	60–75ml
1 tbsp	fresh parsley	15ml
1 1/2 tbsp	lemon juice	22ml
1 tsp	caraway seeds, crushed walnuts or pecans (optional)	5ml
1/4 tsp	paprika	1ml
1/4 tsp	fresh or 1/8 tsp (1/2ml) dried tarragon	1ml
1 tbsp	fresh or 1 tsp (5ml) dried dill	15ml
	black pepper to taste	
1	scallion, finely chopped, or 1 slice of thinly sliced and chopped purple onion	1

☞ Blend until fairly smooth. Use as a dip or spread.

Raita (India)

Very cooling and delicious. Serve along with spicy foods and eat a spoonful or two between fiery bites.

8 tbsp	plain yoghurt	120ml
1	clove garlic, minced	1
1–2-inch	segment of cucumber, finely chopped	2–5cm
2 tbsp	finely chopped lettuce	30ml
1/4 tsp	salt	1ml
1/2 tsp	sugar	2ml
	pinch cayenne pepper	

☛ Mix ingredients well and serve chilled.

Cucumber Raita (India)

The red pepper adds a nice touch of colour to this cooling dish. Serve with spicy food or on its own on a hot day to cool you down.

1 c	plain yoghurt	250ml
	dash cayenne pepper	
	pepper to taste	
4 tbsp	each of red and green pepper, chopped	60ml
1 1/2-inch	segment cucumber, finely chopped	4cm
1	garlic clove	1

☛ Mix all ingredients together, chill and serve. Cooling and delicious, excellent with curries.

Lettuce Raita (India)

Milder than Cucumber Raita and also very cooling.

1 c	plain yoghurt	250ml
1/2 c	tender lettuce, very finely shredded	125ml
	sea salt to taste	
	dash of lemon juice	
1/4 tsp	sugar	1ml
1/4	red pepper, very finely chopped	1/4

☛ Mix together and serve chilled. Also very good with Indian feasts.

Baba Ghanouj (Middle East)

I love the smoky, garlic flavour of this one. As you can see, there are many ways to vary the dish. Great as a spread on bread, with sprouts or as a sandwich.

1	eggplant	1
4–6 tbsp	olive oil	60–90ml
1/2	tomato (optional)	1/2
2–3	scallions	2–3
1	onion, cooked in a little olive oil until tender (optional)	1
1 tbsp	fresh parsley	15ml
4–5 tbsp	lemon juice	60–75ml
	black pepper to taste	
2–3	cloves garlic, finely chopped	2–3
5 tbsp	tahini	75ml
1 tbsp	sesame oil	15ml
1/2 c	chickpeas, cooked (optional)	125ml

☞ Preheat the oven to 375F (190C). Pierce the eggplant several times with a fork. Bake the whole eggplant on a cookie sheet in the oven for 1 hour. Peel and mash the eggplant, discarding the skin.

Or, especially if eggplant is bitter, slice and leave in salted water for 1 hour. Drain and rinse. Sauté lightly in the olive oil at medium heat until very tender. Discard skin, if desired.

Place all the ingredients in a food processor or blender and mix well. Add a little more oil if it seems dry. Refrigerate and serve cool as a dip or spread or by itself. For a different kind of dip, omit the eggplant altogether and blend remaining ingredients (you will need to reduce the amount of oil used).

Hummus (Middle East)

An excellent version of hummus. Nice and lemony and garlicky. Try the options; the slight variations make interesting changes.

19 fl oz	cooked chickpeas, or use canned chickpeas, drained and rinsed	540ml
3–4	cloves garlic, minced	3–4
4–7 tbsp	olive oil (depends on how creamy you want it)	60–100ml
5 tbsp	lemon juice	75ml
1/4 c	tahini	60ml
1 tsp	sesame oil (optional)	5ml
2–4 tbsp	chopped olives (optional)	30–60ml
	salt and pepper to taste	

☞ Blend ingredients well in a blender or food processor. You can spread this on a pita bread and roll with some chopped pepper, onion, zucchini, tomato, sprouts or cucumber, too, and eat it as a sandwich. Or use it as a dip with your next Middle Eastern feast.

Vegetable Dip (Mediterranean)

A delicious, oniony dip. The olives are a nice touch and add an intriguing flavour.

2	green onions (scallions), chopped	2	
1	clove garlic, minced	1	
4	black or green olives, pitted and chopped	4	
4 tbsp	mayonnaise or plain yoghurt	60ml	
1 tbsp	fresh or 1 tsp (5ml) dried dill	15ml	
1/4 tsp	fresh parsley	1ml	

☛ Blend all ingredients well in a blender or food processor and serve with cut vegetables.

Ranch Bean Dip (Mexico)

The degree of spiciness can go up or down in this dip, depending on the amount of chilli powder. If you don't like it hot, substitute green pepper for the jalapeno pepper. The mayo gives it a creamier, tangier taste, more like a ranch-style dip.

19 fl oz	cooked kidney beans, or use canned kidney beans, drained and rinsed	540ml
1/4 tsp	cumin powder	1ml
1/4–1/2 tsp	chilli powder	1–2ml
1/4 c	tomatoes, skinned and well chopped	60ml
1 tbsp	mayonnaise or plain yoghurt (optional)	15ml
1 tbsp	olive oil (optional)	15ml
1/2 tsp	fresh parsley	2ml
1/4 c	cheddar cheese, grated	60ml
1	jalapeno pepper, seeded and chopped	1

☛ Blend all ingredients in a food processor or blender until well blended. Serve with ranch-style nachos, or bread or other chips.

Bean Dip (Mexico)

A slightly different version of a traditional Mexican dip.

19 fl oz	cooked kidney beans or use 1 can red kidney beans, drained and rinsed	540ml
6 tbsp	well-flavoured spaghetti sauce (see pg. 24)	90ml
1/2	jalapeno pepper	1/2
1/4–1/2 tsp	cayenne powder	1–2ml
1/4 c	cheddar cheese, grated (optional)	60ml

☛ Place all the ingredients in a blender or food processor and blend well. Serve as a dip or spread with chopped tomatoes, scallion, or cheese on top if desired.

Mexican Dip (Mexico)

Delicious! I love this one and always end up eating a little before it gets on the table. Every time I serve it at parties, with or without the cheese and yoghurt, it disappears.

19 fl oz	refried beans, or other Mexican beans included in this chapter, mashed, or canned beans, mashed pulp of 1 avocado, mashed	540ml
2 tbsp	lemon juice	30ml
	salt and pepper to taste	
1/4 tsp	chilli pepper flakes	1ml
1 c	plain low-fat yoghurt	250ml
1/4–1/2 tsp	chilli powder	1–2ml
4	green onions (scallions), chopped	4
2–3	small tomatoes, chopped	2–3
	a few olives, pitted and chopped	
3/4–1 c	grated cheese, cheddar or Monterey Jack, or a mixture of both	185–250ml
	a few chilli pepper flakes for garnish	
	nacho chips	

☞ In a dish, layer the beans, then the mashed avocado mixed with the lemon juice, salt and pepper to taste and the hot pepper flakes. Mix the yoghurt with the chilli powder and put it on top of the avocado mixture. Sprinkle the green onions, tomatoes and olives over the top. Then top with the cheese and a few chilli pepper flakes. Serve with nacho chips.

Chickpea Sandwich Filling (France)

This one is very good served on buns with sprouts and cucumber slices. The Dijon and onion pack quite a punch.

19 fl oz	cooked chickpeas or use canned, drained and rinsed	540ml
1/4	small onion, finely chopped	1/4
1 tbsp	mayonnaise	15ml
1/2 tsp	Dijon mustard	2ml
1/8–1/4 tsp	pepper	1/2–1ml
3 tbsp	finely chopped celery	45ml

☞ Mix ingredients well in a food processor and serve on bread or crackers.

Bean Burrito Spread (and the rest) (Mexico)

A very versatile dish. You can eat it in a sandwich, by itself, or hot out of the oven with the sauce.

19 fl oz	cooked kidney beans, or use 1 can kidney beans, drained and rinsed	540ml
1 tbsp	olive oil	15ml
2 tbsp	lemon juice	30ml
2 tbsp	plain yoghurt (optional)	30ml
4 tbsp	salsa (see pg. 21), or 3–4 tbsp (45–60ml) tomato sauce (see pg. 24), or a jalapeno pepper and a tomato chopped together pinch of red pepper flakes, or cayenne powder	60ml
1/2 c	cheddar cheese, grated (optional)	125ml
1	chopped scallion (optional)	1

☞ Put all the ingredients in a food processor or blender and blend until smooth. Serve as is, or add chopped peppers, scallions and tomatoes and eat with nachos, or fill a taco shell or burrito or enchilada shell, or make your own shell (see below).

SHELLS ...		
1 c	whole wheat flour, depending on how many you want	250ml
1 tsp	salt	5ml
	water to moisten	

☞ Mix together flour and salt and then add enough water to moisten the dough without making it sticky. Knead for 3 to 4 minutes. Pinch off small balls, and roll out to a thickness of 1/8" (1/2cm). Cook for 3 to 4 minutes on each side in a well-greased frying pan on medium heat. Shell should no longer be wet, but not too dried out. For cheese enchiladas, stuff shells with 2 1/2 cups (625ml) of grated cheddar/Monterey Jack cheese, 4 chopped scallions and 1/4 tsp (1ml) chilli flakes. Cover with sauce (see below) and bake.

SAUCE ...		
2 c	peeled tomatoes (see pg. 24), chopped	500ml
3	cloves garlic, minced	3
1	jalapeno pepper, seeded and chopped	1
1	stalk celery, chopped	1
1 tsp	dried oregano	5ml
	sea salt and pepper to taste	
1	scallion, chopped (optional)	1
1 c	tomato sauce (see pg. 24)	250ml

☞ Place all the ingredients in a saucepan and cook on medium low heat for about 20 minutes, stirring. Pour over bean or cheese enchiladas and bake for about 20 to 30 minutes at 350F (180C). Serve hot.

For a sandwich, spread bean dip on pita bread and roll with chopped green pepper and scallions.

Chinese White Bean Pâté (Asia)

A spicy sandwich filling or dip.

19 fl oz	cooked white kidney beans, or use canned white kidney beans, drained and rinsed	540ml
3	cloves garlic, minced	3
1 tbsp	extra virgin olive oil	15ml
1 tsp	dried oregano	5ml
3/4 tsp	paprika powder	3ml
2 1/2 tsp	tamari soy sauce	12ml
	dash of vegetarian Worcestershire sauce	
1/2 tsp	powdered ginger	2ml
1 tsp	lemon juice	5ml
1 tsp	honey (optional)	5ml
	chopped green pepper and scallion to taste	

☛ Blend all ingredients in a food processor until well mixed and kidney beans are smooth. Use as a pâté or spread on pita bread and roll with green pepper strips and chopped scallion.

Mediterranean Dip (Mediterranean)

An excellent and tasty mould for parties or just yourself.

19 fl oz	cooked white kidney beans, or use canned kidney beans, drained and rinsed	540ml
3	cloves garlic, minced	3
1 tbsp	extra virgin olive oil	15ml
1 tsp	dried oregano	5ml
3/4 tsp	paprika powder	3ml
2 1/2 tsp	tamari soy sauce	12ml
	dash of lemon pepper	
1/4 tsp	fresh parsley	1ml
1/2 tsp	lemon juice	2ml
1–2 tbsp	grated Parmesan cheese (optional)	15–30ml
	dash of powdered mustard (optional)	

☛ Combine all the ingredients in a food processor or blender and mix well. Place in a bowl or mould lined with plastic wrap and press down with a spatula. Allow to chill in mould for about an hour in the fridge, then remove by placing serving dish on top of bowl or mould and inverting. Remove plastic wrap. Serve with vegetables, bread or crackers.

Tofu-Like Egg Salad Spread (North America)

This is especially good when you're having one of those "I can't find anything to eat" days and need to pack a sandwich. Goes well on crackers too.

1 c	extra firm tofu (put in a sieve or cheesecloth and squeeze all the liquid out first, then mash)	250ml	☛ Mix ingredients well and use as a sandwich spread.
1 tbsp	mayonnaise or yoghurt	15ml	
	sea salt and pepper to taste		
1 tbsp	fresh or 1 tsp (5ml) dried dill	15ml	
1/4–1/2 tsp	garlic powder	1–2ml	
1/4 tsp	mustard powder	1ml	
1/4 tsp	turmeric powder	1ml	
1/4	scallion, chopped (about 1 tbsp/15ml)	1/4	
1/4	green pepper, chopped	1/4	
1 tbsp	shredded carrot (optional)	15ml	
1 tbsp	chopped celery (optional)	15ml	
1/4 tsp	onion powder (optional)	1ml	

Tofu Spread (Asia)

Excellent rolled in Azim bread, or spread on rice crackers or anything else you'd like to try it on.

1/2 c	very dry, extra firm tofu	125ml	☛ Blend all ingredients well in a food processor or blender and serve.
2 tsp	soy sauce	10ml	
	dash of cayenne powder		
	dash of powdered ginger		
1	clove garlic, minced	1	
1	stalk celery, minced	1	
1	scallion, minced	1	
1/4 tsp	dried oregano	1ml	
3/4 tsp	fresh or 1/4 tsp (1ml) dried thyme	3ml	
1/2 tsp	honey (optional)	2ml	

Spicy Dal Roll-Up (India)

A classic Indian dish. I love the black mustard seeds in this one: they have such a satisfying pop when you eat them. This is good served with an Indian dinner.

1 1/4 c	yellow split peas, cooked in boiling water and drained	285ml
1/2–1	green pepper, chopped	1/2–1
2	medium onions, chopped	2
3–4 tbsp	oil or ghee	45–60ml
2–3 tbsp	black mustard seed	30–45ml
1/2–1 tsp	curry powder	2–5ml
1 tsp	turmeric powder	5ml
2–3 tbsp	lemon juice	30–45ml
1/2–1 tsp	cumin powder	2–5ml
1 tsp	coriander powder	5ml
	sea salt to taste	
1/2 tsp	cayenne powder	2ml
2–4 tbsp	olive oil	30–60ml

☛ Sauté the onions on medium heat until tender and add the spices and then the remaining ingredients. Cook 5 minutes on medium heat, stirring. Mix in a food processor or blender until well blended. You may also add a chopped hot chilli pepper or two minced garlic cloves to the blender. Eat hot or cold as is, or spread on a pita bread and roll with chopped celery and green pepper.

Jaji (Armenia)

If you like onions, you'll love this one. Delicious tang to it.

6 oz	firm tofu	185g
1/2 c	plain yoghurt	125ml
1/4	green pepper, chopped	1/4
1/4	yellow pepper, chopped	1/4
4–5	scallions, chopped	4–5
1	stalk celery, finely chopped	1
	a little chopped red pepper	
2 tbsp	fresh or 2 tsp (10ml) dried dill	30ml
2 tbsp	chopped fresh chives	30ml
2–3 tbsp	lemon juice	30–45ml
	sea salt to taste	

☛ Place all the ingredients, except the vegetables, in a blender or food processor and blend until smooth. Stir in the vegetables. Mix well and chill 2 hours. Serve as a dip or a sandwich spread.

Salsa (Mexico)

Everyone knows what salsa is—just get the nacho chips. This one is better for you and fresher tasting than the commercial brands, and it's quite easy to make. Great for parties, in any Mexican dish, or for nights in front of the TV set.

3	large tomatoes, chopped	3
3–4	scallions, chopped	3–4
1/2–1	jalapeno pepper, seeded and chopped	1/2–1
1 tsp	dried oregano	5ml
	sea salt and pepper to taste	
1/2 tsp	cumin powder	2ml
	dash of cayenne powder	
1/4–1/2 tsp	fresh basil, to taste (optional)	1–2ml

☞ Place all the ingredients in a food processor or blender and blend until it reaches the desired consistency, either chunky or smooth.

Ethiopian Spicy Lentil Spread (Ethiopia)

This is one of my favourite dishes. After first eating it, I experimented until I got a really great version. It's good served plain or as a sandwich filling. This spread was a big hit when I was selling my rolled sandwiches. It's traditionally served with injera, a flatbread.

1 1/8 c	dried green lentils	280ml
1–2 tbsp	butter	15–30ml
1	medium onion, chopped	1
1/2	red pepper, chopped	1/2
1 tsp	cayenne powder	5ml
1/4 tsp	pepper	1ml
1/4 tsp	salt	1ml
3–4 tbsp	well-flavoured tomato sauce (see pg. 24)	45–60ml
1 tsp	powdered tandoori masala barbecue spices (optional)	5ml

☞ Cook the lentils in boiling water until tender, about 40 minutes. Drain. Place the butter and onion in a frying pan and sauté on medium heat until tender. Add the red pepper and the spices. Sauté for a few more minutes. Add the lentils and cook for 5 minutes. Remove from heat and blend in a food processor until smooth. Return to heat and add the tomato sauce. Heat for a few minutes. Check the seasoning: it should be spicy. Serve hot with pita bread or cold as a dip or spread, or rolled in Azim, a thin, soft flatbread, with chopped red and green pepper.

Béchamel Sauce (France)

A classic sauce which can be used as a basis for other sauces, or as is with an infinite number of dishes and foods, including vegetables, gratin dishes, and macaroni and cheese.

1/4 c	butter	60ml
2 tbsp	whole wheat flour	30ml
2 c	milk	500ml
1	dried bay leaf	1
	salt and pepper to taste	

☞ In a pan on medium heat, melt the butter. Add the flour and toast for a minute or so, while stirring, until golden. Slowly add the milk, stirring all the while. Add the seasonings and mix until the sauce is smooth and thick. Remove the bay leaf and serve.

VARIATIONS:

To turn it into a **cheese sauce** (France) that's delicious over vegetables or crêpes, add,

5 oz	sharp cheese, like old cheddar, grated	150g
1/2 tsp	mustard powder	2ml
	dash of cayenne powder	

☞ Mix well, melt and serve.

To make a **lemon sauce** (Mediterranean) that's tangy and perfect for that Greek or Spanish mood, add to the original Béchamel Sauce,

3–4 tbsp	freshly squeezed lemon juice	45–60ml
	a little chopped fresh parsley, to taste	

☞ Mix well, melt and serve.

To make a **mushroom sauce** (France) that has a woodsy flavour great over grains or pasta, add to the original Béchamel Sauce,

1 tbsp	butter	15ml
3 c	finely sliced mushrooms	750ml
1 1/2 tbsp	fresh or 1 1/2 tsp (7ml) dried thyme	22ml

☞ Simmer for 5 minutes, or until mushrooms are done. Serve.

To make an **orange sauce** (France), add to the original Béchamel Sauce,

1/4 c	orange juice, fresh squeezed	60ml
1/2–1 tsp	orange zest, not the white part	2–5ml
1 tbsp	orange liqueur	15ml

☞ Mix well, heat and serve.

Mushroom Sauce (France)

A classic sauce over grain dishes, pasta dishes, a sliced loaf dish, or anything else you want to use it on.

1	medium onion, chopped	1
3 tbsp	butter	45ml
2	cloves garlic, minced	2
3 c	sliced fresh mushrooms	750ml
	black pepper	
2 tbsp	soy sauce	30ml
2 1/2 tbsp	fresh or 1 tbsp (15ml) of dried thyme or savoury or 1 tbsp (15ml) dried oregano (optional)	37ml
1 1/2 tbsp	cornstarch or whole wheat flour	22ml
1 c	soy milk or milk	250ml

☛ Sauté the onion in butter on medium heat until tender. Add the garlic, mushrooms and the black pepper, and cook 5 minutes on medium low heat, stirring. Continue stirring, add the soy sauce and cook another 5 minutes. Mix the cornstarch or flour together with the soy milk, and beat until smooth. If you're using herbs, add them now. Slowly add the soy milk mixture, a little at a time, stirring to avoid lumps. Allow to thicken and serve hot over whatever you like.

Sweet and Sour Sauce (Asia)

Perfect for stir-fries or over rice.

2 tbsp	oil	30ml
1	medium onion, chopped	1
2 tsp	cornstarch	10ml
1 c	pineapple juice	250ml
1 c	pineapple chunks, fresh or canned	250ml
1/2	small green pepper, chopped	1/2
2 tsp	tamari soy sauce	10ml
1 tsp	apple cider vinegar	5ml
	pepper and salt to taste	
1 tsp	brown sugar	5ml
1 tsp	honey	5ml
1/2	red pepper, chopped (optional)	1/2
1 c	sliced mushroom (optional)	250ml
2	cloves garlic, minced (optional)	2

☛ Heat the oil in a pan on medium heat. Add the onion and sauté until tender. Mix the cornstarch into the pineapple liquid and add a little to the onions. Stir until thickened. Add the rest of the pineapple liquid and the remaining ingredients and cook, stirring until vegetables are tender and sauce is thickened. Serve hot.

Basic Cooked Tomatoes

A Healthier Equivalent to Canned Tomatoes

Since various forms of tomato are used throughout the book, I've included a basic tomato recipe. This is a healthier equivalent to canned tomatoes, and a tomato sauce recipe that can also be used for spaghetti sauce. If you're in a hurry, use canned or bottled sauces or freeze your own sauces to be used as needed. Using fresh tomatoes is healthier as it provides lots of lycopenes, which are antioxidants, and it avoids excess salt and lead that are found in some canned brands.

Select ripened tomatoes—5 to 6 medium, will yield about 2 cups (500ml). Double or triple the amount as needed. Core tomatoes about 1 inch down, and make two slits running down each side of the tomato, piercing only the skin. Plunge into boiling water for about 1 minute. Wearing rubber gloves, remove tomatoes with a slotted spoon, allow to cool slightly, and peel off the skin, being careful not to burn yourself (the skin should be starting to peel by itself).

If the recipe calls for whole canned tomatoes, this means the tomatoes need to be pre-cooked. In that case, put the tomatoes in a pot and cook them on medium heat for about 5 to 10 minutes, covered, and stirring occasionally, until soft and cooked through.

If you are making a sauce, after peeling, cut each tomato in half and squeeze out the seeds. If chopped tomatoes are required, chop the tomatoes either before or after cooking them.

Basic Tomato Sauce/ Spaghetti Sauce

- Peel the tomatoes as above, cut in half and squeeze out the seeds.
- Peel and chop 1 large onion and sauté in 1 tsp (5ml) olive oil, on low heat, until very soft.
- Add 6 large peeled and minced cloves of garlic.
- If desired, add 1 to 2 cups (250 to 500ml) of sliced mushrooms and/or 1/4 of a chopped green pepper and/or 1 finely chopped celery stalk.
- Sauté everything until soft.
- Add 1/4 tsp (1ml) red chilli flakes, if desired (I usually do).
- Place the tomatoes in a pot with a lid and add 1 1/2 tsp (7ml) each of fresh basil and thyme or 1/2 tsp (2ml) each of dried, 1 tsp (5ml) of dried oregano and 1/8 tsp (1/2ml) of sea salt, and pepper to taste.
- Cook on low for about 5 to 10 minutes, stirring.
- Mix everything together and blend in a blender or food processor until smooth, or leave slightly chunky if desired.
- If you need a thicker sauce, add 1 tsp (5ml) to 1 tbsp (15ml) of tomato paste and mix well.
- If you are in a hurry, you can use canned tomatoes instead of fresh.
- **Yields about 2 cups (500ml).**

Salads and Dressings

Salad Dressings

These dressings provide a variety of flavours and textures.

Lemon, Olive Oil Vinaigrette (Greece)

4 1/2 tbsp	olive oil	67ml	☛ Whisk ingredients together and toss with salad.
2 tbsp	lemon juice	30ml	
1/8 tsp	dry mustard powder (optional)	1/2ml	
	salt and pepper to taste		
1	clove garlic, minced (optional)	1	
3/4 tsp	fresh or 1/4 tsp (1ml) of dried oregano (optional)	3ml	

Red Wine, Olive Oil Vinaigrette (Greece)

4 1/2 tbsp	olive oil	67ml	☛ Whisk ingredients together and toss with salad.
2 tbsp	red wine vinegar	30ml	
1/4 tsp	dry mustard powder	1ml	
	salt and pepper to taste		
1	clove garlic, minced (optional)	1	

Soy Sauce Dressing (Asia)

1 tbsp	olive, or other oil	15ml
1 tbsp	sesame oil	15ml
2 tbsp	tamari soy sauce	30ml
1/4 tsp	ginger powder	1ml
1/8–1/4 tsp	cayenne powder, depending on how tangy you like it	1/2–1ml
1	clove garlic, minced (optional)	1
	honey (optional)	

☞ Whisk ingredients together and toss with salad.

Cheese-Like Italian Dressing (Italy)

1/4 c	olive oil	60ml
1 tbsp	red wine vinegar	15ml
1 tbsp	tahini	15ml
1/4 tsp	dried oregano	1ml
1/2 tsp	fresh basil	2ml
	sea salt and pepper to taste	
1/4 tsp	Dijon mustard	1ml
1 tsp	freshly chopped parsley or scallion, or both	5ml

☞ Whisk ingredients together and toss with salad.

Sesame Garlic Dressing (Italy)

1 tbsp	tahini	15ml
1–2	cloves garlic, minced	1–2
3–4 tbsp	olive oil	45–60ml
2 tbsp	lemon juice	30ml
	pepper and sea salt to taste	
1/2 tsp	dried oregano (optional)	2ml
1 tbsp	water	15ml

☞ Whisk ingredients together and toss with salad.

Tzatziki Dressing (Asia)

1 c	plain yoghurt	250ml
2–3	cloves garlic, minced	2–3
1/2	cucumber (4-inch/10cm segment), grated	1/2
	sea salt to taste	
1 tbsp	olive oil	15ml
	fresh dill, parsley, or mint—as much as you like (optional)	

☛ Blend until smooth and serve over salad or use as a dip for vegetables.

Tahini Dressing (Middle East)

A tangy, smoky tasting dressing.

1/2 c	tahini	125ml
4–5 tbsp	water	60–75ml
2	cloves garlic, minced	2
4 tbsp	lemon juice	60ml
	sea salt and pepper to taste	
1 tbsp	sesame seeds	15ml

☛ Blend ingredients, except the sesame seeds, in a blender until smooth. Stir in seeds and use as a dressing or dip. Thin with water and thicken with lemon juice.

Thousand Island Dressing (North America)

2 tbsp	mayonnaise	30ml
1 tbsp	ketchup	15ml
1 tbsp	pickle relish, or chopped dill pickle	15ml
1 tsp	lemon juice	5ml
	salt and pepper to taste	
1 tsp	soy sauce (optional)	5ml

☛ Whisk ingredients together and toss with salad.

Greek Vinaigrette with Feta (Greece)

Good on both lettuce and spinach salads.

3 tbsp	olive oil	45ml
1 1/2 tbsp	red wine vinegar	22ml
	salt and pepper to taste	
1 tbsp	feta cheese, finely crumbled	15ml

☛ Whisk ingredients together and toss with salad.

Salads

Tabbouleh (Middle East)

A classic salad from the Middle East. Goes very well with other Middle Eastern fare. If you add the chickpeas it's a complete meal on its own.

2 1/2 c	fresh, finely chopped parsley— wash it well	600ml
2 1/2 c	cooked bulgur wheat	600ml
1/2–1	small purple onion, finely chopped	1/2–1
5	scallions, finely chopped	5
4	cloves garlic, minced	4
3	large tomatoes, diced	3
3 1/2 tbsp	olive oil	52ml
2 1/2 tbsp	lemon juice	37ml
	pepper and sea salt to taste	
1/2 c	cooked chickpeas (optional)	120ml
1 tsp	fresh mint (optional)	5ml

☞ Cook the bulgur by placing it in a bowl and covering it with approximately 5 cups (1.25 litres) boiling water. Cover with a plate and let stand for 20 minutes. Stir and fluff with a fork. Drain if necessary. Taste to make sure it's tender. Then combine with all the other ingredients and chill for about one hour. Serve.

Tzatziki Salad (Greece)

Tzatziki is served all over Greece either as a salad or a dip. The first time I tried it was in Methoni, outside under a canopy of grape vines. While we were admiring it, the owner came out and cut some grapes for us to eat. Perfect. It took me a while to figure out whether to eat this salad with a spoon or a fork. Your guess is as good as mine.

1 c	plain yoghurt	250ml
5 inches	cucumber, grated, depending on how thick you want the tzatziki	13cm
3–4	cloves garlic, minced	3–4
1 tbsp	olive oil	15ml
	dash of sea salt	
	dash of pepper (optional)	
1 tsp or more	fresh dill (optional)	5ml or more
1/2 tsp or more	fresh parsley (optional)	2ml or more
1/4 tsp or more	fresh mint (optional)	1ml or more
1/2 c	chopped olives (optional)	125ml

☞ Mix together and allow the flavours to blend for 1/2 hour or longer. Serve chilled.

Spinach Salad (North America)

This is one of my favourite salads. I usually leave out the cheese, bacon bits and croutons for a simpler version.

4 c	freshly washed spinach, gently torn into bite-size pieces	1 litre
1 1/4 c	thinly sliced mushrooms, regular or shiitake	310ml
3–4	scallions, chopped finely	3–4
2–3 tbsp	vegetarian bacon bits (optional)	30–45ml
1 c	mixed greens (optional)	250ml

☛ Place the spinach in a bowl and cover with the dressing and toss, then cover with the mushrooms, scallions, and bacon bits, and mixed greens, as desired.

DRESSING …

3 tbsp	light vegetable oil	45ml
1 tbsp	lemon juice, or red wine vinegar	15ml
1/2 tsp	Dijon mustard	2ml
	pepper and sea salt to taste	
1	clove garlic, minced	1
2	dashes of vegetarian Worcestershire sauce (optional)	2
1/2 c	grated mozzarella or Swiss cheese (optional)	125ml
	croutons (optional)	
	sprinkle with chopped walnuts (optional)	

☛ Mix the dressing ingredients, except the cheese, croutons and nuts, together thoroughly and toss with the salad. Sprinkle the cheese, croutons and walnuts on top if you're using them. Chill for a short time, but it's better served right away.

Tangy Salad Dressing (North America)

Good on both lettuce and spinach salads.

1/4 c	olive oil	60ml	☛ Whisk ingredients together and toss with salad.
1 tbsp	red wine vinegar	15ml	
1 tbsp	vegetarian Worcestershire sauce	15ml	
1 tbsp	lemon juice	15ml	
1/8 tsp	pepper	1/2ml	
1/4 tsp	mustard powder	1ml	

Spicy Spinach Salad (Asia)

Another of my very favourite salads. I always include the garlic and the scallions, although I sometimes leave out the honey. If you don't have sesame oil, it's still good without it.

	4 c	washed spinach, torn into bite-size pieces	1 litre
	1 c	thinly sliced mushrooms	250ml
DRESSING ...	2 tbsp	soy sauce	30ml
		black pepper to taste	
	1/8–1/4 tsp	cayenne powder	1/2–1ml
	1/8 tsp	ginger powder	1/2ml
	1 tbsp	olive oil	15ml
	1 tsp	sesame oil	5ml
	1 tsp	honey (optional)	5ml
	1	clove garlic, minced (optional)	1
		some thinly sliced cucumber (optional)	
		some small broccoli florets (optional)	
	3	scallions, chopped (optional)	3
	2 tbsp	pumpkin seeds (optional)	30ml
		a few chopped walnuts (optional)	

☛ Place the spinach and mushrooms in a bowl. Whisk the dressing well and toss with the salad. Serve right away.

Tomato and Cucumber Salad (Greece)

A simple, refreshing salad served all over Greece, and in my backyard too. If desired, you can serve with olives and feta cheese.

4	large tomatoes, diced in 1" (3cm) pieces	4
1	cucumber, diced in 1" pieces	1
1	scallion, chopped, or	1
	1 small red onion, chopped	
2 tbsp	lemon juice	30ml
2 tbsp	olive oil	30ml
	sea salt and pepper to taste	
1 tbsp	fresh or 1 tsp (5ml) dried oregano	15ml

☛ Place all the ingredients in a bowl and mix well. Serve chilled.

Tomato and Cheese Salad (North America)

A great light lunch. And colourful for entertaining, too.

2–3	large lettuce leaves, torn up	2–3
5–6	tomatoes, finely sliced	5–6
3	scallions, finely chopped	3
2 tbsp	chopped fresh parsley	30ml
2/3 c	grated cheese, either mozzarella, cheddar, or Brie cut in cubes	160ml

☛ Place the lettuce leaves on a small/medium platter, right to the edges, and cover with layered tomatoes, scallions, parsley and cheese.

DRESSING ...		
2 tbsp	olive oil	30ml
3/4 tbsp	lemon juice	12ml
	salt and pepper to taste	
1 1/4 tsp	fresh or 1/2 tsp (2ml) dried oregano	6ml
	splash of apple cider vinegar	

☛ Whisk ingredients well and pour over the salad just before serving.

Chickpea Salad (North America)

This salad is great for picnics. Fast and easy to prepare, and filling too.

19 fl oz	cooked chickpeas, or use canned, drained and rinsed	540ml
1	very large tomato, chopped	1
1/2	cucumber, chopped	1/2
2	scallions, chopped	2
1/8–1/4 tsp	sea salt	1/2–1ml
	lots of pepper	
1 1/2 tbsp	olive oil	22ml
2 tbsp	lemon juice	30ml
1/2 c	fresh chopped parsley	125ml
1/4 c	chopped asparagus (optional)	60ml

☛ Mix well and let the flavours mix for about 1 hour, if possible, before serving.

Black-Eyed Pea Salad (Mediterranean)

I like this salad because it gives me a different way of serving black-eyed peas—in a filling and healthy salad.

1 1/2 c	black-eyed peas	375ml
	or	
1 c	black-eyed peas	250ml
	and	
1/2 c	adzuki beans	125ml
1	large tomato, diced	1
1	stalk celery, chopped	1
3	scallions, chopped	3
1/2	green pepper, chopped	1/2
3 tbsp	olive oil	45ml
2 tbsp	lemon juice	30ml
1 1/2 tbsp	fresh oregano	22ml
	or	
1 1/2 tsp	dried oregano	7ml
3/4 tsp	fresh basil	3ml
1/8 tsp	sea salt	1/2ml
	black pepper to taste	
	a few marinated artichoke hearts, cut in small pieces (optional)	

☛ Cook the black-eyed peas (and adzuki beans, if using) in boiling water until tender. Drain and rinse. Allow to cool. Mix ingredients together and serve chilled.

Pea and Mayonnaise Salad (North America)

A strange but delicious mixture. I love the way the peas pop in your mouth and contrast so well with the mayo.

	lettuce leaves	
1 c	peas, steamed for 3 to 4 minutes and thoroughly cooled	250ml
1/2	green pepper, chopped small	1/2
1/4	cucumber, chopped finely	1/4
1 tbsp	yoghurt or mayonnaise	15ml
2 tbsp	lemon juice	30ml
	pepper and sea salt to taste	
	pinch of chopped fresh parsley	

☛ Tear the lettuce leaves into bite-size pieces and place on a platter. Mix together the remaining ingredients and place in the centre of the platter. Chill for about 20 minutes and serve.

Coleslaw (North America)

A zippy coleslaw that's great for picnics and buffets, or when the fare is fast and simple.

1	very small, or 1/2 small-to-medium green cabbage, cored and shredded	1
1/4	small onion, finely chopped (use more if desired)	1/4
2	large carrots, shredded	2
3–4 tbsp	mayonnaise	45–60ml
	pepper and sea salt to taste	

☛ Mix everything together in a large bowl and chill. Serve.

Waldorf Salad (North America)

I first heard about a Waldorf salad from the television show *Fawlty Towers*, and of course I had to find out what it was. Here it is and it's very good.

2	stalks celery	2
	or	
1/4 c	green pepper, finely chopped	60ml
2	apples with skins on, cored and chopped	2
1 c	green grapes	250 ml
1/4 c	walnuts	60ml
1 1/2–2 tbsp	yoghurt/or mayonnaise	22–30ml
	sea salt and pepper to taste	

☛ Mix everything well and serve, if desired, on lettuce leaves.

Dilled Cucumber Salad (Middle East)

Delicious and simple to prepare. We eat this a lot, especially when we want a salad but don't feel like making one!

1	cucumber, with skin on if organic, sliced very thinly	1
2 tbsp	white vinegar, or apple cider vinegar	30ml
	salt and pepper to taste	
1/2 tsp	paprika powder	2ml
1/4 tsp	white sugar (optional)	1ml
2 tsp	olive oil	10ml
3/4 tbsp	fresh dill (optional)	3ml

☛ Mix well and serve.

Caesar Salad (North America)

An old friend taught me a version of this a long time ago. His had anchovy paste in it but this is a modified version. It's quite garlicky.

1	head romaine lettuce, torn into bite-size pieces	1
1/4 c	+ 2 tbsp freshly grated Parmesan cheese	60ml + 30ml

☛ Place the lettuce in a bowl and toss well with the cheese. It should be well coated. Whisk the dressing well and toss with the salad. Add the croutons and serve immediately.

DRESSING ...		
3	cloves garlic, minced	3
4 1/2 tbsp	olive oil	67ml
1 1/2 tbsp	red wine vinegar	22ml
1/2 tsp	dry mustard powder	2ml
1/8 tsp	garlic salt	1/2ml
	lots of freshly ground pepper	
1/4 c	croutons	60ml

☛ Place the lettuce in a bowl and toss well with the cheese. It should be well coated. Whisk the dressing well and toss with the salad. Add the croutons and serve immediately.

Macaroni Salad (North America)

Another good salad for picnics.

2 c	tubeghetti pasta (little tiny tubes), elbow macaroni or penne, cooked until tender, drained and rinsed	500ml
2 tbsp	mayonnaise, or vegan mayonnaise	30ml
1/2 tsp	salt	2ml
1/4 tsp	pepper	1ml
1/2 tsp	dry mustard powder	2ml
2 tbsp	red wine vinegar	30ml
1	stalk celery, chopped	1
1	small onion, finely chopped	1
1	carrot, finely chopped	1
2	large dill pickles, finely chopped	2
1	scallion, finely chopped	1
	a few pickled artichoke hearts, chopped (optional)	

☛ Mix well and chill for half an hour before serving.

Potato Salad (Version 1) (North America)

A great picnic favourite, or for a buffet. The dill pickles add just the right tang.

4	large potatoes, peeled and cut in quarters, and cooked in boiling water, 20 to 25 minutes, until soft but not mushy. Drain, allow to cool, then cut into 1/2 to 1-inch (2 to 3cm) cubes, depending on how chunky you want the salad	4
2	eggs, hard-boiled 15 to 20 minutes, cooled, peeled and chopped up finely	2
3 tbsp	mayonnaise	45ml
	pepper to taste	
1/8 tsp	salt	1/2ml
1/4–1	Spanish onion, finely chopped, depending on how oniony you like it	1/4–1
1	stalk celery, finely chopped	1
3	dill pickles, finely chopped	3
1/4–1/2 tsp	paprika powder	1–2ml
1 tbsp	green pickle relish	15ml

☞ Mix ingredients together well and chill for an hour or more.
Serve with a sprinkling of paprika on top.

Potato Salad (Version 2) (North America)

A different, equally delicious version of potato salad. The crunchy cauliflower and the steamed peas add a great pop in your mouth.

4	large potatoes, peeled and cut in quarters, and cooked in boiling water, 20 to 25 minutes, until soft but not mushy. Drain, allow to cool, then cut into 1/2 to 1-inch cubes (2 to 3cm), depending on how chunky you want the salad	4
1/2–1	medium onion (preferably a red onion), finely chopped, depending on how oniony you like it	1/2–1
3/4 c	peas, steamed for 3 minutes	185ml
6	finely chopped mushrooms	6
1/2 c	cauliflower or broccoli florets, finely chopped	125ml
2 tbsp	mayonnaise	30ml
3 tbsp	green relish	45ml
	salt and pepper to taste	

☞ Mix everything together and chill before serving.

Lentil Salad (Middle East)

Good hot or cold. Very filling and complete, too. Just add a green vegetable and you've got everything you need. I serve it with the tomato and scallions because I love the juicy, tangy taste they give it.

7–9 c	water	1.75–2.25 litres	☞ Boil the lentils, rice and oil in the water until tender, about 45 minutes, stirring occasionally. Drain and rinse. If eating cold, cool lentil mixture, then mix everything together in a bowl and chill for half an hour or so. If eating hot, mix everything together and serve right away.
1 1/2–2 c	brown/green lentils	375–500ml	
1/2–3/4 c	brown rice	125–185ml	
1 tbsp	oil	15ml	
1	stalk celery, chopped	1	
1	tomato, diced (optional)	1	
1	carrot, diced	1	
1/2	green or red pepper, diced	1/2	
1/4–1/2 tsp	salt, to taste	1–2ml	
2	scallions, chopped	2	
	or		
1	small red onion, chopped	1	
1/4–1/2 tsp	pepper	1–2ml	
3–4 tbsp	olive oil	3ml	
2 tbsp	lemon juice	30ml	
2 tbsp	fresh or 2 tsp (10ml) dried oregano (optional)	30ml	

Bean and Pasta Salad (Italy)

Also great for picnics and buffets. A full meal on its own.

2 c	tri-coloured pasta, cooked until tender, drained and rinsed	500ml	☞ Mix well, chill and serve.
3	scallions, chopped	3	
4 tbsp	well-flavoured spaghetti sauce (see pg. 24)	60ml	
1/2 tsp	Dijon mustard	2ml	
2 tbsp	green pickle relish	30ml	
2 tbsp	fresh parsley	30ml	
1 tbsp	fresh or 1 tsp (5ml) dried oregano sea salt and pepper to taste	15ml	
1/4 tsp	crushed red chilli flakes	1ml	
2 tbsp	olive oil	30ml	
19 fl oz	cooked kidney beans, or use canned, drained and rinsed	540 ml	

The Best Greek Salad (Greece)

This is perhaps my all-time favourite salad. I had versions of it all over Greece, and then I came home and made what I think is the best Greek salad ever. You need very good tomatoes or it won't taste as good. Try to use a feta that's not too dry, but also not too creamy. In Greece, the feta cheese tastes different from village to village and every Greek swears that his village's is the best. I especially like the feta from the Dodoni region. Really good Kalamata olives work best in this salad. Serve it with spanakopita, stuffed peppers and tomatoes, or moussaka, or on its own with some bread, Greek style, to soak up the juices from the salad. Retsina goes very well with this.

4	large, very sweet and ripe tomatoes, chopped in 1" (3cm) pieces, or wedges	4
1	seedless cucumber, peeled and chopped in 1" (3cm) rounds, then cut in quarters	1
1	very small purple onion, sliced finely, the slices then cut in quarters	1
1	green pepper, cut in medium pieces	1
1/4 c	olive oil, less 2 tbsp	45ml
3 1/2 tbsp	lemon juice	52ml
2 1/2 tbsp	fresh or 1 tbsp (15ml) crumbled dried oregano (in Greece they use dried)	37ml
	sea salt and pepper to taste	
7–8 oz	crumbled feta cheese	200–230g
10–12 approx.	Kalamata or green olives	10–12 approx.

☛ Mix everything but the cheese in a bowl or on a large platter. Add the cheese and toss. Serve.

Moroccan Salad (Morocco)

A simple, light-tasting and tangy salad. Serve it with Moroccan-style eggplant, couscous or a favourite Middle Eastern dish.

1/2	large cucumber, diced	1/2
2	medium tomatoes, diced	2
1 1/2 tbsp	olive oil	22ml
1 1/2 tsp	lemon juice	7ml
1/4 tsp	cumin powder	1ml
	sea salt to taste	
	a little fresh chopped parsley	
1 tbsp	tomato juice (optional)	15ml

☛ Mix well and marinate for 1/2 hour or longer before serving.

Asian Rice Noodle Salad (Asia)

Delicious salad with a punch. Use rice noodles if you can get them; they make the salad light and silky.

1	box of cooked brown rice pasta, curly or fettucini or spaghetti (approx. 4 cups/1 litre cooked)	1	☞ Mix all ingredients well and chill before serving.
3 1/2 tbsp	tamari soy sauce	52ml	
3 tbsp	sesame oil	45ml	
1 tbsp	cider vinegar	15ml	
1/4 tsp	cayenne powder	1ml	
1 tbsp	honey	15ml	
1	red or green pepper or	1	
1/2	of each, chopped	1/2	
2	scallions, chopped	2	
1	large stalk celery, chopped	1	
1	clove garlic, minced	1	
	pinch of chilli flakes		
1/8–1/4 tsp	grated fresh ginger	1/2–1ml	
1 1/4 c	mushrooms, sautéed lightly in olive oil until brown	310ml	

African Orange Spice Salad (Africa)

Simple and colourful. This juicy salad looks like Africa—bright and colourful with fruit everywhere.

2	large oranges, peeled and cut into bite-size pieces; squeeze some of the juice into the salad	2	☞ Mix ingredients together and serve, on lettuce leaves if desired.
1 c	sliced radishes	250ml	
1/4 tsp	cumin powder	1ml	
	sea salt and pepper to taste		
	a few fresh dates, chopped (optional)		
	a few pomegranate seeds (optional)		
	lettuce leaves (optional)		

Mango Salad (Thailand)

Spicy, colourful and delicious.

2	mangos, peeled and chopped	2
2	green onions, finely chopped	2
1	red pepper, sliced thinly	1
1/2 c	mung bean sprouts	65ml
1 tbsp	soy sauce	15ml
1/4-1/2 tsp	chilli flakes, depending on how spicy you want it	1-2ml
1/4 c	fresh lime juice	60ml
1 1/2 tbsp	brown sugar	22ml
1	garlic clove, peeled and minced	1

☛ Mix the soy sauce, chilli flakes, lime juice, sugar and garlic together. Toss with remaining ingredients and serve.

Papaya Salad (Indonesia)

A nice refreshing salad on those hot Indonesian days, when all you feel like doing is swimming in that incredible blue water.

1	large papaya, peeled and cut up	1
1/2	of a red onion, finely diced	1/2
1/4	cup lime juice	60ml
1 tbsp	soy sauce	15ml
1 1/2 tbsp	brown sugar	22ml
1	very finely diced hot chilli	1
2 tbsp	fresh cilantro, minced	30ml
1 c	watercress, torn into bite size-pieces	250ml
1/4	of a red pepper, sliced thinly	1/4
1 c	extra firm tofu, cubed	250ml
	a little vegetable oil	
2 tbsp	balsamic or rice vinegar	30ml
1/4 tsp	of cayenne powder	1ml

☛ In a frying pan, place the oil and the tofu on medium-high heat. Stir frequently until browned. Toss with the vinegar and cayenne. Allow to cool and mix with the remaining ingredients. Toss well and serve.

Mediterranean Pasta Salad (Mediterranean)

What really makes this salad is the kitharaki noodles. They are a must. Check out the Greek markets for them. The contrast between the chewy noodles and the chunky vegetables works well with the tangy sauce. This one's a favourite at parties and barbecues. As with all Greek food, you must use very fresh, ripe vegetables.

2 c	kitharaki pasta, cooked until tender (yields 5 cups (1250ml))	500ml
1 1/2	zucchini, chopped medium fine	1 1/2
30	green olives	30
4	scallions, chopped finely	4
	or	
1	very small purple onion, chopped finely	1
1	stalk celery, chopped finely	1
	or	
4 inches	cucumber chopped finely (optional)	10cm
1	tomato, coarsely chopped	1
1	green pepper, chopped medium	1
1	yellow pepper, chopped medium	1
1 tbsp	fresh parsley	15ml
8–10 tbsp	olive oil	120–150ml
1 tbsp	cider vinegar	15ml
2	large cloves garlic, minced	2
2 tbsp	fresh or 2 tsp (10ml) dried oregano	30ml
1 1/2 tbsp	fresh dill	22ml
1/4 tsp	sea salt	1ml
	pepper to taste	
1 tsp	lemon juice	5ml
2 tbsp	vegan mayonnaise	30ml
1/4 c	finely chopped cauliflower florets (optional)	60ml
1/4 tsp	fresh basil	1ml
4–6 oz	feta cheese, crumbled (optional)	120–180g

☞ Mix well and chill for about 30 minutes. I love it with the feta cheese. Serve.

Green Salad (Spain)

The best salad I've ever had was served in the village of Frigiliana. We sat outside among the whitewashed houses on mosaic streets lined with potted plants, overlooking an onion field, and ate fresh lettuce, sweet onions, green olives, wedges of cucumber and tomato in the lightest vinaigrette. Perfect! I liked it so much that I immediately ordered another. And it was served with a Classic Coke in an old Coke bottle.

This salad stands well on its own as a light lunch or equally well as an accompaniment. Make sure the greens are fresh and the tomatoes are really good. Try to use a sweet onion, not a hot one, and don't put the dressing on until you're ready to eat.

2 c	romaine lettuce, torn in pieces	500ml
1 c	spinach, torn in pieces	250ml
2 c	Boston bib lettuce, torn in pieces	500ml
2	tomatoes, cut in wedges	2
1/2	Spanish onion, very thinly sliced	1/2
10–12	green olives	10–12
DRESSING ... 1 tbsp	lemon juice	15ml
3 tbsp	olive oil	45ml
	sea salt and black pepper to taste	

☛ Whisk the dressing well and toss with the salad just before serving.

Green Salad (France)

A classic salad that goes well with anything.

2 c	romaine lettuce, washed, dried and torn into small pieces	500ml
1 c	spinach leaves, washed, dried and torn into small pieces	250ml
2 c	Boston bib lettuce, washed, dried and torn into small pieces	500ml

DRESSING ... 2 tbsp	chopped chives	30ml
1 tsp	fresh tarragon	5ml
3 tbsp	olive oil	45ml
1 tbsp	red wine vinegar	15ml
1/2 tsp	Dijon mustard	2ml
	sea salt and pepper to taste	
	dash of vegetarian Worcestershire sauce	
	cubed Brie cheese (optional)	

☛ Whisk the ingredients, except the cheese, well. Mix in the Brie and toss with the greens. Serve right away.

Spinach Salad (Morocco)

Very North African—fruit always seems to find its way in.

5 c	spinach leaves, washed, dried and torn into bite-size pieces	1.25 litres
10 oz	can mandarin orange pieces, drained, and the juice retained	310ml
1/4 c	chopped dried apricots	60ml
3	scallions, chopped	3
1/4 c	chickpeas, cooked	60ml
1/2	orange, chopped	1/2

DRESSING ...	1 tbsp	vegetable oil	15ml
	1/4	of the juice drained from the mandarin oranges	1/4
	1 tsp	red wine vinegar	5ml
		pepper to taste	

☞ Whisk the dressing well and toss with salad ingredients in a bowl. Serve right away.

Mandarin Orange Salad (North America)

A delicious fruity salad. Great for entertaining. It's a favourite in my house.

1	head of romaine lettuce, torn into bite-size pieces	1
10 oz	can mandarin orange pieces, drained, and the juice retained	310ml
3 tbsp	slivered almonds	45ml

☞ Mix everything well and serve, if desired, on lettuce leaves.

DRESSING ...	1 tbsp	vegetable oil	15ml
	1/4	of the juice drained from the mandarin oranges	1/4
	1 tsp	red wine vinegar	5ml
		pepper to taste	

☞ Place the lettuce in a bowl. Cover the lettuce with the drained mandarins and the almonds. Whisk the dressing well and pour over the salad. Serve.

Asian White Bean Salad (Africa)

A tangy salad that's colourful, especially if you use the red pepper.

19 fl oz	cooked white kidney beans, or use canned, drained and rinsed	540 ml	👉 Mix ingredients well and allow the flavours to blend in the fridge for an hour or so before serving.
2 tbsp	soy sauce	30ml	
1/2 tsp	honey	2ml	
1/8 tsp	grated fresh ginger	1/2ml	
	dash of chilli flakes		
	dash of cayenne powder		
1/2 tsp	red wine vinegar	2ml	
1 tbsp	sesame oil	15ml	
4	chopped scallions	4	
1 tbsp	chopped chives	15ml	
1/2 c	very young snow peas, cut in thirds	125ml	
	a little red pepper, chopped (optional)		
	or		
	a few mushrooms, sliced (optional)		

Bean Salad (North America)

Delicious with any soup or stew.

1 c	cooked red kidney beans	250ml	👉 Mix ingredients well and chill in individual bowls, or on a bed of lettuce. Serve.
1 c	cooked chickpeas, or Romano beans	250ml	
1 c	cooked green lentils	250ml	
1 1/2 c	chopped green beans	375ml	
2–3	scallions, thinly sliced	2–3	
1–2	cloves garlic, minced	1–2	
2 tbsp	chopped fresh chives	30ml	
3 tbsp	slivered red onion	45ml	
5 tbsp	olive oil	75ml	
2 1/2 tbsp	red wine vinegar	37ml	
1 1/4 tsp	Dijon mustard	6ml	
	sea salt and pepper to taste		
3	dashes of vegetarian Worcestershire sauce	3	

Orange Couscous Salad (Africa)

The oranges, pomegranate and radishes contrast with the nutty-tasting couscous. A filling, fragrant salad that's just a wee bit exotic. It's a full meal.

1 tbsp	olive oil	15ml
1	medium onion, chopped	1
1	tomato, chopped	1
1 tsp	cumin powder	5ml
1 tsp	coriander powder	5ml
19 fl oz	cooked chickpeas, or use canned, drained and rinsed	540 ml
1	zucchini, chopped	1
2 1/2 c	raw couscous	625ml
	or	
3 c	couscous, cooked	750ml
	salt and pepper to taste	
4 tbsp	olive oil	60ml
4 tbsp	lemon juice	60ml
2	oranges, peeled and sectioned, then cut in twos	2
5	radishes, sliced	5
1/4 c	orange juice	60ml
1	pomegranate, just the seeds	1

☞ In the 1 tbsp of oil, on medium-low heat, sauté the onion until it's translucent. Add the tomato, cumin, coriander and chickpeas, and cook 3 minutes. Add the zucchini and cook 2 minutes. Cool. Meanwhile, place the raw couscous in a bowl and add boiling, salted water to it 3 times, a little at a time, rubbing with the fingers to help the couscous absorb the water. Then place the couscous in a steamer, lined on the bottom with a muslin cloth, and steam, covered, until the couscous is soft, about 10 minutes. Fluff with a fork. Then mix everything together. Chill for 1/2 hour and serve.

Rice Salad (Mediterranean)

Great for picnics. The first time I had this was at an open-air theatre watching a play. I found myself wishing I had brought twice as much. The fresh air always makes me hungry!

2 1/2 c	cooked brown rice	600ml
	sea salt and pepper to taste	
1 3/4 c	sliced mushrooms, lightly sautéed in oil	420ml
2	cloves garlic, minced	2
5 tbsp	olive oil	75ml
2 tbsp	red wine vinegar	30ml
6	scallions, chopped	6
1/4 tsp	mustard powder	1ml
	chopped fresh chives to taste	
1 tbsp	chopped fresh parsley	15ml
	a few pickled artichoke hearts, chopped (optional)	

☞ Mix ingredients well and marinade for about an hour before serving.

Wild Rice Salad (Middle East)

Filling and similar to Middle Eastern tabbouleh.

3 c	cooked brown rice	750ml
1/2 c	cooked wild rice	125ml
5	large cloves garlic, minced	5
6	scallions, chopped	6
2 c	fresh parsley, finely chopped	500ml
1	large tomato, finely chopped	1
	sea salt and pepper to taste	
3 tbsp	olive oil	45ml
3 1/2 tbsp	lemon juice	52ml
1/2	English cucumber, skin on, cut in quarters lengthwise, then sliced (optional)	1/2

☞ Mix well, chill for 1 hour then serve at room temperature.

Rice Salad (Morocco)

There's that fruit again. A filling and nutritious salad.

3 c	cooked brown rice	750ml
1/2 c	cooked wild rice	125ml
1/4 c	chopped dates	60ml
3 tbsp	olive oil	45ml
2 tbsp	lemon juice	30ml
2	carrots, julienned	2
1/4 c	raisins	60ml
1/4 c	chopped nuts: either walnut, cashew, pecan, or a little of each	60ml
1/4 c	roasted sunflower seeds	60ml

☞ Mix all the ingredients together except the nuts and seeds and chill. Add the nuts and seeds before serving.

Tomato and Currant Salad (North America)

An unusual, tangy salad. I like the different look of a stuffed tomato salad.

2	large tomatoes	2
1/4 c	red currants, fresh	60ml
	sea salt and pepper to taste	
2 tbsp	chopped fresh chives, or scallions, green part only	30ml
1 tbsp	lemon juice	15ml
2 tbsp	olive oil	30ml

☞ Cut the tops off the tomatoes and scoop out the insides. Chop the insides finely and add the remaining ingredients. Mix well and place back inside the tomatoes, mounding them up a little. Serve.

Pasta Salad (Italy)

A healthy salad, with plenty of good stuff in it. Serve it at your next buffet.

3–4 c	uncooked pasta, either penne or spirals	750–1000ml
	or	
4 c	stuffed cheese pasta—when cooked it should make 5 1/2 cups (1,375ml)	1000ml
3 tbsp	olive oil	45ml
1 tbsp	red wine vinegar	15ml
2 tbsp	Parmesan cheese, freshly grated	30ml
	sea salt and pepper to taste	
4	cloves garlic, minced	4
1/4 tsp	Dijon mustard (optional)	1ml
3 tbsp	fresh basil	45ml
2 tbsp	fresh or 2 tsp (10ml) dried oregano	30ml
1 1/2 tbsp	lemon juice	22ml
1	green pepper, chopped (optional)	1
1	red pepper—roasted if possible—and chopped	1
3/4 c	asparagus, chopped, and steamed for 3 minutes	185ml
1 1/4 c	chopped spinach	300ml
3–4 tbsp	pine nuts	45–60ml
2	large scallions, chopped	2
3/4 c	sliced mushrooms	185ml

☞ Cook the pasta in boiling water according to the instructions on the package. Mix the oil, vinegar, Parmesan cheese, salt and pepper to taste, garlic, mustard, basil, oregano and lemon juice together. Toss with the cooked pasta and remaining ingredients in a bowl. Chill briefly and serve.

Grated Carrot Salad (Greece)

A good dish to keep in mind when you want to add some colour to a meal or just want a little something to eat. There's lots of beta-carotene in this salad.

3–4	medium carrots, grated	3–4
1 1/2–2 tbsp	olive oil	22.5–30ml
1–1 1/2 tbsp	lemon juice	15–22ml
	salt and pepper to taste	

☞ In a bowl, mix everything together and allow flavours to blend for 1/2 hour or so before serving.

Tzatziki Pasta Salad (Mediterranean)

This is like tzatziki with a Greek salad thrown in. Serve with retsina.

2 c	penne noodles, cooked al dente	500ml	☞ Mix ingredients together and allow to blend for 10 to 15 minutes before serving.
4–5 tbsp	yoghurt	60–75ml	
5 inches	cucumber, grated	13cm	
4–5	cloves garlic, minced	4–5	
	sea salt and pepper to taste		
1/2	green pepper, chopped	1/2	
1/2	red pepper, chopped	1/2	
2 c	broccoli florets, chopped	500ml	
1 c	cauliflower florets, chopped	250ml	
2 c	mushrooms, sliced	500ml	
3–4 oz	feta cheese, crumbled	90–120g	
1/4 c	olives (optional)	60ml	

Vegetable, Seed and Feta Salad (Greece)

An unusual combination that works very well.

	1 1/2 c	chopped broccoli florets	375ml
	1 c	chopped cauliflower florets	250ml
	1 c	sliced mushrooms	250ml
	1/4 c	finely chopped red onion or scallion	60ml
	1/2 c	chopped green beans	125ml
DRESSING ...	3 tbsp	olive oil	34ml
	1 1/2 tbsp	lemon juice	22ml
		sea salt and pepper to taste	
	2 tbsp	fresh or 2 tsp (10ml) dried oregano	30ml

☞ Whisk the dressing well and toss with the salad ingredients.

Add:

4–6 oz	feta cheese, crumbled	90–120g
2 tbsp	roasted brown sesame seeds	30ml

☞ Toss and serve immediately.

Notes

The Vegetarian Passport Cookbook

Soups and Stews

Tips

- Always be sure to sauté onions until they are completely soft, translucent and have no sharp taste. Also, stir them constantly while they're cooking.
- With all soups, a certain amount of liquid may evaporate, so check the water level frequently, adding more liquid—water or stock—as necessary. Also, be sure to stir soups from time to time, and above all, taste as you go to see if they need a little of this or a little of that.
- I use butter or olive oil for sautéing in some of the soup recipes. If you are trying to cut down on fat you can sauté in a little water or broth instead, or half fat and half broth, in all of the recipes throughout this book. You can use olive oil, a monounsaturated fat, or a non-hydrogenated margarine, instead of butter if you are trying to avoid all animal products and trans-fats. Flax seed oil, a very healthy oil, used uncooked, can also be substituted, as long as it is not heated.
- For soup stock, either make your own or use healthy vegetable stock cubes. If you use homemade stock, you may need to add more salt to the recipe since I have used very little in the stock. For vegetarian chicken or vegetarian beef stock use cubed. See note on purée (pg. XXIII)

Basic Soup Stock

This recipe can be adapted to use whatever needs using up, and altered depending on what you want to use it for.

1–2	peeled, chopped medium onions	1–2
1–4	cloves garlic, peeled—this will make the stock stronger tasting (optional)	1–4
2	potatoes, roughly chopped	2
1	small zucchini, sliced (optional)	1
1 c	squash or yam, peeled and chopped—this will make it sweeter (optional)	250ml
1–2	stalks celery, chopped	1–2
2	carrots, roughly chopped	2
1 tsp	of fresh parsley, added near the end of cooking time (optional)	5ml
1/2 –1 inch	dried kombu—this has a strong taste and will make it saltier and taste a little like consommé, but it's loaded with minerals (optional)	1 1/2–3cm
1	dried bay leaf	1
	a good grinding of black pepper	
1	small apple, peeled seeded and chopped—this will make it sweeter (optional)	1
1/4 tsp	salt or more to taste	1ml
9–10 c	water	2–2 1/2 litres

* Put all ingredients in a large pot, cover, bring to a boil, then simmer for 45 minutes. Strain and discard the vegetables. The stock will last in the fridge, sealed, for about 3 days.

- If you want a sweeter stock, use apple, squash or yam.
- If you want a tomato stock, throw in a small amount of skinned tomato near the end of the cooking time, after the onion is cooked, and continue cooking until the tomato is done.
- For a more Italian flavour, throw in fresh herbs like basil, thyme (about 1 tbsp/15ml total) and dried oregano (1/2 to 1 tsp/2 to 5ml), near the end of cooking time.
- For an Asian flavour, add fresh ginger, shiitake mushrooms, scallions and tamari sauce (optional).
- For a dill-flavoured stock, throw in fresh dill, 1/4 cup (60ml) or more to taste, near the end of cooking time.
- Yellow split peas can also be added in for thicker stock. Use 1/4–1 cup (60–250ml).
- To make an onion stock, use four onions. I like to sauté them first in a little olive oil, then I make the stock as above.
- To make a mushroom stock, use 2–4 cups (500–1000ml) of sliced mushrooms. I also like to sauté the mushrooms in a little olive oil, and then make the stock as above.
- To make celery stock, use 4 stalks celery.

Basic Broth (North America)

Keep this one in mind when someone is sick and needs a little something to get their strength back. Makes an excellent soup stock.

2	potatoes, cut up, and peeled if desired	2
1 c	mushrooms, sliced	250ml
1	small zucchini, chopped up	1
1/2 c	yellow split peas	125ml
1	stalk celery, chopped	1
	some green beans, chopped (optional)	
	some carrots, chopped (optional)	
	some spinach	
	anything that needs using up (optional)	
	salt (optional)	

☛ Place all the vegetables in a pot, except the spinach if you're using it, cover with water and bring to boil. Then reduce heat and simmer, covered, until the vegetables are tender. Add the spinach near the end. Strain or purée. Keep in mind the balance of the broth when adding vegetables, i.e., carrots and squash will sweeten the sharp ones, like spinach. This will keep in the fridge for about three days.

Red Lentil Soup (Middle East)

Fast and easy and high in protein, too, especially if you serve it with a whole grain bread. Don't forget it at your next Middle Eastern feast or when you have very little time but need something warm and filling.

1 tbsp	butter or olive oil	15ml
2	large onions, chopped	2
4	cloves garlic, minced	4
1 1/4 c	red lentils	280ml
5 1/2–7 c	vegetable stock, enough to cover	1375–1750ml
1 c	chopped tomatoes	250ml
1 1/2 tsp	cumin	7ml
1 tsp	dried sumac herb (optional)	5ml
	pepper and sea salt to taste	
1 tbsp	fresh parsley	15ml
1 tsp	butter	5ml

☛ Place the butter/oil and onions in a pot and sauté on medium heat until tender. Add the garlic and the lentils and cook 2 minutes while stirring. Add vegetable stock, bring to a boil and then simmer 10 minutes. Add remaining ingredients, except parsley and butter. Bring to a boil again and then simmer 20 to 25 minutes. Add the parsley in the last few minutes. Check water level and add more if necessary. Purée. Add butter and melt. Serve.

Peruvian Soup (Peru)

I was surprised when in Peru to find that a soup provided a totally different experience. It was a whole meal in the bowl, with all kinds of big pieces of delicious foods just thrown in. Very good and very filling.

6 c	well-flavoured vegetable stock	1.5 litres
1 c	finely chopped green beans	250ml
1	carrot, diced	1
1	celery stalk, diced	1
2–3	kinds of potatoes diced	2-3
1 c	cooked lima beans	250ml
2 c	greens like spinach or chard or other green	500ml
	pepper, salt to taste	
1	cob of corn, cut up	1
1 c	cut up pumpkin with the skin left on	250ml

☛ Place everything, except the greens, into a large soup pot, cover, boil and then simmer on medium low until everything is tender, about 45 minutes to an hour. Add the greens and cook a few more minutes. Serve hot.

Green Pea Soup (Eastern Europe)

This soup is loaded with flavour. I'm not a huge fan of the green split pea, but I like this one. Hearty and filling, all you need with this soup is good bread, like dark rye or water-bread, and a salad.

1 tbsp	butter	15ml
2	large onions, chopped	2
2–3	cloves garlic, minced	2–3
2	carrots, chopped	2
2–3	stalks celery, chopped	2–3
2	potatoes, chopped	2
1 1/2 c	green split peas	375ml
	vegetable stock to cover	
1	bay leaf	1
	pepper to taste	
1 tbsp	fresh parsley	15ml
1 tsp	butter	5ml
	sea salt to taste	
1/2 c	very finely chopped celery, or green beans or both	125ml
1 tsp	fresh dill (optional)	5ml

☛ Sauté the onion in the butter until translucent. Add vegetables and sauté 2 to 3 minutes on medium heat, stirring. Add split peas, vegetable stock, bay leaf and pepper. Bring to a boil and then simmer until vegetables are tender. Check water level and add more if necessary. Continue stirring as soup cooks. Remove the bay leaf. Purée and add the remaining ingredients. Simmer 5 minutes more. Serve hot.

Chickpea Soup (Spain)

When I was in Spain, I looked in every restaurant for this soup. But it was the wrong season. They only make this soup when the chickpeas are in season and fresh, which is what Mediterranean cooking is all about.

3 tbsp	olive oil	45ml
2	medium onions, finely chopped	2
1	large carrot, chopped	1
2 1/2 c	chickpeas, cooked	625ml
approx. 2–3 c	vegetable stock to cover	500–750ml
	pepper and salt to taste	
1	bay leaf	1
1 1/2–2 tbsp	butter	22–30ml
3–4 tbsp	lemon juice, to taste	45–60ml

☞ Put the oil and the onions in a medium pot and sauté on low heat, stirring, until very well done. Add the carrot and the chickpeas and sauté 2 minutes, stirring.

Add stock and bring to a boil. Add the seasoning and simmer on low heat, checking the water and stirring occasionally. When the vegetables are tender, approximately 35 minutes, remove the bay leaf. Purée. Add butter and lemon juice and heat through. Serve hot. This soup goes very well with stuffed peppers, Spanish Salad and Chocolate-Orange Mousse or Sabra Squares for dessert.

Red Pepper and Chickpea Soup (North America)

A fragrant and unusual tasting soup, especially if you add the tarragon.

1 tbsp	butter	15ml
1	medium onion, chopped	1
2	carrots, chopped	2
1	red pepper, chopped	1
4 c	vegetable broth	1 litre
19 fl oz	cooked chickpeas, or use canned chickpeas, drained and rinsed	540ml
	salt and pepper to taste	
1/4 tsp	cayenne powder	1ml
2 tbsp	lemon juice	30ml
1	tomato, diced	1
1	small pinch of chopped fresh or dried tarragon, to taste (optional)	1

☞ Place the butter and the onions in a soup pot and sauté on low heat, stirring, until tender. Add the carrots and the red pepper and sauté 2 minutes. Add the stock and bring to a boil. Reduce heat to low and keep covered, stirring and checking the stock level as it cooks. Add the remaining ingredients and simmer until tender, approximately 10 to 15 minutes. Purée and check seasonings, adding more lemon if desired. Add the tarragon right at the end and heat. Serve hot.

Chinese Soup with Noodles (Asia)

A whole meal in a bowl. Filling and fun to eat, full of contrasting colours and textures.

1 tbsp	toasted sesame oil	15ml
1 1/2 c	button or shiitake mushrooms (or both), sliced	375ml
2	cloves garlic, minced	2
5 c	vegetarian chicken (use cubed) or vegetable stock	1250ml
1	can water chestnuts, drained	1
1 1/2–2 c	very thin Chinese noodles, cooked and sautéed briefly in 1/2 tsp (2ml) sesame oil	375–500ml
1 c	mung bean sprouts	250ml
1 c	bamboo shoots	250ml
1 c	green peas	250ml
3	scallions, chopped	3
3 tbsp	soy sauce	45ml
1/4 tsp	fresh or	1ml
1/8 tsp	dried ginger	1/2ml
	dash of cayenne powder	
1 c	cubed lightly fried tofu (optional)	250ml
	a little sea salt (optional)	
1 c	freshly chopped spinach, or snow peas (optional)	250ml

☛ In a soup pot, put the oil, mushrooms and garlic. Sauté 2 minutes on medium low heat. Add stock, water chestnuts, noodles, bamboo shoots, scallions, spices and seasonings. Bring to a boil, stirring, then simmer for 5 to 10 minutes. Add the remaining ingredients and simmer for 3 minutes. If using spinach, put this in at the last minute. Serve hot.

Cauliflower Soup (North America)

A pale white soup with just a pinch of paprika over it. Keep this one in mind when you're serving pasta and need a light soup to go with it.

2 tbsp	butter	30ml
3	medium onions, chopped	3
4	large cloves garlic, minced	4
3 1/2 c	cauliflower	875ml
2–3 c	vegetable stock	500–750ml
1 c	milk or soy milk	250ml
	salt and pepper to taste	
1/4 tsp	paprika powder	1ml
1/4 c	cauliflower chopped into small pieces (optional)	60ml

☛ Put the butter and the onions in a soup pot and sauté on medium heat until very tender. Add the garlic and the cauliflower and sauté 2 minutes. Add stock and bring to a boil, stirring. Reduce heat and simmer until tender, stirring occasionally and checking the water level. Purée and add the remaining ingredients. Heat through and serve hot. Sprinkle with extra paprika.

Spicy Noodle Soup (Asia)

Spicy and delicious. A meal in a bowl.

7 c	vegetarian chicken stock (use cubed) 1.75 litres	
1	chopped leek, green part only	1
2	scallions, chopped	2
2 c	mushrooms, chopped	500ml
1/4 c	tofu, cubed	60ml
1/4 c	dried adzuki beans	60ml
2	dashes of powdered ginger	2
1	dash of cayenne powder, or more if desired	1
1 1/2 tbsp	Szechwan sauce, available in food stores and some grocery stores	22ml
1	stalk celery, chopped	1
	pepper and sea salt to taste	
1 tbsp	sesame oil	15ml
1 c	very thin rice noodles	250ml
1 c	frozen peas	250ml

☛ In a soup pot, put the stock, leeks, scallions, mushrooms, tofu, adzuki beans, ginger, cayenne, Szechwan sauce, celery, salt and pepper to taste, sesame oil and rice noodles. Bring to a boil, then reduce heat and simmer, partially covered, stirring occasionally, until tender, about 30 to 40 minutes. Add peas and heat through. Serve hot.

Broccoli and Herb Soup (North Africa)

I love dill, so this one's a winner with me.

1 tbsp	olive oil	15ml
2	small onions, chopped	2
1/2 c	white wine (optional)	125ml
2	cloves garlic, minced	2
3 c	broccoli, stalk and florets	750ml
3–4 c	vegetarian chicken stock (use cubed), or vegetable stock, enough to cover the vegetables	185ml
4–5 tbsp	fresh or 4–5 tsp (20–25ml) dried dill	60–75ml
1 tsp	fresh parsley	5ml
	salt and pepper to taste	
2 tbsp	butter	30ml
1 c	soy milk, milk or light cream	250ml
1/2 c	finely chopped broccoli florets	125ml
3	scallions, green parts only, finely chopped	3
1/4 c	chopped red pepper (optional)	60ml

☛ Put the onions and oil in a pot and sauté on medium heat until tender. Add the wine if you're using it. Add the garlic, broccoli and stock, and bring to a boil, then simmer until tender. Purée and return to the pot. Add the remaining ingredients and simmer for a few more minutes. Serve.

For Cauliflower Soup: Omit broccoli and use cauliflower. Use 3 cups (750ml) of stock and omit dill. You can also sprinkle some grated Parmesan cheese on top at the end.

French Onion Soup (France)

It took me a while to get a well-flavoured broth for this one. The secret is in the sautéing of the onions. Make sure you do them slowly until they're completely golden and tender. Very filling and almost a whole meal in itself—just add a salad.

2 tbsp	butter	30ml
3–4	medium cooking onions, thinly sliced	3–4
1 tbsp	flour	15ml
4 c	vegetable stock, or cubed vegetarian beef stock	1 litre
	salt and pepper to taste	
1 tbsp	apricot brandy or other brandy or sherry	15ml
1 tbsp	Parmesan cheese, grated	15ml
	toasted French or whole wheat bread, broken into pieces	
1/4–1/2 c	half and half mixture of grated cheddar and mozzarella cheese	60–120ml
	Parmesan cheese for garnish	
	pepper to taste	

☞ In a saucepan or soup pot, melt the butter on low heat. Add the onions and cook very slowly, stirring constantly, until the onions are completely soft and tender (approx. 45 minutes). Add the flour and brown, stirring, for 2 minutes. Slowly add the stock, stirring to prevent lumps forming. Add the salt and pepper to taste and the brandy. Bring to a boil and then simmer for 25 to 30 minutes, stirring occasionally. Add 1 tbsp (15ml) grated Parmesan cheese. Ladle the soup into ovenproof bowls and cover each one with the broken bread and the cheddar-mozzarella cheese mixture. Sprinkle liberally with Parmesan cheese and lightly pepper each bowl. Toast in the oven at 350F/180C until cheese melts, about 10 minutes. Serve hot.

Mushroom Zucchini Soup (North America)

A light, silky soup. Unusual tasting, but very good.

3 1/2 c	vegetable broth	875ml
2	medium-large zucchini, sliced	2
1 tsp	fresh parsley	5ml
1 tbsp	fresh or 1 tsp (5ml) dried dill	15ml
3 c	mushrooms, sliced and sautéed in 1 tbsp (15ml) butter until tender	750ml
	salt and pepper to taste	
1 tsp	butter	5ml
1/4 tsp	paprika powder	1ml

☞ Place all ingredients, except fresh herbs and mushrooms, in a soup pot and bring to a boil. Then simmer until vegetables are tender, on low heat for about 20 to 30 minutes. Purée, add mushrooms and fresh herbs, and heat a few minutes. Serve hot.

Potato, Leek and Chive Soup (North Africa)

A rich, onion-flavoured, classic soup. You can serve it hot or cold.

2 tbsp	butter	30ml
2 c	leeks, carefully washed and chopped, white part only	500ml
1	small onion, chopped	1
2	large cloves garlic, minced	2
2 1/2	cubed peeled potatoes	2 1/2
approx. 3–3 1/2 c	stock or vegetarian chicken stock (used cubed) to cover	approx. 750–875ml
1/4 c	white wine	60ml
1/4 c	soy milk or milk	60ml
2–3 tbsp	chopped fresh chives	30–45ml
	pepper and salt to taste	
1 1/4 tsp	dried oregano	6ml
	dash of cayenne powder	
1 tsp	butter	5ml
	chopped roasted red pepper, for garnish (optional—see right)	

☞ In a soup pot, on medium heat, put the butter, leeks, onion, and garlic. Sauté until very tender. Add potatoes and stock and bring to a boil, stirring. Then simmer, partially covered, until potatoes are tender, checking water level. Purée. Add the wine and the soy milk, adding more if the soup seems too thick, less if it's too thin. Add the remaining ingredients and simmer for a few minutes. Serve hot or cold.

For roasted pepper hold the pepper with a long fork (wear gloves) over the gas element of your stove or barbecue and blacken, turning. Place in a brown paper bag to cool. Peel off skin and it's ready to use.

Potato, Cauliflower Soup (North America)

Warming, thick and delicious. The soy milk adds a nice touch of sweetness.

1 tbsp	butter	15ml
1	large onion, chopped	1
2	medium potatoes, peeled and chopped	2
3 c	cauliflower, chopped	750ml
	stock or cubed vegetarian chicken stock to cover	
	pepper to taste	
1 tsp	butter	5ml
1/4 c	soy milk	60ml
1/2 c	very finely chopped cauliflower	125ml

☞ Place the butter and the onion in a soup pot, and sauté, stirring, until tender. Add the potato and the cauliflower and sauté for a few more minutes. Add the stock and bring to a boil and then reduce the heat. Simmer until vegetables are tender, about 20 to 25 minutes, and then purée. Add the remaining ingredients and heat for a few more minutes. Serve hot.

Pumpkin Soup/Pepper Squash Soup (Caribbean)

Delicious. A favourite of mine and even of people who don't like pumpkin. The soy milk adds a nice sweetness.

3 tsp	butter	45ml
2	large onions, chopped	2
2	cloves garlic, minced	2
2	potatoes, peeled and cut up	2
2 1/2–3 c	pumpkin or pepper squash, peeled and cut into cubes	625–750ml
approx. 5 c	vegetable stock, enough to cover	approx. 1250ml
1 tbsp	butter	15ml
	pepper and salt to taste	
1/4–1/2 c	soy milk	60–125ml

☛ Put the butter and the onions in a soup pot. Sauté, while stirring, on medium heat until completely soft and tender with no sharp taste. Add the garlic and the potatoes, and sauté 1 minute, stirring. Add the squash, and sauté 2 minutes, stirring. Add stock and bring to a boil, and then simmer, partially covered, until vegetables are tender, about 30 minutes. Stir occasionally and check water level, adding more stock if necessary. Purée. Add remaining ingredients and heat through. Serve hot. This soup is very good served with the Caribbean rice and bean dish (pg. 99).

Chilled Cucumber Soup (Morocco)

An excellent, light, chilled soup. I first had this soup in a Moroccan restaurant and I loved it. It took me a while to figure out how to make it. I don't know how traditional my version is, but it tastes a lot like the one I ate in Morocco.

2–3 tbsp	olive oil	30–45ml
1	cucumber, peeled and diced	1
4 tsp	lemon juice	20ml
1/2 c	white wine	125ml
2	lettuce leaves (leaf lettuce)	2
1/4–1/2 tsp	ground cumin powder	1–2ml
	sea salt to taste	
1 c	water	250ml
2 tsp	lemon juice	10ml
1 tsp	olive oil	5ml
1/4 tsp	white sugar	1ml

☛ Put the olive oil and the cucumber in a soup pot and sauté, stirring, for 5 minutes. Add the lemon juice, wine, lettuce, cumin, sea salt and water and bring to a boil, stirring. Then simmer gently for 15 minutes. Remove lettuce leaves and purée the soup until smooth. Add the remaining ingredients and mix well. Chill and serve with Moroccan fried eggplant and couscous for a traditional Moroccan meal.

Gazpacho (Spain)

My first experience with this soup was in Ubeda, Spain. The day was hot and sunny and the soup—almost a drink—was cool and refreshing. Perfect. Keep it in mind for hot days, and if you can, eat outside in the garden. It'll seem even better in the sunshine.

1	medium onion, chopped and sautéed in 1 tsp (5ml) of oil until tender (optional)	1
2	cloves garlic, minced	2
1	green pepper, chopped, removing all white parts	1
5	tomatoes, preferably peeled, and chopped	5
1/2	medium cucumber, chopped	1/2
2	scallions, chopped	2
1 c	tomato juice	250ml
1 tsp	red wine vinegar	5ml
3–4 tbsp	lemon juice	45–60ml
2 tbsp	olive oil	30ml
1 tsp	dried oregano (optional)	5ml
	salt and pepper to taste	
5 tsp	each of finely chopped cucumber, tomato, scallion, and green pepper, for garnish	25ml

☛ Place all the ingredients, except the finely chopped vegetables for garnish, in a blender or food processor and blend until desired consistency is reached. Add the seasonings. I like it lemony, so you may not want as much lemon as I use here. Mix well and add the garnishes. Serve chilled. Some people add crunchy French bread cut in cubes when serving.

Cool Yoghurt and Cucumber Soup (Middle East)

Even if you don't like yoghurt, try this one. My husband claims to hate yoghurt but he loves this dish, although it took me a while to coax him to try it. Now he frequently asks me to make it.

1 c	light yoghurt	250ml
1	cucumber, chopped finely	1
	sea salt and pepper to taste	
1 1/2 tbsp	fresh or 1 1/2 tsp (7ml) dried dill	22ml
1 tbsp	fresh parsley	15ml
1 1/4 tsp	fresh or 1/2 tsp (2ml) dried mint	6ml
1/2	green pepper, chopped (optional)	1/2

☛ Mix ingredients together and serve chilled.

Minestrone Soup (Italy)

This soup is perfect because you can do almost anything with it. Just keep a basic background of tomatoes and put in almost anything you have around—that you can eat, that is!

1 tbsp	oil	15ml
2	medium onions, chopped	2
3	cloves garlic, minced	3
1	carrot, chopped	1
2	stalks celery, chopped	2
1–2	small potatoes, finely chopped	1–2
1 c	mushrooms, sliced	250ml
	water to cover	
15 fl oz	fresh cooked peeled tomatoes (see pg. 24) or canned tomatoes, chopped, or	450ml
1	can tomato paste	1
	salt and pepper to taste	
1–2 tsp	fresh basil or dried oregano	5–10ml
1/2 c	broccoli or cauliflower or both	125ml
1/2 c	corn	125ml
1/2 c	peas	125ml
1 c	cooked spaghetti noodles, or other grain	250ml
1 c	cooked kidney beans, or other bean	250ml
1/2 c	chopped green beans, or green, red or yellow peppers (optional)	125ml

☛ Put the oil and the onions in a soup pot and sauté on medium heat until tender. Add the garlic, carrot, celery, potato and mushrooms and sauté for a few minutes. (The longer-cooking vegetables should always be added near the beginning of the cooking time.) Cover with water and bring to a boil, then simmer for 10 minutes. Add the tomatoes and seasoning, except fresh herbs, and simmer until tender. Add the remaining ingredients and simmer until all the vegetables are tender, about 5 minutes. Stir occasionally and check water level, adding more if necessary. Serve hot.

Zucchini Soup (Italy)

A perfect silky and heavenly soup. Great for entertaining. Its pale green colour looks beautiful, like spring. It's not too filling so you can serve other delightful courses with it.

4 c	vegetarian chicken stock (use cubed)	1 litre
	pinch of salt and pepper to taste	
4	small to medium zucchini, chopped roughly	4
1 tsp	dried dill	5ml
1/2 tsp	butter	2ml
1 1/2 tbsp	fresh or 1 1/2 tsp (7ml) dried dill	22ml
2 tsp	butter	10ml

☛ In a soup pot, place the stock, salt, pepper, zucchini, dried dill and butter. Bring to a boil and then simmer until tender, about 20 minutes. Purée and add the rest of the dill and butter. Heat a few minutes and serve hot. The texture should be silky.

Tomato, Vegetable Soup (North America)

A quick and easy well-flavoured soup. Makes a nice change from canned tomato soup.

1 tbsp	olive oil	15ml
1	medium onion, chopped	1
1	tomato, chopped	1
1	stalk celery, chopped	1
1	carrot, chopped	1
1/2 c	cabbage or lettuce, chopped	125ml
1	scallion, chopped	1
1	clove garlic, minced	1
1/4 c	green beans, finely chopped	60ml
1 c	vegetable broth	250ml
3 c	tomato juice	750ml
1 tsp	soy sauce (optional)	5ml
	pepper to taste	
1 c	cooked pasta or rice— kitharaki noodles are nice	250ml
1/4 c	corn or cooked baby lima beans (optional)	60ml
2 tsp	dried oregano or 1 tbsp (15ml) fresh basil (optional)	10ml
1/2 tsp	vegetarian Worcestershire sauce	2ml

☛ Put the olive oil and onion in a soup pot and sauté on medium low heat until tender. Add the tomato, celery, carrot, cabbage, scallions, garlic and green beans. Sauté for a few minutes, stirring. Add the rest of the ingredients, except the cabbage or lettuce, and the corn and fresh basil if you are using them. Bring to a boil, then simmer, covered, stirring occasionally, for about 45 minutes to 1 hour or until vegetables are tender. Add the corn, basil and the lettuce or cabbage, and heat through for a few minutes. Serve hot.

Broccoli, Zucchini, Celery and Chickpea Soup (North America)

Unusual and very good. Healthy, too. The chickpeas give it an earthy flavour.

4 c	strong vegetable broth	1 litre
1/8 tsp	pepper	1/2ml
2 c	broccoli, stalks and florets, chopped	500ml
1	medium zucchini, chopped	1
1	stalk celery, chopped	1
1 c	chickpeas, cooked	250ml
3 1/2 tbsp	lemon juice	52ml
1 tbsp	olive oil	15ml
1/8 tsp	sea salt	1/2ml

☛ Place the stock and all the vegetables, including the chickpeas, in a soup pot and bring to a boil, then simmer, stirring, until tender. Keep partially covered. Purée and add the remaining ingredients. Heat and serve hot.

Cabbage, Vegetable Soup (North America)

Excellent. This was one of my grandmother's most favourite soups. It was good and hearty and well flavoured. It reminded her of her Russian mother's cabbage soup. This 92-pound woman could eat seconds and sometimes even thirds—and that was before the potato latkes that were traditionally served after the soup!

2 tbsp	olive oil	30ml
3	large onions, chopped	3
4	stalks celery, chopped	4
2	carrots, chopped	2
1	green or red pepper, chopped	1
1	small green cabbage, chopped	1
	water to cover	
5 c	canned tomatoes and liquid, chopped, or use fresh peeled and cooked (see pg. 24)	1.25 litres
2	envelopes powdered onion soup mix—slightly less than enough for the amount of water you added	2
1 tsp	vegetable stock powder	5ml
	salt and pepper to taste	
4–5 tbsp	soy sauce	60–75ml
1 tsp	fresh parsley	5ml
1 tbsp	fresh or 1 tsp (5ml) dried thyme	15ml

☞ Put the oil and the onions in a large Dutch oven. Sauté on medium-low heat until tender. Add vegetables and sauté for a few more minutes, stirring frequently. Add remaining ingredients, except fresh herbs and bring to a boil, stirring. Then reduce heat to low and simmer for 1 hour, or until the vegetables are tender, stirring occasionally. Check the water level as you go. Add the fresh herbs at the end of cooking. Serve hot. This recipe makes a lot, but it freezes well for next time.

Tomato, Rice Soup (North America)

A rich red soup. Filling, too.

2 tbsp	olive oil	30ml
2	medium onions, chopped	2
4	cloves garlic, minced	4
1	red pepper, finely chopped	1
4–5	tomatoes, preferably peeled, and chopped	4–5
	salt and pepper to taste	
	water or vegetable broth to cover	
2 tbsp	olive oil	30ml
1 1/2 c	cooked brown rice	375ml
	handful of cooked wild rice	
	freshly chopped basil	

☞ Put the oil and the onions in a soup pot, on medium heat, and sauté until very tender. Add the garlic, red pepper, tomatoes, salt and pepper to taste. Sauté for a few minutes. Add water or stock and bring to a boil, then simmer, covered and stirring occasionally, until vegetables are tender. It should take about 25 minutes. Add olive oil and purée. Add remaining ingredients and heat through for 5 minutes. Serve hot.

Mushroom Soup (France)

My husband's favourite soup, and he always insisted he didn't like mushrooms or cream soups. This one looks fancy and is great for company. It's a bit tricky to make, but that's where the strainer comes in—if you make mistakes you can strain them out.

1	large package of powdered onion soup mix	1
1 tbsp	butter	15ml
1	medium onion, chopped	1
20	large mushrooms, chopped	20
1 tbsp	margarine or butter	15ml
1 tbsp	flour	15ml
1/2 c	milk or soy milk	125ml
1 tbsp	butter	15ml
1/4 c	grated Parmesan cheese	60ml
	pepper to taste	
1 tbsp	fresh or 1 tsp (5ml) dried thyme (optional)	15ml

☛ Make the soup mix as directed on the package. In another pan, sauté the onion in 1 tbsp (15ml) butter until tender. Add the mushrooms and sauté until tender. Then add onions and mushrooms to the soup mix. In another pot, melt the 1 tbsp (15ml) margarine or butter, add the flour and brown it, stirring on low heat for 1 minute. Slowly add the milk, stirring to prevent lumps forming. Mix until smooth and thick. Pour slowly into the soup mixture through a fine mesh strainer to get rid of any lumps. Simmer for 2 minutes. Add remaining ingredients and heat though. Serve.

Barley Soup (Eastern Europe)

Another satisfying soup from Eastern Europe. They know how to make a meal out of soup, although they often eat soup as a first course, followed by a lot of other heavy food. I prefer this soup with just salad and bread. I love barley and the silky, slippery feel it has in the mouth.

1 tbsp	olive oil	15ml
1	medium onion, chopped	1
2	carrots, finely chopped	2
2	stalks celery, chopped	2
1	potato, cubed	1
1/2 c	cabbage, finely chopped	125ml
9 c	mushroom or onion stock	2250ml
1 1/2 c	pearl barley	375ml
2 tbsp	soy sauce (optional)	30ml
	sea salt and pepper to taste	
	serve with grated Parmesan cheese (optional)	

☛ Put the oil and the onion in a large Dutch oven and sauté on low heat, stirring, until tender. Add the rest of the vegetables and sauté 2 minutes. Add the barley and the stock and bring to a boil. Reduce heat to low and simmer, partially covered, stirring, adding more stock if necessary. When the vegetables and barley are tender, about 1 hour, add the remaining ingredients and heat through. Serve hot.

Bean and Barley Soup (Eastern Europe)

Another hearty and flavourful soup from Eastern Europe.

3 tbsp	olive oil	45ml
1 tsp	butter	5ml
2	medium onions, chopped	2
2	medium carrots, chopped finely (optional)	2
3	stalks celery, chopped finely (optional)	3
2 c	mushrooms, chopped	500ml
1 1/4 c	dried navy beans	300ml
1 c	barley	250ml
8–10 c	well-flavoured stock, or onion or mushroom stock (add as much as needed)	2–2.5 litres
	salt and pepper to taste	
1 tsp	soy sauce (optional)	5ml

☛ In a soup pot, sauté the onions in the oil and butter, stirring on low heat until tender. Add the other vegetables and sauté for a few more minutes. Then add the beans, barley and stock and bring to a boil. Reduce the heat and simmer on low until tender, stirring occasionally and checking the liquid level. Keep it partially covered. It should be tender in about the 3 hours. Add the seasonings and serve hot.

Yellow Spilt Pea Soup (Eastern Europe)

My mom loves this one, and so does her friend who's from Hungary. He always told me that it reminded him of the soups he had back home. My mother even learned to make this one. A hearty, easy to make, all-purpose soup.

2 tbsp	olive oil	30ml
1	medium onion, chopped	1
1	large carrot, chopped	1
1	stalk celery, chopped	1
	or	
3/4 c	chopped green beans	185ml
1	large potato cubed, or 2–3 small	1
1	clove garlic, minced (optional)	1
1 1/2 c	yellow split peas	375ml
40–60 fl oz	vegetable stock, depending on how much boils away	1250–1875ml
3–4	bay leaves	3–4
	pepper to taste	
1–2 tbsp	butter or olive oil	15–30ml

☛ Put the oil and the onion in a soup pot, and sauté until tender. Add the vegetables and sauté for about 5 minutes on low heat, stirring. Add the split peas and sauté 2 minutes, stirring to coat with the oil. Add stock, starting with less and adding more if necessary, bay leaves and pepper. Bring to a boil and then reduce to low heat and simmer for 40 to 60 minutes, stirring occasionally. When the vegetables and split peas are tender, remove the bay leaves and purée. Add the butter and check the seasoning, adding more pepper and salt if necessary. Also, add more stock if it's too thick, or simmer longer if it's too thin. Serve hot.

Peasant Stew (Eastern Europe)

A rich-tasting, warming stew. Just serve with a salad.

4	potatoes, sliced	4
4	carrots, sliced	4
4	onions, sliced	4
2 1/2 c	canned mushrooms, drained or	600 ml
2 c	sliced fresh mushrooms	480ml
3 c	spaghetti sauce (see pg. 24), or use canned or bottled	720 ml
2	dried bay leaves	2
6 tbsp	olive oil	90ml
	salt and pepper to taste	
1 tbsp	paprika powder	15ml
1 tsp	soy sauce	5ml
1–1 1/2 c	water	250–375ml

☛ Layer the sliced vegetables in a large, greased, ovenproof dish in the order they are listed, starting with the potatoes. Pour the spaghetti sauce, seasonings and water over the top and cover. Bake at 350F (180C) for 1 1/2 to 2 hours or until the vegetables are tender. You may need to add a little water throughout the cooking if it gets too dry. Remove the bay leaves. Serve hot.

Spicy Stew (Cuba)

Fabulous. A thick, rich, heady broth and plenty filling, too.

2–3 tbsp	butter	30–45ml
2	large onions, chopped	2
3	cloves garlic, minced	3
3	small red potatoes, peeled and chopped	3
6–8 c	vegetable broth, or cubed vegetarian chicken broth: you may need to add more if it seems too thick	1.5–2 litres
1/2 c	dried black beans	125 ml
1 c	dried navy beans	250ml
3/4 c	barley	185ml
1/2 tsp	chilli powder	2ml
1 tsp	cumin powder	5ml
2	bay leaves	2
2	carrots, chopped in rounds	2
	salt and pepper to taste	
5 1/2 oz	can tomato paste	156ml
2–4 tbsp	soy sauce	30–60ml

☛ Put the butter and the onions in a soup pot and sauté until tender. Add the garlic and the potatoes and sauté for a few more minutes. Add the stock and bring to a boil. Add the black beans, navy beans, barley, chilli powder, cumin, bay leaves and carrots. Simmer until tender, stirring and adding more liquid if necessary. When everything is tender, about 2 1/2 to 3 hours, add the remaining ingredients and heat through. Remove the bay leaves. Serve hot.

Italian Bean Soup (Italy)

Another one of my husband's favourites. Mine too. I love the little Greek noodles that are like rice, and the mashed beans add the perfect texture. Filling and delicious—just add a salad and bread.

2 tbsp	olive oil	30ml
1	medium onion, chopped	1
1	shallot, finely chopped	1
2	cloves garlic, minced	2
4 c	vegetarian chicken stock, use cubed 1 litre	
19 fl oz	cooked Romano beans, or use canned beans, rinsed and drained— mash about 3/4 of the beans with a potato masher	540ml
	sea salt and pepper to taste	
1 1/2–2 c	cooked kitharaki pasta	375–500ml
1/8–1/4 c	Parmesan cheese	30–60ml
1 tbsp	fresh parsley	15ml

☛ In a soup pot, place the olive oil, onion and shallot and sauté on low heat until very tender. Add the garlic and sauté 1 minute. Add the stock and bring to a boil. Reduce heat and add the beans, salt and pepper to taste, and pasta. Simmer on low heat for 10 minutes, stirring. Add the cheese and parsley and ladle into bowls. Pass around freshly grated Parmesan cheese at the table and let everyone sprinkle as much as they want on the soup. I buy the kitharaki pasta in the Greek market, but you could use other small pasta if you can't find it.

Vegetarian Chicken Noodle Soup (North America)

A good one to keep in mind when you're under the weather. It soothes and nourishes when your stomach can't take too much. If you're really feeling terrible, leave out the onion and especially the cheese. And if you can't even handle that, just make a simple stock. Bring to a boil 4 cups (1 litre) of water and then simmer for 25 minutes with 1 chopped zucchini,1 potato, chopped, 1/4 cup (60ml) yellow split peas, and 1/4 cup (60ml) mushrooms, chopped. Strain and eat only the broth. You'll soon feel better.

4 c	vegetarian chicken stock, use cubed 1 litre	
1/4 tsp	kelp (optional)	1ml
1/4 tsp	pepper	1ml
1 tsp	olive oil	5ml
1	scallion, green part only, chopped	1
1/2 c	frozen green peas	125ml
1 c	cooked noodles, kitharaki or other	250ml
2 tbsp	fresh parsley	30ml
2 tbsp	grated Parmesan cheese (optional)	30ml

☛ In a soup pot, bring the stock to a boil and add the seasonings, except the parsley, and olive oil. Reduce heat and add the onions. Cook for 10 minutes. Add the peas, noodles, parsley and cheese and simmer for 4 minutes. Serve hot.

Portuguese Potato Soup (Portugal)

Everywhere I ate in Portugal there was a version of this soup. I fell in love with it, first because it tasted so good with their lighter cabbage and freshly grown beans, and second because it was hard to find vegetarian food. As soon as I came home, I experimented until I got it right. I recommend adding the finely chopped cabbage.

2 tbsp	olive oil	30ml
1	medium onion, chopped	1
3	large potatoes, peeled and chopped	3
2	medium-large carrots, chopped	2
1	stalk celery with the leaves, chopped	1
3/4–1 c	green beans, chopped	185–250ml
1/4–1/2 tsp	sea salt	1–2ml
	water to cover	
1/2 c	finely chopped green beans	125ml
1/2–1 c	finely chopped delicate cabbage (optional)	125–250ml

☛ Put the oil and the onion in a soup pot and sauté on low heat, stirring, until tender. Add the vegetables, except the finely chopped green beans and the cabbage, if you're using it, and sauté for a few more minutes, stirring. Add the salt to taste and water to cover. Bring to a boil, then reduce heat and simmer, stirring and checking water level for about 20 to 25 minutes. Purée and add the 1/2 cup (125ml) of finely chopped beans, and the cabbage. Simmer for 5 to 10 more minutes. Serve hot.

Broccoli, Potato, Dill Soup (North America)

An unusual version of broccoli soup. The dill and the scallions add an interesting twist.

1 tsp	butter	15ml
1	onion, chopped	1
1	very large potato, or 2 medium potatoes, chopped and peeled	1
2	broccoli stalks, flowers and leaves	2
approx. 3 c	stock or vegetarian chicken stock (use cubed)	approx. 750ml
	salt and pepper to taste	
2 tbsp	fresh dill	30ml
1 c	finely chopped broccoli flowers the tops only of 2 scallions, chopped	250ml
1 tsp	butter	5ml

☛ Put the butter and the onion in a soup pot and sauté until tender. Add the other vegetables, except the final cup of broccoli flowers. Sauté for a few minutes. Add the stock and the salt and pepper to taste. Bring to a boil and then reduce heat and simmer for about 15 to 20 minutes. When vegetables are tender, purée. Add the remaining ingredients and heat for about 5 minutes. Serve hot.

Thick and Rich Lentil Soup (North America)

A thick, rich and delicious version of lentil soup. Almost a stew. Smells great and tastes even better. A meal in itself—just add a salad and bread, or baked potato.

2 c	dried green lentils	500ml
6–8 c	water, start with less and add more if necessary	1.5–2 litres
1	medium onion, chopped	1
2 tbsp	olive oil	30ml
5–6	cloves garlic, minced	5–6
1	carrot, finely chopped	1
1	stalk celery, finely chopped	1
1/4–1/2 tsp	pepper	1–2ml
2 tbsp	red wine vinegar	30ml
2 tbsp	olive oil	30ml
1 1/4 c	well-flavoured spaghetti sauce (see pg. 24)	300ml
	or	
5 fl oz	chopped cooked tomatoes (see pg. 24)	150ml
	and	
6 fl oz	tomato sauce (see pg. 24)	185ml
1 tsp	garlic powder	5ml
1/2 tsp	onion powder	2ml
4 tbsp	soy sauce	60ml

☛ Put the lentils and the water in a pot and bring to a boil, then let simmer. Meanwhile, sauté the onion in the olive oil until tender. Add the garlic, carrot and celery and sauté for a few more minutes. Add vegetable mixture to the lentils and simmer for 55 minutes. Check the water level and stir occasionally. Add the remaining ingredients and simmer until everything is tender and hot, about 15 minutes. Serve hot.

Curried Lentil Soup (India)

A very good curried soup. Serve it on its own, with a salad and bread, or with other Indian dishes.

2 tbsp	olive oil	30ml
1	medium onion, chopped	1
5–6	cloves garlic, minced	5–6
2	carrots, chopped	2
1	potato, peeled and chopped	1
1 1/2 c	diced pepper squash	375ml
3/4 c	green beans, finely chopped	185ml
3 tsp	coriander powder	15ml
2 tsp	cumin powder	10ml

☛ Put the oil and the onion in a pot and sauté until tender. Add the other vegetables, except tomato, and sauté for a few minutes. Add the spices and the ghee or oil and sauté for a few more minutes. Add the lentils and the stock and bring to a boil.

1 tsp	turmeric powder	5ml
1 tsp	ghee or oil	5ml
1/4 tsp	dried ginger, or freshly grated ginger to taste	1ml
	pepper and sea salt to taste	
1 1/2 c	green lentils	375ml
5–6 c	water or onion broth (you can use cubed or fresh onion broth)	1250–1500ml
1	large tomato, chopped	1
4 tbsp	tomato paste	60ml

Reduce heat and simmer, stirring until tender, about 40 to 50 minutes, adding the tomato in the last 20 minutes. Check the water level as it cooks. Add the tomato paste, heat and serve hot.

Barley Lentil Soup (Eastern Europe)

I love to make use of barley, especially in soups, because I love its texture. This is another complete meal—just add a salad or some steamed vegetables.

1 tbsp	oil	15ml
1	carrot, chopped	1
2	stalks celery, chopped	2
1	potato, peeled and chopped	1
1 1/4 c	green lentils	300ml
7–8 1/2 c	stock, either vegetarian beef (use cubed), mushroom or onion. Start with less and add more if necessary: you may need even more than I've suggested if it seems too thick.	1750–2125ml
2	bay leaves	2
1-inch	stick of dried kombu, broken in pieces (optional)	3cm
3/4 c	barley	185ml
2–3 c	mushrooms, sliced	500–750ml
	sea salt and pepper to taste	
2–4 tbsp	soy sauce	30–60ml
2 tbsp	fresh or 3/4 tbsp (12ml) dried savoury tiny bit of freshly grated ginger (optional)	30ml

☛ Sauté the vegetables in the oil in a soup pot for a few minutes and then add everything else except the seasonings and bring to a boil. Reduce heat and simmer, stirring and checking the water level, for about 1 1/2 hours until everything is tender. Remove bay leaves and add the seasonings. Heat a few more minutes and serve.

Lentil Soup (Greece)

A delicious, not as thick version of lentil soup. We ate several versions of this soup all over Greece. I particularly remember two occasions—once at Olympia after a horrible rainstorm in the ruins, where we spent most of the day under a tree, waiting for the rain to stop. We were freezing and this soup felt great. The second time was in Cephalonia. The woman we were staying with asked us in for soup. Her son translated it as "some kind of little vegetables." I had four or five bowls and loved it. They use a lot more olive oil, so go ahead if you want to.

3 tbsp	olive oil	45ml
2	medium onions, chopped	2
4	large cloves garlic, minced	4
4	stalks celery with the leaves, finely chopped	4
1	carrot, finely chopped	1
1	medium potato, peeled and finely chopped	1
1	bay leaf	1
1 3/4 c	green lentils	420ml
6–7 c	water, check as you go and add more if necessary	1.5–1.75 litres
	sea salt and pepper to taste	
2 tbsp	olive oil	30ml
2 1/2 tsp	red wine vinegar	12ml
1 tsp	dried oregano	5ml
1 tbsp	fresh parsley	15ml

☞ Put the oil and the onion in a soup pot and sauté, stirring until tender. Add the garlic, celery, carrot and potato and sauté for 2 minutes. Add the bay leaf, lentils and water and bring to a boil. Reduce heat and simmer, stirring occasionally, until vegetables and lentils are tender, about 45 minutes. Add remaining ingredients and heat through. Remove bay leaf and serve hot. Goes very well with a Greek salad, spanakopita and baklava, if you can eat all that.

Spicy Baked Bean and Pasta Soup (North America)

A slightly different version of this soup. Thick, rich and delicious.

1–2 tbsp	olive oil	15–30ml
1	medium onion, chopped	1
3	cloves garlic, minced	3
1	green chilli, diced	1
4 1/2–5 c	water	1125–1250ml
14 oz	can baked beans	398 ml
1 1/2–2 c	cooked mini shell macaroni	375–500ml
	pepper and salt to taste	
1 1/2–2 tbsp	vegetarian Worcestershire sauce	22–30ml
2 tbsp	tomato paste	30ml
1 tbsp	fresh or 1 tsp (5ml) dried rosemary	15ml
1/2 c	corn (optional)	125ml

☞ Put the oil and the onions in a soup pot and sauté, stirring, until tender. Add the garlic and the chilli and sauté 1 minute. Add the water and bring to a boil. Reduce heat and add the remaining ingredients, except the corn and fresh rosemary if you are using it, and cook on low heat, stirring occasionally, for about 25 minutes. Add the corn and rosemary and heat through. Serve hot.

Lima Bean Soup (Eastern Europe)

I thought I hated lima beans until I tried a version of this soup in a Jewish dairy restaurant in Toronto. It was so good that I went right out and got some lima beans and started experimenting. This is my version, and it passed with my mother's approval. She grew up in a Jewish household with a grandmother from Russia who made lima bean soup. Incidentally, my great-grandmother lived to be 101 years old. Perhaps it was the soups …

2 tbsp	oil	30ml
1	medium onion, chopped	1
2 c	finely chopped celery	500ml
1–2	small potatoes, chopped and peeled	1–2
3/4 c	dried lima beans	185ml
1/2 c	dried navy beans	125ml
1/2 c	barley	125ml
8–10 c	stock or cubed vegetarian chicken stock or celery stock—start with less and add more if it gets too thick	2–2.5 litres
	salt and pepper to taste	
3/4 c	fresh dill, or 3 tsp (15ml) dried	185ml

☞ Place the oil and the onion in a soup pot and sauté over medium heat until tender. Add the celery, potato, beans and barley and sauté, stirring, for a few more minutes. Add the stock and bring to a boil, then reduce heat and simmer, checking water level and stirring occasionally until tender, about 2 1/2 hours. Add the seasonings and fresh dill and heat for a few more minutes. Purée about 1/4 of the soup and pour it back into the pot. Heat through and serve hot. This soup is much better with fresh dill.

Greek White Bean Soup (Greece)

I love Greece and anything to do with it. In Greece they would use large white beans for this soup, but as they are sometimes hard to get here, I use navy beans. Check out the Greek markets; you might find the large white beans.

approx. 8 c	water	approx. 2 litres
2 c	uncooked white beans	500ml
2–3	carrots, diced	2–3
4	stalks celery, diced	4
3	medium onions, chopped	3
	pepper and salt to taste	
2 1/2 tbsp	tomato paste	37ml
2	cloves garlic, minced	2
1/4 c	olive oil	60ml
1 tbsp	fresh parsley	15ml
1 tbsp	red wine vinegar	15ml

☞ Place the water and the beans in a pot and bring to a boil, then simmer for 2 1/2 hours, stirring and checking the water level. Place the rest of the ingredients in the pot, except the vinegar and parsley, and bring to a boil, stirring. Simmer until tender, about 1 hour, stirring occasionally and checking the water level. Add the parsley in the last few minutes. Add the vinegar before serving. Serve hot.

Bean Soup, with Shells and Rosemary (Italy)

Keep this one in mind when someone is sick and needs a little something to get their strength back. Makes an excellent soup stock.

1–2 tbsp	olive oil	15–30ml
2	large onions, chopped	2
1	jalapeno pepper, minced (optional)	1
1	large clove garlic, minced	1
1	bay leaf	1
approx. 3 c	water, or stock	approx. 750ml
1 1/4 c	finely chopped celery	300ml
	a little finely chopped green cabbage (optional)	
5 1/2 oz	can tomato paste	156ml
1 1/2 tbsp	vegetarian Worcestershire sauce	22ml
2 tbsp	soy sauce	30ml
	pepper to taste	
1 1/2 c	cooked pasta shells	375ml
19 fl oz	can baked beans, or other beans (like white beans), cooked	540ml
1 tbsp	fresh parsley	15ml
1 1/2 tbsp	fresh or 1 1/2 tsp (7ml) dried rosemary	22ml

☛ Put the oil and the onion in a soup pot. Sauté on medium heat until tender, stirring. Add the jalapeno pepper and the garlic. Sauté another 2 minutes. Add the remaining ingredients, except the fresh herbs, bring to a boil, then simmer for 20 minutes on low heat, stirring occasionally. Check water level as it cooks. Add fresh herbs in the last five minutes. Remove bay leaf and serve.

Many Bean Soup (North America)

Soups are great. They're delicious, healthy and filling, and require very little effort. Just put everything in the pot, stir now and then, and let time take over. If you have a crock pot, you can use it to make most of the soups and stews. (I think crock pots take away a bit of the flavour, but they're great when you have to go out or you're just plain busy.)

2 tbsp	olive oil	30ml
1	medium onion, chopped	1
2–3	large cloves garlic, minced	2–3
1	carrot, chopped	1
2	stalks celery, chopped	2
1	potato, peeled and chopped	1
1/2 c	each of dried pinto, black and navy beans	125ml
1/2 c	yellow split peas	125ml
3/4 c	Scotch barley	185ml
8–10 c	stock, or cubed vegetarian chicken stock	2–2.5 litres

☛ Sauté the onion in the oil, in a soup pot on medium heat, until tender. Add the garlic, carrot, celery and potato and sauté for a few more minutes. Now add the beans, yellow split peas, barley and the stock and bring to a boil. Boil for 10 minutes, stirring, then reduce heat and simmer until vegetables and beans are tender, stirring and checking the liquid level.

⇨

1 1/2 tsp	paprika powder	7ml
1 tbsp	fresh or 1 tsp (5ml) dried dill weed	15ml
1	bay leaf	1
1 tsp	fresh parsley	5ml
1/2 tsp	chilli powder	2ml
1 c	cauliflower, chopped (optional)	250ml
	salt and pepper to taste	
2 tbsp	lemon juice	30ml
2 tbsp	soy sauce	30ml

It should take about 3 hours. After 1 hour add the seasonings, except the salt and pepper to taste, soy sauce and lemon juice. When everything is tender, remove the bay leaf and purée about 1/3 of the soup. Pour it back in the pot and add the cauliflower and cook for 10 minutes. Add the remaining ingredients and heat through. Serve hot.

If you're using a crock pot, sauté the onion and the garlic and place all the ingredients, except salt and pepper to taste and fresh herbs, in the crock pot and let it cook. Add the salt and herbs at the end.

Black Bean Soup (Caribbean)

This is one of my mom's favourites. Every time she comes back from the Caribbean she raves about black bean soup. So I made this one for her, and she loves it. I like it lemony, but you don't have to use this much lemon if you don't like it.

2 tbsp	olive oil	30ml
2	medium onions, chopped	2
5	cloves garlic, minced	5
3	stalks celery with the leaves, chopped	3
2–3	small to medium potatoes, peeled and chopped	2–3
1	large carrot, chopped	1
2 c	dried black beans	500ml
6–7 c	vegetable stock	1.5–1.75 litres
1	bay leaf	1
2 tsp	dried oregano	10ml
1 tsp	fresh parsley	5ml
	pepper to taste	
1 tsp	sea salt	5ml
1 tsp	dried oregano	5ml
7 tbsp	lemon juice	100ml

☞ Place the oil and the onions in a soup pot and sauté, stirring, until tender. Add the garlic and the vegetables and sauté 1 minute. Add the black beans, stock, bay leaf, oregano, parsley and pepper and bring to a boil. Partially cover and simmer, on medium-low heat, for about 3 hours, or until tender, stirring occasionally and checking the water level. Remove the bay leaf and purée. Stir in the remaining ingredients. Serve hot.

Rasam (India)

In India this spicy broth is said to cure colds and, given the amount of garlic, cayenne, cumin, coriander, turmeric, pepper, and ginger, it certainly should, since these herbs have immune-enhancing properties. It tastes wonderful and my husband swears it burns the colds right out of him in one day flat. They wouldn't dare hang around for more fire! I don't find it too hot, just delicious. I'm told by a friend from India that they sometimes let the soup separate and serve the thin part over rice and eat the thick part as a separate dish.

2 tbsp	ghee or butter	30ml
5	cloves garlic, minced	5
3 tsp	black mustard seeds	15ml
1/2 tsp	black pepper	2ml
1 tsp	cumin powder	5ml
1 tsp	coriander powder	5ml
	dash of cayenne powder, up to 1/2 tsp (2ml) if you like it really hot	
	dash of ginger powder	
1	dried bay leaf	1
1/2 tsp	turmeric powder	2ml
1/2 tsp	salt	2ml
3	tomatoes, chopped finely	3
2 tbsp	oil	30ml
2–3 c	cooked yellow split peas, or mung beans, or half and half	500–750ml
3 c	water, or part tomato juice (I like using about 250ml (1 cup) tomato juice)	750ml
5 tbsp	lemon juice	75ml
1/2 c	peas (optional)	125ml

☞ Put the ghee and the garlic and the mustard seeds in a pot and sauté for a few minutes, stirring. Watch for popping mustard seeds, and cover if necessary. Add the rest of the spices and the tomatoes and sauté for 5 minutes. Add the oil and the cooked split peas or mung beans, water and tomato juice and bring to a boil. Reduce heat and simmer stirring for 10 minutes. Strain for colds and use the liquid, or purée lightly for a meal, removing the bay leaf first. Add the remaining ingredients and heat through. Serve hot.

Beet Borscht Soup (Eastern Europe)

This is one of the dishes I taught my husband to make. Now it's his specialty, and he usually invites his mother-in-law over for it. It's delicious and it looks pretty, too. Last summer we grew beets in our garden. Ted would make this soup and bring it to the table with a huge smile, saying how great it was to be able to grow and eat our own vegetables—organically too.

4 tsp	olive oil	20ml
1	medium onion, chopped	1
3	cloves garlic, minced	3
1	potato, cut up and peeled	1
1	carrot, chopped	1
2	stalks celery, chopped, with the leaves	2
4 c	vegetable stock	1 litre
3–4	medium beets, grated (use the whole beet, including the leaves and stems, chopped)	3–4
2	bay leaves	2
	sea salt and pepper to taste	
1 1/2 tsp	honey (optional)	7ml
1/2 c	spaghetti sauce (see pg. 24)	125ml

☛ Put the oil and the onion in a soup pot and sauté, stirring, until tender. Add the garlic and sauté 1 minute. Add the potato, carrot and the celery and sauté for another 2 minutes, stirring. Add the stock and bring to a boil. Add the beets, roots only, and the bay leaves and reduce heat to a low boil. After about 10 minutes add the remaining ingredients, including the beet leaves and stems. Simmer until everything is tender, about 10 minutes. Remove the bay leaves and purée. Serve hot. I like it with lots of pepper. Potato latkes go great with this soup.

Cheesy Cauliflower Soup (North America)

A delicious cauliflower soup that tastes like cauliflower in a good cheese sauce. Serve it with light dishes, such as a salad and steamed greens, since it's quite rich.

3 tbsp	butter	45ml
3 c approx.	cauliflower, cut in small pieces	750ml approx.
2 c	vegetable stock, enough to cover vegetables	500ml
1 c	soy milk or milk	250ml
1/2 tsp	dry mustard	2ml
	pepper and sea salt to taste	
1/4 c	very finely chopped cauliflower	60ml
2/3 c	grated old cheddar cheese	165ml
3 tbsp	freshly grated Parmesan cheese	45ml
	a little finely chopped red or green pepper and fresh parsley for garnish	
	dash of paprika	

☛ Put the butter and the cauliflower in a soup pot and sauté on low heat for 2 minutes. Add the stock, soy milk, mustard, pepper and salt and bring to a boil. Lower heat and simmer for 20 to 25 minutes, stirring occasionally. Add the cauliflower and cheeses and heat through. Ladle into bowls and add the finely chopped pepper and parsley as a garnish. Sprinkle with paprika and serve hot.

Hungarian Stew (Eastern Europe)

This one is inspired by a Swiss friend of my mother who cooks for a Hungarian husband. One summer she invited us over and served up a wonderful vegetarian meal in our honour. I loved it and decided to experiment a little. This is what I came up with. If you like mushrooms–or even if you don't–you'll love this. Yum!

2–4 tbsp	butter	30–60ml
2	medium onions, chopped	2
5 c	button mushrooms	1250ml
1	green pepper, chopped and seeded	1
1	red pepper, chopped and seeded	1
3	cloves garlic, minced	3
2 1/2–3 1/2 tsp	paprika powder, depending on how spicy you like it	12–17ml
	salt and pepper to taste	
1 tsp	sugar	5ml
2 c	chopped fresh or canned tomatoes and their liquid	500ml
2 tbsp	red wine	30ml
	dumplings or noodles	

☞ Put the butter and the onions in a frying pan and sauté until tender. Add the mushrooms and sauté for a few more minutes, adding more butter if necessary. Add the peppers and sauté for about 5 minutes, until the mushrooms are soft and brown. Add the garlic and sauté another 2 minutes. Add the spices, sugar, tomatoes and red wine and simmer gently, covered, for about 30 minutes, stirring occasionally. Serve hot over dumplings or noodles.

Ranch Bean Stew (North America)

Simple, fast and filling.

1 tbsp	oil	15ml
1	medium onion, chopped	1
2	large cloves garlic, minced	2
2	stalks celery with the leaves, chopped	2
approx. 1 1/2 c	each, carrot, corn, zucchini and cooked rice	approx. 375ml
	some green beans, chopped (optional)	
10 oz	can of vegetable soup and one can of water	284ml
	or	
3 c	vegetable stock	750ml
	pepper to taste	
14 oz	can of baked beans	398ml
1–2 tsp	vegetarian Worcestershire sauce	5–10ml
1 tbsp	fresh or 1 tsp (5ml) dried thyme	15ml
1/2 tsp	cumin powder	2ml

☞ Put the oil and the onion in a soup pot and sauté until tender. Add the garlic cloves and the celery and other vegetables and rice, if you are using them. Add the soup, or stock, and bring to a boil. Add the pepper, beans, Worcestershire sauce, thyme, unless you are using fresh, and cumin. Simmer for about 25 minutes or until everything is tender. Add fresh thyme, heat and serve hot.

Thick and Rich Bean Stew (North America)

I made this once and left it simmering in a crock pot, where my visiting mother found it, ate it and left me a note saying it was delicious! Rich and filling—just add a salad.

2 tbsp	olive oil	30ml
1	medium onion, chopped	1
4	large cloves garlic, minced	4
2 c	sliced mushrooms	500ml
1 c	dried navy beans	250ml
1/4 c	dried black beans	60ml
1/2 c	yellow split peas	125ml
1 c	pearl barley	250ml
8–10 c	vegetarian beef-flavoured stock (use cubed)	2–2.5 litres
2 tsp	paprika powder	10ml
1 tsp	cumin powder	5ml
	pepper to taste	
1/8 tsp	chilli powder	1/2ml
	salt to taste	
2 tbsp	soy sauce	30ml
1 tbsp	red wine	15ml
2 tbsp	ketchup	30ml
1 c	well-flavoured spaghetti sauce (see pg. 24)	250ml

☛ Place the oil and the onion in a soup pot, and sauté on medium heat until very tender. Add the garlic and the mushrooms and sauté for a few minutes. Add beans, peas, barley, stock (enough to cover and add as you go, if necessary), paprika, cumin, pepper and chilli powder. Bring to a boil, then reduce heat to low and simmer, partially covered, for about 3 hours, stirring occasionally and checking the water level. Add the remaining ingredients and simmer for about 1/2 hour. Serve hot.

Spicy Bean and Macaroni Soup (North America)

A very filling and flavourful soup.

2 tbsp	olive oil	30ml
1	medium onion, chopped	1
1	green pepper, chopped (optional)	1
1	jalapeno pepper, chopped (optional)	1
1/8 tsp	cayenne pepper	1/2ml
2	cloves garlic, minced	2
	black pepper	
19 fl oz	cooked kidney beans, or use canned kidney beans, drained and rinsed	540ml
2 tsp	dried oregano	5ml
1 tsp	paprika powder	5ml
	sea salt to taste	
3 c	vegetable stock	750ml
1 c	fresh cooked (see pg. 24) or canned tomatoes, chopped up, and liquid	250ml
1 c	cooked macaroni	250ml
1/2 c	spaghetti sauce (see pg. 24)	125ml
1/2 c	corn (optional)	125ml

☛ Place the oil and the onion in a soup pot and sauté until tender. Add the peppers, if using, the cayenne and the garlic. Sauté 1 minute. Add remaining ingredients, except the corn, and bring to a boil. Then reduce heat and simmer for about 20 minutes, or until everything is tender, stirring. Add the corn and heat through. Serve hot.

Cream of Celery Soup (Eastern Europe)

Even if you don't like creamed soups, try this one. My husband, Ted, swore he'd hate it, and he ended up asking for seconds and thirds, and then if I could possibly make some more.

1–2 tbsp	olive oil	15–30ml
1	medium onion, chopped	1
3	cloves garlic, minced	3
1 1/2 tbsp	whole wheat flour	22ml
2	large potatoes, peeled and chopped	2
5 c	vegetable broth	1250ml
3 1/2 c	diced celery	875ml
1/4 tsp	garlic powder	1ml
	sea salt and pepper to taste	
1 tsp	fresh chopped parsley	5ml
1/2 c	soy milk	125ml
5 tbsp	very finely chopped celery	75ml

☛ Put the oil and the onion in a soup pot and sauté on low heat, stirring, until tender. Add the garlic and the flour and brown, stirring, for 1 minute. Add the potatoes and slowly add the stock, stirring to avoid lumps. Bring to a boil and add the celery and seasoning, except the parsley. Simmer on low heat until the vegetables are tender, about 20 to 25 minutes. Add the parsley and purée. Add the soy milk and the 5 tbsp (75ml) celery and heat through. Serve hot.

Pasta, Rice and Grains

• Note: See Grain and Bean Chart (pg. XXI-XXII) for cooking times and amounts.

Rice with Cabbage (Greece)

Rice is served many different ways in Greece, and not just as a side dish. If you have the wine, I recommend adding it. It gives a wonderful flavour and aroma.

2 tbsp	butter	30ml
1	medium onion, chopped	1
1/2	very small green cabbage, finely shredded	1/2
3	large tomatoes, chopped	3
	or	
3/4-1 c	fresh cooked (see pg. 24) or canned tomatoes with liquid	185-250ml
1/4 c	fresh parsley, chopped	60ml
	pepper and salt to taste	
1-3 tbsp	fresh or 1-3 tsp (5-15ml) dried basil	15-45ml
1/2 c	wine, preferably red	125ml
1 1/2-2 c	cooked rice	375-500ml
	lemon juice, or grated cheese (optional)	

☛ Sauté the onion in the butter until completely tender. Add the cabbage and sauté 5 minutes, on medium heat, stirring. Add the remaining ingredients, except the lemon juice and grated cheese, and cook for about 5 to 10 minutes. Serve hot, sprinkled with lemon juice and/or grated cheese if you're using them.

Pasta with Sesame Seeds (Italy)

An unusual, woody taste.

	whole wheat spaghetti noodles, enough for two—about 2 inches (5cm) around—cooked and drained	
2 tbsp	butter	30ml
	pepper and salt to taste	
1 c	brown sesame seeds	250ml
1/2 c	grated Parmesan cheese	125ml
	pinch each of ground nutmeg and ground cinnamon	

☛ Mix ingredients together well, heat quickly and serve hot.

Rice with Mushrooms, Tomatoes and Peas (Italy)

A classic dish served all over Italy. Don't let the peas get mushy—cook them no more than 3 minutes!

1 c	brown rice	250ml
2 tbsp	butter	30ml
2	medium onions, chopped	2
2 1/2–3 c	sliced mushrooms	625–750ml
2	large tomatoes, chopped	2
	or	
8–10 fl oz	canned tomatoes, broken up	250–310ml
2 tbsp	olive oil	30ml
	salt and pepper to taste	
2 tsp	dried oregano	10ml
1 1/2 tbsp	fresh or 1 1/2 tsp (7ml) dried basil	22ml
1 1/2 c	frozen peas	375ml
1 tbsp	fresh parsley	15ml
2 tbsp	olive oil	30ml
	grated cheese, cheddar or Parmesan, or both (optional)	

☞ Cook the rice. Meanwhile, place the butter and onions in a pan and sauté until tender. Add the mushrooms and sauté 5 minutes or until they begin to brown. Add the tomatoes, 2 tbsp (30ml) olive oil, spices and dried herbs. Sauté 5 to 10 minutes, stirring. Add the rice, peas, fresh herbs and 2 tbsp (30ml) olive oil and heat through. Add the cheese and serve. If desired, you can use all olive oil instead of butter.

Ziti with Zucchini (Italy)

I discovered this delicious yet simple dish in a little village full of stone fountains. As I ate I could hear the sound of running water. Use young, fresh zucchini so that it doesn't taste bitter.

4	hard-boiled eggs, shelled and sliced in half	
	ziti pasta cooked according to the package, approx. 4 cups (1 litre) cooked	
1 tbsp	olive oil	15ml
1	medium onion, chopped and sautéed in olive oil until tender (optional)	1
2	zucchini, thinly sliced	2
3 tbsp	fresh or 3 tsp (15ml) dried dill	45ml
	salt and pepper to taste	
2 tbsp	olive oil	30ml
1/4 c	grated Parmesan cheese	60ml

☞ Cook the pasta and drain. Meanwhile, sauté the onion in 1 tbsp (15ml) of oil until translucent. Add the zucchini, sauté for 2 minutes. Add the dill, salt, pepper, olive oil and pasta and heat. Add the cheese and serve hot.

Kitharaki Noodles and Sauce (Greece)

I first had this in my backyard with retsina and sunshine, which went very well together. A good dish for entertaining.

2 1/2 c	kitharaki noodles, cooked as directed on package	625ml
3–4 tbsp	olive oil	45–60ml
2	medium onions, finely chopped	2
2	yellow peppers, chopped	2
2	red peppers, chopped	2
3	tomatoes, diced	3
1	stalk celery, chopped	1
2–3	cloves garlic, minced	2–3
	pepper and salt to taste	
1 tbsp	fresh parsley	15ml
2 tsp	dried oregano	10ml
2 tbsp	olive oil	30ml
2 tbsp	lemon juice	30ml
	sprinkle of dried oregano	
5 oz	crumbled feta cheese	150g
	olives	

☞ Cook the noodles as directed on package, drain and rinse. Meanwhile, sauté the onions in the oil until tender. Add the peppers and tomatoes and sauté 5 minutes, stirring, on low heat. Add the remaining ingredients, except the noodles, cheese and olives, and sauté 3 to 5 minutes. Add the remaining ingredients and heat through. Serve.

Greek Spaghetti with Kefalotiri Cheese (Greece)

The first time I had this dish was on a beach in Methoni when I ordered spaghetti, which is called macaronia. The cheese is strong-tasting and takes some getting used to, but it's simple and delicious, and manages to do what Greek cooking does best—a few fresh ingredients and you've got a great meal!

	enough spaghetti for two, about 2 inches (5cm) around, cooked according to the package	
2–3 tbsp	butter	30–45ml
	pepper and salt to taste	
1 1/2 c	kefalotiri cheese, grated	375ml
1 tsp	dried oregano (optional)	5ml

☞ Cook the pasta, drain, and add the remaining ingredients to it. Heat quickly and serve hot.

Ziti Pasta (Italy)

I first had this dish in a garden, under a mountain, in a little village in Italy, while getting a small lesson in the importance of pasta and learning a few more words of Italian. The cheese gets chewy, the pepper gives the dish a bit of fire, and the olives give it a nice tang.

approx 4 1/2 c	enough ziti pasta for two, cooked prepared according to the package	(1,125ml)
2 tbsp	butter	30ml
3 tbsp	grated Parmesan cheese	45ml
1 c	cubed mozzarella cheese	250ml
1	sliced zucchini (optional)	1

SAUCE ...

19 fl oz	tomato sauce (see pg. 24), or use canned	540ml
3	cloves garlic, minced	3
1	medium onion, finely chopped and sautéed until tender in 1 tsp (5ml) olive oil	1
1	hot pepper, chopped	1
1 tsp	garlic powder	5ml
	dash each of dried rosemary and dried thyme	
1 tsp	dried oregano	5ml
	sprinkle of grated Parmesan cheese	
1 c	chopped green olives	250ml

Cook the pasta and place it in a buttered casserole dish with the butter, Parmesan cheese, mozzarella cheese, and zucchini, if you're using it. Mix the sauce ingredients together and pour over the pasta. Sprinkle with the Parmesan cheese and bake at 375F (190C) for 20 to 30 minutes. Serve hot.

Shells and Peppers (Italy)

Italy is famous for its pasta and every night I'd try a different kind. Even the slightest variations make a huge difference. As in all Mediterranean cooking, the secret is to use very fresh ingredients.

3 c	dried shell pasta, 5 cups (1.25 litres) cooked	750ml
2–3 tbsp	olive oil	30–45ml
2	medium onions, chopped	2
4	cloves garlic, minced	4
2	red peppers, chopped	2
1	yellow pepper, chopped	1
1	small hot pepper, minced (optional)	1
2	large tomatoes, chopped	2
1/4 c	white wine (optional)	60ml
2 1/2 tsp	fresh basil, chopped	12ml
	salt and pepper to taste	
2 tbsp	olive oil	30ml

☛ Cook the pasta according to the directions on the package. Meanwhile, sauté the onions in the oil, on low heat, until they're translucent. Add the garlic and peppers and sauté for 2 more minutes. Add the remaining ingredients and sauté for about 10 minutes, stirring. Toss with the pasta and serve hot.

Rice with Spinach (Middle East)

Another healthy and hearty grain dish. For a change, try some of the variations below.

1 c	brown rice, cooked in 3 1/2 c (875ml) water for 45 minutes, or until tender	250ml
2 tbsp	olive oil	30ml
2	medium onions, chopped	2
2 c	chopped fresh spinach	500ml
3 1/2 to 4 tbsp	fresh or 3 1/2–4 tsp (7–20ml) dried dill	52–60ml
3	scallions, chopped	3
2–4 tbsp	olive oil	30–60ml
	salt and pepper to taste	

☛ Sauté the onions in the oil until tender. Add the spinach, dill and scallions and cook 1 minute. Add the rice and the remaining ingredients and heat through.

VARIATIONS:
- add cut up tomatoes to the onions
- serve with lemon juice
- omit the dill and use either – basil (2–3 tbsp/30–45ml fresh or 2–3 tsp/10–15ml dried)
  – oregano (2–3 tsp/10–15ml dried)

Spaghetti with Pesto (Version 1) (Italy)

Everyone knows pesto, and that must mean that it's really good, considering how expensive pine nuts are. It's worth it. And if you grow your own herbs this dish will taste even better. The walnuts add a nice earthy bite.

3 c	cooked whole wheat spaghetti	750ml
3 tbsp	fresh chopped basil	45ml
4 tbsp	fresh chopped parsley (optional)	60ml
2–3	cloves garlic, minced	2–3
4–5	walnuts	4–5
2 tbsp	pine nuts	30ml
6–7 tbsp	olive oil	90–100ml
1–2 tbsp	cooking water from the pasta	15–30ml
1 tbsp	grated Parmesan cheese	15ml
	pepper to taste	
1/4 c	grated Parmesan cheese	60ml
1 tbsp	butter	15ml

☛ Cook the pasta according to the directions on the box. Meanwhile, place everything but the 1/4 cup (60ml) Parmesan cheese and 1 tbsp (15ml) butter in the blender and blend until fairly smooth. Add the Parmesan and the butter to the cooked pasta and mix well. Toss the pesto sauce from the blender with the pasta and heat 1 minute. Serve hot.

Spaghetti with Pesto (Version 2) (Italy)

Another version of a traditional dish that's popular in Italy and North America.

8 oz	whole wheat spaghetti	230g
2–3	cloves garlic, minced	2–3
8–10 tbsp	olive oil	120–150ml
1 tbsp	fresh parsley, chopped	15ml
2 tbsp	fresh, chopped basil	30ml
4 tbsp	pine nuts	60ml
2 tbsp	grated Parmesan cheese	30ml
	pepper to taste	
1 tbsp	pasta water	15ml

☛ Cook the pasta until al dente. Place all the other ingredients in a blender and blend until smooth. Add to the hot cooked pasta and toss. Serve immediately.

Spaghetti with Garlic (Italy)

A garlic lover's dream. And very simple, too.

	cook enough whole wheat spaghetti pasta for two, approx. 4 cups (1 litre) cooked	
3 1/2 tbsp	olive oil	50ml
4–5	cloves garlic, minced	4–5
	pepper and salt to taste	
2 tbsp	chopped fresh parsley	30ml
1/4 c	Parmesan cheese, grated	60ml

☛ Cook the pasta according to the directions on the box. Place the oil and the garlic in a pan and sauté, stirring, on low heat, for 3 minutes. Add the very well drained pasta and sauté until it's well coated in the mixture. Add the remaining ingredients and heat through. Serve hot.

Pasta Casserole (Italy)

A nice, mild tasting pasta. This is a good dish if you're busy. You can just pop it in the oven and let it cook while you're doing other things. Serve with a green salad or a steamed green vegetable. In Italy they bake this in a clay dish and put it right on the table.

2–3 c	uncooked egg noodles	500–750ml
2 tbsp	butter	30ml
2 tbsp	whole wheat flour	30ml
1 1/2 c	milk or soy milk	375ml
2	eggs, beaten	2
1 1/4 tsp	mustard powder	6ml
1/2 c	grated Parmesan cheese	125ml
1/4 c	cheddar cheese	60ml
	salt and pepper to taste	
1 tbsp	dried parsley	15ml

☛ Cook the pasta according to the directions on the box. Meanwhile, melt the butter and add the flour to toast it lightly, stirring on low heat. Slowly add the milk, stirring to prevent lumps, and allow it to thicken. Remove from the heat and add the eggs, mustard powder, cheeses, salt and pepper to taste and parsley. Mix well. Place the pasta in an ovenproof buttered dish and pour the sauce over the top. Sprinkle with pepper and more grated Parmesan cheese. Bake at 400F (200C) for about 25 minutes or until lightly browned on top. Serve hot.

Corkscrew Noodles with Pine Nuts (Italy)

The spinach is very nice in this dish and it makes it healthier. You can vary the "bite" by the amount of red pepper flakes you use.

5 c	cooked tri-coloured corkscrew noodles	1.25 litres
2–4 tbsp	olive oil	30–60ml
6 or more	green olives, pitted and chopped	6 or more
	dash of red pepper flakes	
1 tsp	dried oregano	5ml
1 tbsp	fresh or 1 tsp (5ml) dried basil	15ml
1 tbsp	fresh parsley	15ml
	pepper to taste	
3	cloves garlic, minced	3
3	chopped tomatoes	3
3 tbsp	pine nuts	45ml
1/2 tbsp	fresh or 1/2 tsp (2ml) dried basil	7ml
	Parmesan cheese, grated	
2 c	chopped spinach (optional)	500ml

☞ Cook the pasta according to the package. Meanwhile, in a pan, put the oil, olives, dried herbs, spices and garlic and sauté two minutes. Add the tomatoes and sauté 15 minutes, stirring, on low heat. Add the remaining ingredients, including the cooked pasta, and heat through. If you're using the spinach, allow it a few minutes to turn bright green. Serve hot.

Bulgur Pilaf (Mediterranean)

Simple and good. Try serving with red lentil soup and Middle Eastern cucumber and yoghurt salad.

1 1/2 c	bulgur	375ml
1–2 tbsp	oil or butter	15–30ml
1	medium onion, chopped	1
1	red pepper, chopped	1
1 c	fresh mushrooms, sliced	250ml
2 tbsp	fresh or 2 tsp (10ml) dried basil	30ml
2 tbsp	fresh or 2 tsp (10ml) dried thyme	30ml
1/2 tsp	pepper	2ml
	sea salt to taste	
1 tsp	olive oil	5ml

☞ Place the bulgur in a large bowl and cover with 4 1/2 cups (1125ml) of boiling water. Cover with a plate and allow to stand for about 20 minutes. Fluff with a fork. Drain if necessary. Meanwhile, sauté the onion in the butter until tender. Add the red pepper and the mushrooms and sauté on low heat for about five minutes. Add the herbs and spices and the cooked bulgur. Heat through for a few minutes, add the olive oil and serve hot.

Rice Loaf (North America)

All this dish needs is a salad or some soup to make a meal.

2 1/2–3 c	cooked brown rice	625–750ml
7 oz	grated cheese, cheddar or other	200g
5 oz	corn (fresh or frozen are best)	150g
2	medium onions, chopped and sautéed in 1 tbsp (15ml) olive oil until tender	2
3	cloves garlic, minced	3
2 tbsp	olive oil	30ml
1	small red pepper, chopped	1
1	small zucchini, chopped (optional)	1
1	small green pepper, chopped	1
1 c	sliced mushrooms (optional)	250ml
2–3	medium tomatoes, chopped	2–3
2	eggs, beaten	2
1/4 c	tomato juice	60ml
	salt and pepper to taste	
1/4 tsp	cayenne powder	1ml
1 tsp	dried parsley	5ml
	dash of lemon juice (optional)	

☞ Cook the rice for 45 minutes, or until tender, in about 7 1/2–9 cups (1875–2250ml) water, depending on how much rice you're using. Mix together everything except the lemon juice, press into a casserole dish and cover. Bake at 350F (180C) for about 1 hour. Serve with lemon juice, if desired.

Sweet Indian Rice (India)

A sweet, barbecue-flavoured version of Indian rice. Good with curries.

1 tbsp	vegetable oil	15ml
2	medium onions, chopped	2
1 c	brown rice	250ml
3 1/4 c	water	800ml
	salt and pepper to taste	
1/4 c	coconut, finely shredded	60ml
1 tsp	powdered tandoori masala, barbecue flavour	5ml
2 tbsp	lemon juice	30ml
	cashews and/or raisins (optional)	

☞ Sauté the onions in the oil until tender. Add the rice and sauté for a few minutes. Add the water, salt and pepper to taste, bring to a boil, then turn heat to low, cover and simmer for 45 minutes, or until tender, stirring occasionally. Add the remaining ingredients, mix well, and serve hot.

Spaghetti with Eggplant (Italy)

A simple merging of some classic tastes of Italy.

2 c	cooked whole wheat spaghetti noodles	500ml
4 tbsp	olive oil	60ml
1	medium onion, chopped	1
3	cloves garlic, minced	3
1	red pepper, chopped	1
2	tomatoes, chopped	2
1	eggplant, chopped and soaked in salted water for 1 hour, drained well and rinsed	1
1 tbsp	fresh or 1 tsp dried basil	15ml
1 tsp	dried oregano	5ml
1/4 tsp	red pepper flakes (optional)	1ml
	sea salt and pepper to taste	
1 c	white wine	250ml
	olive oil	
	grated Parmesan cheese (optional)	

☛ Cook the noodles according to the package. In the meantime, sauté the onion in the oil until tender. Add the garlic, red pepper and tomatoes and sauté for a few minutes. Add the eggplant (that has been soaking in salt water for 1 hour to remove all the bitter juices, drained and rinsed). Add the herbs and spices and the wine and cook on low heat until everything is tender. If you are using fresh herbs, add them in the last few minutes of cooking time. Drain the pasta and coat with a little olive oil. Toss. Serve with the sauce on top and with a sprinkle of grated Parmesan cheese, if desired.

Tomato Macaroni (England)

A slightly different version of a classic. They traditionally used a milder English cheese, but I like it better with a sharp cheddar to liven up the taste.

1 1/4–1 1/2 c	cooked macaroni	300–360ml
1 tbsp	butter	15ml
2	medium onions, chopped	2
28 fl oz	cooked tomatoes, chopped, or use canned	875ml
	salt and pepper to taste	
1 c	aged cheddar cheese, grated	250ml
	wheat germ for topping	
4 tbsp	grated Parmesan cheese	60ml

☛ Cook the noodles until tender, according to package. Sauté the onions in the butter until tender. Then place the cooked noodles, onions, chopped tomatoes and liquid, salt and pepper to taste and cheese in a casserole dish. Top with a thin layer of wheat germ and sprinkle with grated Parmesan. Bake at 350F (180C) for 30 minutes. Serve hot.

Spicy Rice with Cashews (India)

A tasty, filling dish from India. This is a well-spiced dish with lots of good stuff in it.

1 c	long grain brown rice	250ml
3 c	water	750ml
2 tbsp	ghee, or butter	30ml
2	medium onions, chopped	2
2	cloves garlic, minced	2
1	potato cut in tiny cubes	1
1	dried bay leaf	1
1/4 tsp	turmeric powder	1ml
1 tsp	cumin powder	5ml
1/2 tsp	cayenne powder	2ml
1/2 tsp	cinnamon powder	2ml
1	clove (optional)	1
1/4 tsp	ground ginger	1ml
1/2 tsp	salt	2ml
	black pepper to taste	
1/2–1 c	vegetable stock	125–250ml
2 c	finely chopped green beans, or peas	500ml
1	carrot cut in matchsticks	1
1/4 c	roasted cashews	60ml
2	mandarin oranges, sectioned (optional)	2

☛ Bring the water and rice to a boil, then turn it down to low and cook for about 45 minutes, covered, until tender. Meanwhile, sauté the onions in the butter until tender. Add the garlic, potato, seasonings, and about half of the stock. Cook 10 minutes, on low heat, stirring. If you're using beans, add and cook for a few minutes. Add the rest of the stock, the carrots, peas, if you're using them, and the cooked rice and heat through for a few minutes. Add the nuts and oranges, and remove the bay leaf and the clove. Serve hot.

Peppers with Macaroni (Italy)

For a healthier version, use whole wheat pasta.

1 3/4 c	cooked whole wheat macaroni pasta	420ml
2 tbsp	olive oil	30ml
2	medium onions, chopped	2
2	large yellow, red or green peppers, chopped	2
3	tomatoes, chopped	3
	salt and pepper to taste	
1 1/4 c	grated cheddar cheese	300ml
1 c	sliced olives (optional)	250ml

☛ Cook the noodles according to the package. While the pasta is cooking, sauté the onions in the oil until tender. Add the peppers, tomatoes, salt and pepper to taste and cook on low heat, stirring, for about 5 minutes. Add the pasta, cheese and olives and mix well. Heat and serve.

Cannelloni (Italy)

This is still one of my very favourite dishes, and I serve it often when company is coming, especially because I have a certain brother-in-law who won't eat anything vegetarian except tomato sauce, pasta and cheese. Serve with a Caesar salad, minestrone soup and garlic bread, and, of course, some wine. A nice red Valpolicella or Chianti goes well with this dish. Fudge or Sabra squares finish off the perfect meal.

4 1/2 c	shredded mozzarella cheese	1125ml
20	no-boil cannelloni noodles	20
38 fl oz	well-flavoured spaghetti sauce (see pg. 24), or use canned	1185ml
	Parmesan cheese, grated	

OPTIONAL STUFFINGS:
- mozzarella cheese, or other, and spinach
- kidney beans and fried onions
- well-flavoured rice or bread crumbs
- fried mushrooms, onions and pepper

☞ Stuff the cannelloni noodles with the mozzarella cheese and place them in an oblong 12" x 9" (30cm x 24cm) baking dish. Pour the sauce over the noodles, making sure a little bit gets underneath them. Sprinkle liberally with grated Parmesan, cover and bake at 350F (180C) for about 50 minutes to an hour, or until the noodles are soft. Serve. If you use one of the optional stuffings, the cooking method is the same.

Cheesy Macaroni with Tomato (North America)

A variation on macaroni and cheese.

9 oz	whole wheat elbow macaroni noodles	260g
1 tbsp	oil	15ml
1/2	green pepper, chopped	1/2
1	red pepper, chopped	1
3	cloves garlic, minced	3
4	scallions, chopped	4
1 1/2 c	fresh or canned tomatoes, chopped	360ml
1 c	tomato sauce (see pg. 24)	250ml
1/4 tsp	each black pepper, dried thyme, basil and oregano	1ml
2 1/2 c	grated cheddar cheese	625ml
1/4 c	grated cheddar cheese	60ml
2 tbsp	wheat germ	30ml
1 tbsp	fresh parsley	15ml

☞ Cook the macaroni noodles until tender. Meanwhile, sauté the peppers, garlic and scallions in the oil for a few minutes on low heat. Add the tomatoes, tomato sauce, herbs and spices and simmer for 5 minutes, stirring. Mix with the cooked macaroni and the 2 1/2 cups (625ml) cheddar cheese. Place in a greased 11" x 8.5" (27.5cm x 21.25cm) casserole dish and sprinkle with the 1/4 cup (60ml) of cheddar cheese and the wheat germ. Bake covered for 35 minutes at 325F (170C). Serve hot. Serve with a good grinding of pepper and fresh chopped parsley.

Spaghetti with Meat-like Sauce (Italy)

This one is very filling and looks, tastes and smells a lot like spaghetti with meat sauce. Even if you don't like tofu, give it a try because the tofu takes on the taste and texture of the sauce. Just make sure you squeeze all the water out of the tofu.

2 c	spaghetti noodles	500ml
1 tbsp	olive oil	15ml
2	large onions, chopped	2
6	large cloves garlic, minced	6
1	red or yellow pepper, chopped	1
1 c	extra firm tofu	250ml
2 c	chopped tomato, fresh or canned	500ml
5 1/2 oz	can tomato paste	156ml
1 c	vegetable stock	250ml
3 tsp	dried oregano	15ml
2 tbsp	fresh or 2 tsp (10ml) dried basil	30ml
	pepper and sea salt to taste	
1/4 tsp	chilli flakes, or more	1ml
	a little chopped fresh parsley	
1	stalk celery, chopped small	1
2	medium carrots, diced	2
	a few sun-dried tomatoes (optional)	
1/2	jalapeno pepper, diced (optional)	1/2
1/2 c	red wine (optional)	125ml
2 c	fresh spinach, chopped (optional)	500ml

☛ Cook the pasta al dente. Meanwhile, sauté the onions in the oil until tender. Add the garlic and red pepper and sauté for a few minutes. Squeeze all the water out of the tofu and process in a food processor until it is the texture of ground beef. Add to the onion mixture and sauté until all the excess liquid evaporates. Add the remaining ingredients, except the spinach and parsley, and simmer for 20 to 30 minutes, stirring, or until the vegetables are tender. Add the spinach, if you're using it, and the parsley and heat for 2 minutes. Serve hot over pasta, in Sloppy Joes, in lasagna, or on pizza.

Fettucini Alfredo (Italy)

A classic, and I believe this is the perfect version. Even finicky eaters will eat this one, and I often use it for the ones who hate everything, including tomato sauce.

2 1/2–3 c	wide egg noodles	625–750ml
3 tbsp	butter	45ml
3/4–1 1/4 c	whipping cream	185–300ml
1/2–3/4 c	grated Parmesan cheese	125–185ml
1/4–1/2 tsp	pepper	1–2ml
1/8–1/4 tsp	cayenne powder	1/2–1ml
	sprinkle of nutmeg powder (optional)	

☛ Cook the noodles according to the package instructions. Drain. Add the remaining ingredients, starting with the smaller amounts and adding more if necessary. Heat through. Serve hot.

Lasagna (Version 1) (Italy)

Another one of my very favourite dishes that I serve often to company. I think this is one of the very best. Serve with a salad and zucchini soup, wine and dessert for a completely stuffing meal.

9	lasagna noodles, cooked in boiling water until tender	9
1 tbsp	oil	15ml
1	large onion, chopped	1
3–4	large cloves garlic, minced	3–4
1	green pepper, chopped	1
10 oz	can sliced mushrooms, drained	284 ml
28 fl oz	cooked tomatoes (see pg. 24) or use 1 can of tomatoes, chopped	875ml
5 1/2 oz	can tomato paste	156ml
2 1/2 tsp	dried oregano	12ml
1 tsp	dried basil	5ml
1 tsp	dried thyme	5ml
1 tsp	garlic powder	5ml
1/8 tsp	pepper	1/2ml
1/2 tsp	onion powder	2ml
	sea salt	
3 1/2 c	shredded mozzarella	875ml
	Parmesan cheese, grated	

☛ Cook the lasagna noodles according to the package instructions and drain. In the meantime, sauté the onion in the oil, on low heat, until tender. Add the remaining ingredients, except the noodles and the cheeses, and cook, stirring, for about 15 to 20 minutes. In an oblong 12" x 9" (30cm x 24cm) ovenproof dish, spread a little of the sauce on the bottom, then layer ingredients as follows: 3 of the cooked noodles, trimmed if necessary, 1/3 of the mozzarella cheese, 1/2 of the sauce, 3 noodles, 1/3 of the mozzarella cheese, the rest of the sauce, 3 noodles, the rest of the mozzarella. Top with lots of Parmesan cheese. Bake covered at 350F (180C) for 20 minutes. Uncover and bake until top is golden, about 20 minutes. Cut into squares and serve hot.

Cream-Style Chinese Noodles (Asia)

A creamy, mushroomy noodle dish with a distinct Asian flavour. Serve with a salad with lots of greens.

5–6 c	cooked broad egg noodles	1.25–1.5 litres
10 oz	can condensed mushroom soup	284 ml
4 tbsp	soy sauce	60ml
	slightly more than 1/4 cup (60ml) soy milk, but less than 1/2 cup (125ml)	
1/8 tsp	pepper, or more if desired	1/2ml
10 oz	can sliced mushrooms, drained	284 ml
1/4 c	Parmesan cheese (optional)	60ml

☛ Cook the noodles according to the package instructions and drain. Meanwhile, mix everything, except the Parmesan cheese, if you're using it, in a bowl, until smooth. Heat, stirring, and then pour over the noodles. Add the cheese if desired. Serve hot.

Lasagna (Version 2) (Italy)

A slightly different version of lasagna. I often use one of these two lasagna recipes for entertaining, because they taste good, look great, and can be assembled in advance and then baked in the oven later. The last stage can even be delayed if need be.

9	lasagna noodles, whole wheat or regular, or rice lasagna noodles	9
1 1/4 c	broccoli florets, chopped small	300ml
1 1/4 c	cauliflower florets, chopped small	300ml
1	small green pepper, chopped	1
2 c	spinach, washed, dried and chopped	500ml
19 fl oz	well-flavoured spaghetti sauce (see pg. 24), or use canned	540ml
5 1/2 oz	can tomato paste	156ml
3 c	ricotta cheese	750ml
1/2 c	grated Parmesan cheese	125ml

☛ Cook the noodles according to the package instructions. Meanwhile, chop the vegetables up very small. Combine the vegetables with the tomato sauce and tomato paste in a bowl and mix well. In a 12" x 9" (30cm x 24cm) oblong dish, place three noodles, then layer as follows: 1/2 of the vegetable-tomato mixture, 1/2 of the ricotta, 3 noodles, the rest of the vegetable-tomato mixture, and the remaining ricotta. Top with 3 more noodles and the grated Parmesan cheese. Bake for 50 minutes at 350F (180C), covered for the first 30 minutes, and then uncovered to brown. Serve hot.

Italian Pasta with Zucchini (Pasta Salina) (Italy)

I first tried this in a restaurant called Luciano's in the Aeolian Islands in Italy. It was so superb I figured out my own version when I came home. Every night Luciano brought us a different pasta that he made specially, knowing we were vegetarians. Each one was wonderful and made even better by the surrounding gardens, mountains and sea.

4 1/2 c	tri-coloured rotini pasta, cooked	1125ml
1 tbsp	olive oil	15ml
5–6	large cloves garlic, minced	5–6
4	zucchini, quartered and sliced thinly	4
1/2 c	whipping cream	125ml
3/4 c	grated cheddar cheese	185ml
	sea salt and pepper to taste	
1/4 c	grated Parmesan cheese	60ml
1 tbsp	olive oil	15ml

☛ Cook the noodles according to the package instructions. While the pasta is cooking, sauté the garlic in the oil for 30 seconds, on low heat, stirring. Add the zucchini and sauté for 1 to 2 minutes. Add the cooked pasta and the remaining ingredients, mix well, and heat through. Serve hot.

Thai Fried Rice (Thailand)

A staple that I had all over Thailand. It's filling too.

1-2 tbsp	oil	15-30ml
	extra firm tofu, cubed, about 8 pieces	
1	carrot, thinly sliced	1
1	red pepper, thinly sliced	1
1/2 c	canned baby corn	125ml
1 c	green peas, frozen	250ml
	a little each of nappa, broccoli, cauliflower, cut up	
1 c	mung bean sprouts	250ml
3 c	cooked brown rice	750ml
2 to 3 tbsp	soy sauce	30-45ml
1 tbsp	vegetable oil	15ml
1/4-1/2 tsp	hot chilli flakes	1-2ml
1	egg, scrambled	1
2 tbsp	crushed peanuts	30ml
	lime wedges	

☞ In a frying pan, place the oil and tofu and brown on medium heat. Add the egg, scramble and cook, stirring until set then break apart. Add in the carrots and red pepper and sauté for 3 minutes. Add in the other vegetables and sauté for 3 to 5 minutes. Vegetables should be cooked but not mushy. Add the cooked rice and remaining ingredients, except lime and peanuts and heat through. Serve hot topped with the peanuts and with lime squeezed over the top.

Fried Rice (Asia)

This is a classic that adapts to endless variations. Add whatever vegetables you like—frozen peas or corn, bok choy, snow peas, different kinds of mushrooms, crumbled tofu, bean sprouts, and scallions. It's popular in our house and Ted makes if often. Eat with chopsticks, and serve with Chinese tea and some greens steamed in a little soy sauce, garlic and ginger. Or serve as part of an Oriental buffet with soup, spring rolls, egg fu yung and a stir-fry.

4 c	cooked brown rice	1 litre
1 tbsp	butter	15ml
1	large onion, chopped	1
1	green or red pepper, chopped	1
12	mushrooms, sliced	12
1–2 tbsp	walnuts, peanuts or almonds (optional)	15–30ml
1 tbsp	soy sauce	15ml
2	eggs, lightly beaten (optional)	2

☞ Cook the rice for about 40 minutes, or until tender. You'll need to use about 1 1/3 cups (335ml) dry rice in 4 1/2 cups (1125ml) of water. Check the water level and stir it as it cooks. When it's done, drain if necessary. Meanwhile, sauté the onion in the butter on low heat, stirring, until tender. Add the green or red pepper, mushrooms, nuts (if using) and 1 tbsp (15ml) soy sauce. Sauté 3 to 5 minutes.

⇨

1	stalk celery, sliced on the diagonal	1
1	carrot, cut in matchsticks	1
1/4–1/2 tsp	pepper	1–2ml
1/4–1/2 tsp	cayenne powder	1–2ml
6 tbsp	soy sauce	90ml
3 tbsp	vegetarian Worcestershire sauce	45ml
1 tbsp	sesame seeds (optional)	15ml

Add the eggs if you're using them and cook, breaking them apart, until dry and loose. Add the celery and the carrots and cook 1 minute. Add any other vegetables you are using according to the amount of time needed to cook them: harder, longer-cooking ones before softer, quick-cooking ones like peas. Don't overcook the vegetables; keep them crunchy. Add the remaining ingredients, including the rice, mix well and heat through. Serve hot.

Szechwan Fried Rice (Asia)

Spicy and delicious, this recipe adapts to a lot of variations. Try snow peas, bok choy, broccoli, peppers, or whatever you like. The secret is in the sauce and the vegetables–don't overcook them–they should be tender crisp.

2 1/2 c	cooked brown rice	625ml
1 tbsp	oil	15ml
1	medium onion, chopped	1
2	scallions, chopped	2
14	mushrooms, chopped (any kind, or use a variety)	14
1	red pepper, chopped	1
2	stalks celery, sliced	2
2	cloves garlic, chopped	2
1/4 c	peanuts (optional)	60ml
1/4 c	slivered almonds (optional)	60ml
1/4 c	grated cheddar cheese (optional)	60ml

SAUCE ...

1	pkg powdered Szechwan sauce	1
3 tbsp	soy sauce	45ml
1 tsp	brown sugar	5ml
1/4 c	water	60ml
or		
4 tbsp	bottled Szechwan flavouring	60ml
4 tbsp	soy sauce	60ml
1 tbsp	sesame oil	15ml

☞ Cook a little less than 1 cup (250ml) raw rice in about 3 cups (750ml) water until tender, about 45 minutes. Meanwhile sauté the onion in the oil until tender. Add the scallions, mushrooms, pepper, celery and garlic and cook 2 minutes, stirring. Add the nuts, if using, and cook 3 minutes. Add one of the sauces and heat through, about 2 minutes. Add the cooked rice and cheese, if you're using it, and mix well. Heat and serve hot.

Bulgur Pilaf with Melted Cheese (Middle East)

I love the contrast between the texture of the melted cheese and the chewy texture of the grain. Quick and easy to make, too.

1 1/2 c	bulgur	375ml
2 tbsp	butter	30ml
2	medium onions, chopped	2
2	cloves garlic, minced	2
1	green pepper, chopped	1
1 1/4 c	mushrooms, sliced	300ml
	dash of cayenne powder	
	salt and pepper to taste	
1 c	diced mozzarella cheese	250ml

☞ Place the bulgur in a bowl and cover with lots of boiling water— about 5 cups (1.25 litres). Let stand, covered, for 20 minutes, then drain and fluff with a fork. In the meantime, sauté the onions in the butter until tender. Add the garlic, green pepper and mushrooms and sauté for 5 minutes or so, or until the mushrooms begin to brown. Add the remaining ingredients, including the bulgur, but not the cheese, and sauté for a few minutes until heated through. Mix in the cheese and allow to melt slightly. Serve hot.

Rice and Spinach Casserole (France)

A delicious way to eat spinach. You don't need to add much to make a meal, perhaps a yellow vegetable, some steamed cauliflower or a light soup.

3 1/2 c	cooked brown rice	875ml
4 c	chopped fresh spinach	1 litre
4	cloves garlic, minced	4
	a little freshly chopped parsley	
4	scallions or shallots, chopped, then lightly sautéed in a little oil	4
1	egg, well beaten	1
	lots of pepper, sea salt	
2 tbsp	red wine vinegar	30ml
1 c	grated cheddar cheese	250ml
2 tbsp	grated Parmesan cheese	30ml
2 tbsp	grated mozzarella cheese	30ml
5 tbsp	olive oil	75ml
	additional grated Parmesan cheese for topping	
	sprinkle of wheat germ	

☞ Cook about 1 cup (250ml), plus a little, of raw rice in 4 cups (1 litre) of water for about 45 minutes, or until done. Drain, if necessary. Mix everything in a bowl, including the rice, but not the wheat germ. Place in a large buttered casserole dish and top with an additional sprinkling of grated Parmesan and the wheat germ. Cover and bake at 350F (180C) for about 25 minutes. Serve hot.

Couscous with Stew (Morocco)

A traditional national dish of Morocco. It's healthy and delicious and can adapt to variations, using different vegetables, and adding or omitting nuts and seeds. Serve with pita bread, Moroccan eggplant, cucumber soup, and Moroccan salad for a feast.

1 1/4 c	couscous	300ml
2–3 tbsp	olive oil	30–45ml
2	large onions, chopped	2
2	cloves garlic, minced	2
1	carrot, sliced into thin rounds	1
1/4	chopped yam (optional)	1/4
1	small potato, peeled and diced	1
2	large tomatoes, chopped	2
1/2 c	tomato juice	125ml
1/2 tsp	ground cinnamon	2ml
1 tsp	ground cumin	5ml
2 tsp	ground coriander	10ml
2 tbsp	lemon juice	30ml
1 c	cooked chickpeas, or use canned	250ml
	a little freshly chopped parsley	
	sea salt and pepper to taste	
2 tbsp	brown sesame seeds	30ml
2 tbsp	almonds, with skins on	30ml

☛ Place the couscous in a bowl and slowly add 1 1/4 cups (300ml) of warm, lightly salted water to it. Rub with your fingers to coat the grains, allowing the couscous to absorb the water, and separating the grains. Let stand for 5 minutes. Repeat the process 2 more times. Then place the couscous in a steamer on a piece of muslin cloth and steam for about 20 minutes, covered. Fluff with a fork and make sure it's cooked. Meanwhile, prepare the stew.

Sauté the onions in the oil until tender. Add the garlic, carrot, yam, if you're using it, potato, tomatoes, tomato juice and spices and cook for 20 minutes. Add the lemon juice and the chickpeas and cook for about 5 to 10 minutes. Meanwhile, place the nuts and seeds in the oven and roast them on a cookie sheet, stirring often, until browned. Watch them because they burn. Place the couscous on a platter and pour the stew over top of it. Add some chopped parsley and the roasted nuts and seeds. Serve hot.

Paella (Spain)

Another national dish. This is served all over Spain in endless variations and often contains fish. It's usually served right at the table in a large pan so everyone can see how magnificent it looks.

1 1/4 c	brown rice	300ml
1	packet of dried saffron, about 1 tsp (5ml)	1
2–3 tbsp	olive oil	30–45ml
2	medium onions, chopped	2
1 c	finely diced pepper squash	250ml
3	large cloves garlic, minced	3
1/2 c	finely chopped green beans	125ml
1	large red pepper, sliced in rings	1
1	green pepper, chopped	1
1	yellow pepper, sliced in rings	1
3	large tomatoes, chopped	3
2 tbsp	tomato juice	30ml
	sea salt and pepper to taste	
1/4 c	frozen corn	60ml
1/2 c	frozen peas	125ml
1/2 c	cooked chickpeas, or use canned	125ml
1/2	small hot pepper, minced very finely (optional)	1/2
4 tbsp	olive oil	60ml
	roasted sunflower seeds and pistachios	

☛ Cook the rice in 4 1/4 cups (1060ml) of boiling, lightly salted water. Add the packet of saffron and cook for 45 minutes, or until tender. Check to see if it needs additional water. When cooked, drain if necessary. Meanwhile, sauté the onion in the oil until tender. Add the squash and cook for 10 minutes, stirring. Add the garlic, green beans, the peppers, tomatoes, tomato juice and the salt and pepper to taste. Cook until vegetables are tender but not mushy (about 10 minutes). Add the corn, peas, chickpeas and hot pepper, and cook for 3 minutes. Add to the rice along with the remaining ingredients. Mix well. Serve hot.

Mild Indian Rice (India)

The mild tanginess of this rice dish adds a nice contrast to spicy curries.

2 1/2 c	cooked basmati rice, white or brown	625ml
2 tbsp	ghee, or butter	30ml
	salt to taste	
1 tbsp	olive oil	15ml
1/2	chopped green pepper	1/2
1/2	chopped tomato	1/2
	pinch of turmeric powder	
1/4 c	apple juice	60ml
	top with chopped walnuts, cashews, sunflower or sesame seeds (optional)	

☛ Cook the rice, using about 1 cup (250ml) raw to 3 cups (750ml) water, for 40 minutes. Mix it with the other ingredients, except the nuts and seeds. Heat. Top with nuts or seeds. Serve hot.

Rice With Tomatoes, Peppers and Beans (Jamaica)

One of my favourite dishes. I first had it at a buffet in Jamaica and was told that its origin is Rastafarian. It's colourful, spicy and delicious. And filling, too. Just add a green salad.

1 1/2 c	cooked brown rice	375ml
22 fl oz	cooked red kidney beans, or use canned	685ml
2–3 tbsp	butter, or olive oil, but butter gives it a better taste	30–45ml
2–3	medium onions, chopped	2–3
3	cloves garlic, minced	3
1	red or yellow pepper, chopped	1
3	large tomatoes, chopped	3
4 tsp	powdered coriander	20ml
1/4 tsp	chilli powder	1ml
2 dashes	cayenne powder	2
	sea salt and pepper to taste	
1/4 tsp	garlic powder (optional)	1ml
1–1 1/2 c	tomato juice, depending on how much liquid you want	250–375ml
	a little chopped parsley	
1 tbsp	olive oil	15ml

☞ Cook the rice and the kidney beans ahead of time. For the rice, use approximately 1/2 cup (125ml) rice to 2 cups (500ml) water, and cook for about 45 minutes. For the beans, use about 1 1/4 cups (300ml) dry beans to 4 1/2 cups (1125ml) of water, and cook for about 1 1/2 hours. (You don't need to cook the canned beans, if you're using them.) Sauté the onion in the butter until tender. Add the garlic, red or yellow pepper, tomatoes and spices, and cook for about 5 to 10 minutes. Add the remaining ingredients, including the rice and the beans, and mix well. Heat through and serve hot.

Noodles and Kale (England)

A creamy, delicious way of eating kale, one of the best "super" veggies you can get.

3 1/2 c	cooked penne noodles, preferably spinach penne	875ml
2 tsp	oil	10ml
1	medium onion, chopped	1
	salt and pepper to taste	
4 c	chopped kale	1 litre
1	egg, beaten	1
1 c	milk	250ml
10 oz	can condensed cream of mushroom soup	284 ml
1/4 c	grated cheddar cheese	60ml
1/4 c	grated Parmesan cheese	60ml
	a little paprika powder	

☞ Cook the noodles according to the package instructions. Meanwhile, sauté the onion in the oil, on low heat, until tender. In a 12" x 9" (30cm x 24cm) lasagna pan, place the cooked pasta, onion, salt and pepper to taste, and kale. Mix well. Mix the remaining ingredients together in a bowl and pour over the mixture in the lasagna pan. Mix well. Sprinkle with paprika. Cover and bake at 350F (180C) for about 30 to 40 minutes. Serve hot.

Lentils with Pasta (Middle East)

A very unusual tasting pasta dish. The cinnamon and cumin, combined with red lentils, blends well with the pasta. All you need is a green salad full of fresh vegetables.

4 1/2 c	cooked ziti or shell pasta	1125ml
1–2 tbsp	olive oil	15–30ml
2	medium onions, chopped	2
4	cloves garlic, minced	4
2 c	red lentils	500ml
3/4 c	tomato juice	185ml
2	large tomatoes, finely chopped	2
3/4 tsp	cinnamon, ground	3ml
1 tsp	dried sumac (optional) (available in Middle Eastern grocery stores)	5ml
1 tsp	cumin, ground	5ml
2 tbsp	lemon juice	30ml
	sea salt to taste and lots of pepper	
1/2 tsp	garlic powder	2ml
1/2 tsp	onion powder	2ml
4 tbsp	grated cheddar cheese	60ml
	grated Parmesan cheese, or soy Parmesan cheese	
	wheat germ	

☛ Cook the noodles al dente. While the pasta is cooking, sauté the onions in the oil until tender. Add the garlic and the lentils and sauté 1 minute. Add water to cover and bring to a boil, then simmer until tender, about 15 to 20 minutes. Add the remaining ingredients, except the noodles, cheeses and wheat germ, and simmer for a few minutes. In a greased 11" x 8.5" (27.5cm x 21.25cm) casserole dish, layer 1/2 the noodles, 1/2 the lentil mixture, then 2 tbsp (30ml) grated cheddar cheese. Repeat the layers, and top liberally with Parmesan cheese, and a little wheat germ. Dot with olive oil. Bake at 350F (180C) for 30 to 40 minutes, covered. Uncover during the last 10 minutes. Serve hot.

Spaghetti with Garlic and Chickpeas (Italy)

Delicious garlic flavour, and simple, too.

5 oz	spaghetti noodles	150g
1/4 c	olive oil	60ml
4	cloves garlic, minced	4
2 tbsp	fresh chopped parsley	30ml
	pepper and sea salt to taste	
19 fl oz	cooked chickpeas or 1 can chickpeas, drained and rinsed	540ml
1 tbsp	olive oil	15ml
2 tbsp	red wine vinegar	30ml
1 tbsp	lemon juice	15ml
1/4 c	grated Parmesan cheese	60ml

☛ Cook the noodles al dente. Meanwhile, sauté the garlic in the olive oil, on low heat, for 1 minute. Add the parsley, cooked pasta, pepper and salt and sauté for a few minutes. Add the remaining ingredients, mix well, heat and serve.

Italian Pasta (Italy)

A different healthy spaghetti. A favourite of one of my friends, who claims she doesn't like spinach.

3-4 oz	whole wheat spaghetti pasta, enough for two	90-120g
1 tbsp	butter	15ml
1	medium onion, slivered	1
1	clove garlic, minced	1
1 1/4 c	chopped tomatoes, fresh or canned	300ml
1 1/2 c	chopped fresh spinach or broccoli (or both), or asparagus	375ml
1/2 c	tiny peas, or snow peas	125ml
	lots of pepper	
2 1/2 tbsp	cornstarch	37ml
1 c	soy milk	250ml
3 tbsp	soy sauce	45ml
2 tbsp	chopped walnuts (optional)	30ml

☞ Cook the pasta al dente. Meanwhile, sauté the onion in the butter in a large pan until tender. Add the garlic, tomatoes, greens and pepper. Heat for a few minutes, stirring. Mix together the remaining ingredients, except the pasta, and add slowly to the pan, stirring. Heat, stirring, to cook off some of the liquid, and allow to thicken. Serve hot with the noodles and the walnuts, if desired.

Brown Beans and Bulgur (North America)

This one may not look great but it tastes superb. Give it a try. It's filling, delicious and nutritious.

1 c	bulgur	250ml
	boiling water	
1-2 tbsp	butter	15-30ml
2	medium onions, chopped	2
2 c	sliced mushrooms (optional)	500ml
1 tbsp	fresh or 1 tsp (5ml) dried thyme	15ml
1 tbsp	fresh or 1 tsp (5ml) dried basil	15ml
1/2 tsp	pepper, or more if desired	2ml
1 1/4 tsp	paprika powder	6ml
5 1/2 oz	can tomato paste	156ml
4 tbsp	soy sauce	60ml
4 tbsp	water	60ml
14 oz	can baked beans, or cooked white beans	398 ml

☞ Place the bulgur in a bowl and cover with about 3 cups (750ml) of boiling water. Cover and let stand for about 20 minutes. Drain and fluff. Meanwhile, sauté the onion in the butter on low heat, until tender, and sauté the mushrooms if you are using them. Add the remaining ingredients, including the bulgur, and heat, stirring for about 5 minutes. Serve hot.

Spanish Rice (Spain)

Another classic dish that's eaten all over Spain and Mexico. You can vary the vegetables if you like, but keep the spices the same. Serve with refried beans and a salad and maybe some grilled peppers or nacho chips.

5 1/2 c	water	1375ml
1 1/2 c	uncooked brown rice	375ml
1–2 tbsp	olive oil	15–30ml
2	medium onions, chopped	2
4	cloves garlic, minced	4
1	green pepper, chopped	1
1	red pepper, chopped	1
1	stalk celery, chopped	1
2	large tomatoes, chopped	2
1 c	tomato juice	250ml
1/4 tsp	paprika powder	1ml
3 1/2 tsp	dried oregano	52ml
1/2–1 tsp	chilli powder	2–5ml
	sea salt and pepper to taste	
3 tbsp	olive oil	45ml
2 tbsp	lemon juice	30ml
1/4–1/2 c	grated cheddar cheese (optional)	60–125ml
	a little diced jalapeno pepper	
	or	
1	small green or red pepper (optional)	1

☞ Cook the rice in the water for 40 to 45 minutes, or until soft. Drain if necessary. Meanwhile, sauté the onions in the oil until tender, on medium low heat. Add the garlic, peppers, celery, tomatoes and tomato juice, and the seasonings. Cook for about 10 minutes, stirring. Add the rice, olive oil and lemon juice and heat through. Garnish with options, if desired, and serve hot.

Noodles with Onions and Bread (Italy)

This is a delicious variation of an Italian dish.

3 c	wide egg noodles, enough for two	750ml
2–4 tbsp	butter	30–60ml
2	large onions, chopped	2
1/2 tsp	onion powder	2ml
2 1/2 c	whole wheat bread, torn into little pieces	625ml
1 tbsp	butter	15ml
1/4–1/2 c	Parmesan cheese	60–125ml
	pepper and sea salt to taste	
2 tsp	fresh parsley for garnish	10ml

☞ Cook the noodles al dente. Meanwhile, sauté the onions in the butter until tender. Add the onion powder and the bread and sauté for a few minutes. Add the noodles and the remaining ingredients, except the parsley. Stir well and heat. Garnish with the parsley. Serve hot.

Grain Stuffing (U.S.A.)

A delicious, woodsy version of stuffing. It's good as it is or stuffed into various vegetables such as peppers or tomatoes.

2–3 tbsp	olive oil	30–45ml
3	medium onions, chopped	3
3	cloves garlic, minced	3
4	stalks celery, chopped	4
3 c	sliced mushrooms	750ml
	pepper and sea salt to taste	
3 1/2 tsp	dried oregano	17ml
1 tbsp	fresh or 1 tsp (5ml) dried basil	15ml
1 tbsp	fresh or 1 tsp (5ml) dried thyme	15ml
1/2 tbsp	fresh or 1/2 tsp (2ml) dried sage	7ml
1/4 c	chopped fresh parsley	60ml
1/4–1/2 c	vegetable stock	60–125ml
5 c	cubed whole wheat bread	1.25 litres
1/4 c	roasted sunflower seeds	60ml
1/2 c	sliced roasted almonds	125ml
1 c	cooked black-eyed peas, with or without a little chopped tomato (optional)	250ml

☛ Put olive oil and the onions in a pan and sauté until tender. Add the garlic, celery, mushrooms, spices and dried herbs and cook 5 minutes, or until the mushrooms are browned. Add the fresh herbs and cook 2 to 3 minutes. Add the stock and the bread cubes; mix well and heat. If you're using the peas, add them with the bread cubes. Serve hot or cold, topped with roasted sunflower seeds and almonds.

Lemon Asparagus with Fettucini (Italy)

This is one of my mom's favourites, and mine too. The tang of the lemon and the crunch of the asparagus go very well with the creamy fettucini noodles.

3 c	fettucini noodles	750ml
1–2 tbsp	olive oil	15–30ml
3	large cloves garlic, minced	3
1 1/4 c	whipping cream	300ml
	pepper and sea salt to taste	
3–4 tbsp	lemon juice	45–60ml
1 1/2 c	chopped fresh asparagus	375ml
	grated Parmesan cheese for garnish	

☛ Cook the noodles al dente. While the pasta is cooking, sauté the garlic in the olive oil for a few minutes, stirring, on low heat. Add the remaining ingredients and cook for 3 to 5 minutes, or until hot. Do not let the asparagus get mushy. Pour over the hot noodles. Sprinkle with grated Parmesan cheese. Serve hot.

Pasta with Mushrooms (Italy)

A great dish to serve company. The woodsy, intoxicating fragrance of the mushrooms floats all over the house, inviting you and your guests to dinner. Serve with a salad and maybe a little soup.

3 c	wide egg noodles, enough for two people	750ml
1 tbsp	olive oil	15ml
1/4 c	grated Parmesan cheese	60ml
2–4 tbsp	butter	30–60ml
3	cloves garlic, minced	3
4 c	sliced mushrooms, including some wild ones if you can get them	1 litre
2 tsp	dried oregano	10ml
1 tbsp	fresh or 1 tsp (5ml) dried basil	15ml
1 tbsp	fresh or 1 tsp (5ml) dried thyme	15ml
3/4 tsp	fresh or 1/4 tsp (1ml) dried rosemary	3ml
1/2 tsp	paprika powder	2ml
	dash of cayenne powder	
1/4 tsp	dried savoury	1ml
	sea salt and pepper to taste	

☛ Cook the pasta al dente, and toss with olive oil and the grated Parmesan cheese. In the meantime, sauté the other ingredients, except the fresh herbs, if you're using them, on low heat, stirring, for about 15 to 20 minutes, or until the mushrooms are brown and fragrant. Add fresh herbs, if you're using them. Make the sauce.

SAUCE ...	2 c	well-flavoured spaghetti sauce (see pg. 24)	500ml
	2	cloves garlic, minced	2
	1/2 tsp	garlic powder	2ml
	1/2 tsp	onion powder	2ml
	1/2 tsp	dried oregano	2ml
		pepper to taste	
	4 tbsp	red wine (optional)	60ml

☛ Mix ingredients well in a saucepan and simmer on low heat for about 15 minutes, stirring. Place the cooked pasta on plates and spoon the sauce over top. Add the mushroom mixture. Garnish with grated Parmesan cheese and, if desired, some chopped olives. Serve hot.

Fettucini in Spicy Tomato Cream Sauce (Italy)

A striking, tasty version of fettucini with a punch. Excellent, and great for entertaining.

2 c	fettucini noodles	500ml
1–2 tbsp	olive oil	15–30ml
1 tbsp	butter	15ml
5 c	sliced mushrooms	1.25 litres
4	large cloves garlic, minced	4
1/4 tsp	chilli flakes	1ml
	dash of cayenne powder	
1 1/2 c	diced tomatoes, fresh or canned, with liquid, or add 1/2–3/4 cup (125–185ml) tomato juice if using fresh tomatoes	375ml
3/4 c	whipping cream	185ml
1/2–3/4 c	white or red wine, excellent if you have it, but reduce amount of tomato liquid if you're using the wine (optional)	125–185ml
	pepper and sea salt to taste	
2–3 tbsp	grated Parmesan cheese	30–45ml
2 c	finely chopped cauliflower or broccoli florets, or spinach, or a little of each (optional)	500ml

☞ Cook the pasta al dente. Meanwhile, sauté the mushrooms and garlic in the olive oil and butter. Add the chilli flakes and cayenne powder and sauté for a few minutes, until the mushrooms begin to brown. Add the remaining ingredients and cook 3 to 5 minutes, stirring until the vegetables are tender but still crisp. Add the cooked pasta, stir, heat and serve.

Couscous Pilaf (Middle East)

A nice light-tasting couscous, spiked with dill.

1 3/4 c	well-flavoured vegetable stock	435ml
1 c	couscous	250ml
1 tbsp	olive oil	15ml
2	medium onions, chopped	2
2	cloves garlic, minced	2
1 c	sliced mushrooms	250ml
3/4 c	chopped snow peas	185ml
1 c	frozen peas	250ml
2 1/2 tbsp	fresh or 1 tbsp (15ml) dried dill	37ml
	sea salt and pepper to taste	
1–2 tbsp	olive oil	15–30ml

☞ Bring the stock to a boil. Add the couscous and bring back to the boil. Cover and remove from the heat. After about 5 minutes, fluff with a fork. In the meantime, sauté the onions in the olive oil until tender. Add the garlic and the mushrooms and sauté for a few minutes, until tender. Add the remaining ingredients, except the olive oil, and heat through. Add the cooked couscous and the olive oil, and mix. Serve hot or cold.

Pasta Stir-Fry (Asia)

A zingy pasta that's also great for entertaining. Try the rice noodles. They add to the flavour and texture of the dish. Better yet, try all the variations–they're good.

2 c	thin or spiral noodles, rice pasta or other noodles	500ml
1–2 tbsp	sesame oil	15–30ml
2	cloves garlic, minced	2
3 c	sliced mushrooms	750ml
1	red pepper, chopped	1
1/4	green pepper, chopped (optional)	1/4
1 c	finely chopped green beans or snow peas (or both), or broccoli	250ml
1/4–1/2 c	very firm tofu cut in small cubes (optional)	60–125ml
	pepper to taste	
1	medium carrot, cut in matchsticks (optional)	1
2 tbsp	soy sauce	30ml
1/8 tsp	cayenne powder	1/2ml
2	dashes of powdered ginger (optional)	2
2 tbsp	brown sesame seeds	30ml
2 tbsp	cashew pieces, or slivered almonds (optional)	30ml
1 tbsp	soy sauce	15ml

☞ Cook the noodles al dente. Meanwhile, in a wok, place the sesame oil, garlic, mushrooms, peppers, beans, tofu and pepper. Sauté for about 5 minutes, making sure everything gets coated. Add the remaining ingredients and sauté for 2 to 3 minutes. Mix in the cooked pasta, and serve hot or cold.

Spicy Lentil Rice (Middle East)

Spicy! You can tone it down by using fewer hot peppers, but I like it hot.

4 c	cooked brown rice	1 litre
1 1/2 c	uncooked red lentils	375ml
2 c	vegetable stock or cubed vegetarian stock, chicken-flavoured	500ml
5 1/2 oz	can tomato paste	156ml
	sea salt and pepper to taste	
2–4 tbsp	olive oil	30–60ml
1 1/2 tsp	cumin powder	7ml
1/4 tsp	cinnamon powder	1ml
1/4 tsp	cayenne powder	1ml
1–3	hot jalapeno peppers, fresh or canned, chopped	1–3

☞ Combine the above ingredients and place in an 11" x 8.5" (27.5cm x 21.25cm) casserole dish. Cover and bake at 375F (190C) for 30 to 40 minutes. Serve hot.

Couscous Bake (Middle East)

A great dish when you don't have a lot of time. Just assemble it in advance and pop it in the oven when you're ready. A complete grain dish.

1 1/4 c	couscous	300ml
approx. 2 c	well-flavoured vegetable stock, boiling	500ml approx.
3	dashes cumin powder	3
2	dashes cinnamon powder	2
	pepper and sea salt to taste	
1–2 tbsp	butter	15–30ml
2	medium onions, chopped	2
3	cloves garlic, minced	3
3 c	sliced mushrooms	750ml
1/2 tsp	cumin powder	2ml
1/8–1/4 tsp	cinnamon powder	1/2–1ml
	sea salt to taste and lots of pepper	
1–1 1/2 tbsp	dried basil	15–22ml
2–3	tomatoes, chopped, plus 3/4 cup (185ml) tomato juice	2–3
1 c	cooked chickpeas	250ml
1 1/4 c	grated cheddar cheese (optional)	300ml
3 c	chopped fresh spinach	750ml
2 tbsp	olive oil	30ml
	handful of dried currants (optional)	

☛ Place the couscous in a bowl and pour the boiling stock over it. Cover. Allow to stand for 15 minutes. Then fluff with a fork and add the seasonings. Sauté the onions in the butter until tender. Add the garlic and mushrooms and sauté for 5 minutes. Add the spices, herbs, tomatoes and tomato juice, and the chickpeas, and cook for a few minutes. Remove from the heat and add the remaining ingredients, including the couscous, mixing well. Place in a greased 12" x 9" (30cm x 24cm) oblong dish and cover. Bake at 325F (170F) for 30 minutes. Serve hot.

Mushroom Rice (Eastern Europe)

An easy dish that cooks itself in the oven. Serve as a side dish or as a main dish with a salad and some accompanying vegetables.

1 c	brown rice, uncooked	250ml
10 oz	can condensed mushroom soup	284 ml
1	large package powdered onion soup mix	1
3–3 1/2 c	milk or soy milk	750–875ml
1/4–1/2 tsp	pepper	1–2ml
10 oz	can mushrooms, drained	284 ml

☛ Put everything into an 11" x 8.5" (27.5cm x 21.25 cm) ovenproof casserole dish that has a lid. Mix well and cover. Bake at 350F (180C) for 1 1/2 hours, or until the rice is tender. Check the liquid level as it cooks and add more milk if necessary. Serve hot.

Notes

The Vegetarian Passport Cookbook

Beans and Lentils

Note

Many beans can be pre-soaked to cut down on the cooking time—up to 40 minutes for harder beans. There are a couple things you can add to beans to make them more easily digestible, such as red wine or apple cider vinegar. Add them near the end of the cooking time. Kombu, a sea vegetable, can be added as the beans cook. This sea vegetable will also give the beans a richer flavour and add nutrients as well. Use dried beans when you can, but, if you're in a hurry, use canned beans that are low in salt. Make sure the cans are lined to prevent ingesting lead. You can also freeze cooked beans to have on hand when you need them.

Kidney Bean, Red Lentil, Pepper Medley (Middle East)

A warming, rich stew that's perfect for those cold days. Serve with a salad and good crusty bread or scones.

4 tbsp	olive oil	60ml
2	medium onions, chopped	2
3 c	fresh tomatoes, cooked and chopped (see pg. 24) or use canned tomatoes, chopped	750ml
1 1/2 tsp	pepper	22ml
1 tsp	cumin powder	5ml
1/2 tsp	onion powder	2ml
2/3 c	dried red lentils	160ml
2 c	vegetable stock	500ml
19 fl oz	cooked kidney beans or 1 can kidney beans, drained and rinsed	540ml
2	red peppers, chopped	2
1	yellow pepper, chopped	1

☞ Sauté the onions in the oil on low heat until tender. Add remaining ingredients and bring to a boil, then simmer for about 1/2 hour or until everything is tender. Serve hot.

Romano Bean Casserole (North America)

Simple to prepare and delicious, too. You can assemble everything in advance and cook it when you need it.

1	red or green pepper, chopped	1
1 c	chopped green beans	250ml
1 1/2 c	mushrooms, cut in half	360ml
1/2	very small red onion, chopped	1/2
19 fl oz	cooked Romano beans or 1 can Romano beans, drained and rinsed	540ml
5 1/2 oz	can tomato paste plus 1 can water	156ml
1/4 c	red wine (optional)	60ml
1/4–1/2 tsp	red pepper flakes	1–2ml
1 tsp	dried oregano	5ml
1 tsp	dried thyme	5ml
1 tsp	dried basil	5ml
	salt and pepper to taste	
1/2 tsp	brown sugar	2ml

☞ Place everything in an 11" x 8.5" (27.5cm x 21.25cm) casserole dish and mix well. Cover and cook for about one hour, or so, at 375F (190C). Uncover during the last 10 minutes of cooking time. Serve hot.

Chickpea Loaf (North America)

Excellent for entertaining. It's delicious and looks great on a plate with steamed vegetables, rice or roasted potatoes. Serve with Dijon mustard, horseradish or another favourite sauce, or just eat it as is.

19 fl oz	cooked chickpeas or 1 can chickpeas, drained and rinsed	540ml
1 tbsp	olive oil	15ml
1	medium onion, chopped	1
6	mushrooms, chopped	6
1 tsp	each, dried thyme, basil, parsley	5ml
3 tbsp	soy sauce	45ml
1 1/2 tbsp	ketchup	22ml
1	stalk celery, chopped (optional)	1
1/4 c	wheat germ	60ml
2	eggs, beaten	2
	salt and pepper to taste	
	sesame seeds for garnish	

☞ Mash the chickpeas. Sauté the onion in the oil on medium heat until tender. Add the mushrooms to the onions and sauté for a few minutes. Mix in the rest of the ingredients, except the sesame seeds, and press into a greased 4.5" x 8.5" (11.25cm x 21.25cm) loaf pan. Sprinkle with sesame seeds and press them down into the loaf. Bake, covered, at 350F (180C). After 15 minutes, uncover and bake until a little browned on top, about 20 to 30 minutes. Serve hot or cold. It also makes a good sandwich filling, with Dijon mustard.

Asian Chickpea Burgers (Asia)

Good for lunch or dinner or whenever you feel like a burger. They are also great cold for lunch the next day. You can also mix everything together, uncooked, to use as a spread on crackers or pita.

19 fl oz	cooked chickpeas or 1 can, drained, rinsed and mashed	540ml
1/2 tsp	powdered vegetarian chicken broth (use cubed)	2ml
3 tbsp	soy sauce	45ml
2 tbsp	hot water	30ml
1	stalk celery, finely chopped	1
	salt and pepper to taste	
4 tbsp	wheat germ	60ml
	Dijon mustard, lettuce, cucumber, sprouts for garnish (optional)	

☞ Mix together everything, except the optional garnishes, and form into patties. Fry the patties in a little oil until browned on both sides or brush lightly with a little oil and bake in the oven on a cookie sheet until golden, at 350F (180C), for 15 to 25 minutes. Serve on a bun with or without the garnishes.

Bean Loaf (North America)

Good served with roast potatoes, spicy squash and a spinach salad.

19 fl oz	cooked kidney or Romano beans, or 1 can kidney or Romano beans, drained, rinsed and mashed	540ml
1	medium onion, chopped	1
1 tbsp	oil	15ml
1/2 c	cooked rice	125ml
2	eggs, beaten	2
2	cloves garlic, minced	2
1/4 c	wheat germ	60ml
5 tbsp	well-flavoured tomato sauce (see pg. 24) or barbecue sauce (use bottled)	75ml
2 tsp	dried oregano	10ml
1/2 tsp	dried basil	2ml
1/2 tsp	dried thyme	2ml
1 c	tomato sauce (see pg. 24) flavoured with 1/2 tsp each of garlic and dried oregano, 1/4 tsp each of onion powder and fresh basil, and pepper to taste (optional)	250ml

☞ Sauté the onion in the oil on medium heat until tender. Mix with the rest of the ingredients, except the final cup of flavoured tomato sauce. Press into a greased 4.5" x 8.5" (11.25cm x 21.25cm) loaf pan and bake at 350F (180C) for 30 to 40 minutes. Serve with heated tomato sauce spooned over top, if desired.

Bean Pie (Mexico)

Spicy and delicious. The cheese helps hold everything together, but you can leave it out if you want. I use the whole teaspoon of cayenne powder because I like it spicy.

3	large potatoes, peeled and cubed	3
1/2 c	vegetable broth	120ml
	pepper and salt to taste	
1 tsp	butter	5ml
1 1/2 tbsp	oil	22ml
2	medium onions, chopped	2
3	cloves garlic, minced	3
1/4 tsp	pepper	1ml
1/2	zucchini, sliced in rounds (optional)	1/2
2	fresh tomatoes, diced	2
1/4–1 tsp	cayenne powder	1–5ml
1 1/2 tsp	dried oregano	7ml
19 fl oz	cooked kidney or Romano beans, or 1 can kidney or Romano beans, drained and rinsed	540ml
3/4 c	grated cheddar or Monterey Jack cheese (optional)	185ml
1/2 tsp	dried oregano (optional)	2ml

☞ Cook the potatoes in boiling water until tender. Drain and mash them well with the vegetable broth, salt, pepper and butter. Press into a greased 9" (23cm) diameter pie plate, to form a crust. Sprinkle lightly with cayenne and bake at 375F (190C) until slightly golden. In the meantime, sauté the onions in the oil on low heat until tender. Add the garlic and sauté for a few minutes. Add the remaining ingredients, except the cheese, and cook for 7 minutes, stirring. Mash lightly and pour into the potato crust in the pie plate. If you like, you can top with another layer of potatoes, in which case double the amount of potatoes, vegetable broth, salt, pepper and butter you use. Top with the cheese and bake at 325F (170C) for 20 to 30 minutes. Slice into wedges and serve hot.

Peasant Beans (North America)

Simple and delicious. Use the wine if you have it. It makes it smell and taste incredible.

2 tbsp	oil	15ml
1	medium onion, chopped	1
2	cloves garlic, minced	2
1 1/2 c	chopped green cabbage	375ml
1 c	canned tomato juice, or canned tomatoes and juice	250ml
1/2 c	red wine (optional)	125ml
19 fl oz	cooked white beans or 1 can baked beans, or other type	540ml
	salt and pepper to taste	

☞ Sauté the onion in the oil, on low heat, stirring, until tender. Add the garlic and sauté 1 minute. Add the cabbage and sauté 2 minutes. Add the remaining ingredients and cook on low heat, stirring, for about 15 to 20 minutes. Serve hot.

Bean and Rice Balls (North America)

These are a reworking of an old meatball recipe. If you want to spice them up, add chilli powder. Serve with salad, steamed vegetables and rice.

1 tbsp	oil	15ml
1	medium onion, chopped	2
2	cloves garlic, minced	
19 fl oz	cooked kidney beans or 1 can kidney beans, drained, rinsed and mashed	540ml
1/2 c	cooked brown rice	125ml
2 tbsp	breadcrumbs or wheat germ	30ml
1/2 tsp	chilli powder (optional)	2ml
4 tbsp	well-flavoured spaghetti sauce (see pg. 24)	60ml
1 c	well-flavoured tomato sauce, (see pg. 24) mixed with 1/2 tsp (2ml) garlic powder and 1/4 tsp (1ml) cumin powder	250ml

☞ Sauté the onion in the oil on medium heat until tender. Add the garlic and sauté for a few minutes. Mix together the beans, onion-garlic mixture, cooked rice, breadcrumbs, chilli powder and the spaghetti sauce. Roll into small—approximately 2-inch (5cm)—but firm balls. Place in an 11" x 8.5" (27.5cm x 21.25cm) casserole dish and bake, uncovered, at 350F (180C) for 15 minutes. Then cover the balls with the tomato sauce and bake uncovered for another 20 minutes. Serve hot.

Lentil Noodles Casserole (England)

A delicious, warming casserole that can be prepared in advance and then just popped into the oven when you're ready to eat. Serve with steamed vegetables or salad.

1 c	green lentils	250ml
1 c	whole grain macaroni	250ml
1 tbsp	oil	15ml
1	medium onion, chopped	1
19 fl oz	fresh tomatoes, cooked and chopped (see pg. 24) or canned tomatoes, chopped	540ml
1/2 c	spaghetti sauce (see pg. 24)	125ml
1 1/2 tsp	pepper	7ml
3	slices whole wheat bread, lightly buttered and torn into 1" (2.5cm) pieces	3

☞ In a large saucepan, place the lentils in about 3 cups (750ml) water, bring to a boil, then simmer for 50 minutes to an hour, until tender. Meanwhile, cook the macaroni according to the package instructions. Sauté the onion in the oil on low heat until tender. Add the tomatoes, spaghetti sauce, pepper, cooked lentils and cooked macaroni and mix well. Put into a 12" x 9" (30cm x 22.5cm) baking dish and top with the bread. Bake at 300F (150C) for about 30 minutes. Serve hot.

Chilli (Mexico)

People who try this think it's the best chilli they've ever had. We eat if often in our house. You can vary the degree of heat by the amount of chilli powder you add. In Mexico, they often use a different kind of bean for chilli, such as a black bean or red bean. And there's always fresh salsa and nachos on the table.

1 tbsp	oil	15ml
1	medium onion, chopped	1
3	large cloves garlic, minced	3
1	green pepper, chopped	1
1/2–1 c	tomato juice, depending on how much liquid you like	125–250ml
1 1/4–1 1/2 tsp	chilli powder	6–7ml
2 1/2 tsp	dried oregano	12ml
1/8 tsp	salt	1/2ml
1/4–1/2 tsp	cumin powder (optional)	1–2ml
19 fl oz	cooked kidney beans (you can use canned, but make sure you rinse them well)	540ml
1 1/2 c	cooked brown rice	375ml
1/2 c	frozen corn	125ml
1/2 c	grated cheddar cheese (optional)	125ml
1/4 c	sliced olives (optional)	60ml

☞ Sauté the onion in the oil on low heat until tender. Add the garlic and the green pepper and sauté 2 minutes. Add the tomato juice, using a small amount first, the chilli powder, oregano, salt, and cumin, if you're using it. Add the kidney beans and cook for 5 minutes on low heat, stirring. To get 1 1/2 cups (375ml) of cooked rice you will need 1/2 cup (125ml) of raw rice and about 2 cups (500ml) of water. Bring to a boil and then simmer until the rice is tender, about 45 minutes. Add the cooked rice and corn, and the rest of the tomato juice if desired, and cook for about 2 minutes, or until hot. Serve as is, or top with the options, and serve hot.

Kidney Beans with Spicy Pineapple (North America)

Hawaiian-style chilli.

19 fl oz	cooked kidney beans or 1 can red kidney beans, drained and rinsed	540ml
1/4 c	barbecue sauce (use bottled)	60ml
1/4 tsp	mustard powder	1ml
1 c	cooked rice	250ml
1 3/4 c	fresh or canned pineapple plus 1/4 cup (60ml) pineapple juice	420ml
1/4–1/2 tsp	Dijon mustard	1–2ml

☞ Place all ingredients in a heavy saucepan and cook on low heat, stirring, for 10 minutes to heat through. Serve hot.

Romano Chilli (Mexico)

A delicious, different version of chilli. You control the spiciness by the amount of chilli powder you add.

1 tbsp	olive oil	15ml
1	onion, chopped	1
2–3	cloves garlic, minced	2–3
10–14	green beans, finely chopped	10–14
1–2	stalks celery, chopped finely	1–2
6	mushrooms, sliced	6
19–28 fl oz	fresh tomatoes, cooked and chopped (see pg. 24) or canned tomatoes, chopped up– the amount depends on how much liquid you prefer	540–875ml
2 tsp	dried oregano	10ml
1/2–1 tsp	chilli powder, depending on how hot you like it	2–5ml
1/8 tsp	pepper tiny pinch of kelp powder	1/2ml
1/4 tsp	salt	1ml
19 fl oz	cooked Romano beans, or 1 can Romano beans, drained and rinsed	540ml
1–1 1/2 c	cooked bulgur	250–375ml
1 tsp	fresh parsley	5ml
1/4–1/2 c	grated cheddar cheese (optional) dollop of plain yoghurt (optional)	60–125ml

☛ Sauté the onion in the oil on low heat until tender. Add the garlic and sauté 1 minute. Add the green beans, celery and mushrooms and sauté for 2 minutes. Add the tomatoes and spices and herbs, except the parsley, and cook for 5 minutes, stirring. Add the beans and bulgur and heat through for 5 minutes, stirring. Serve hot, with parsley and the options if desired.

Oniony Kidney Beans and Barley (North America)

Oniony and good. I like to use the barley because it has such a nice slippery texture.

19 fl oz	cooked kidney beans, or 1 can red kidney beans, drained and rinsed	540ml
1/2 c	strong onion soup stock, or use powdered stock mixed with water	125ml
2 c	chopped tomatoes, fresh or canned	500ml
1/2 c	tomato juice	125ml
1 1/2 c	cooked rice or barley lots of pepper	375ml

☛ Place all ingredients in a heavy saucepan and cook, stirring, on medium heat for 12 minutes to heat through. Serve hot.

Curried Lentils (India)

Another great dish for your next Indian feast. Serve with raita for a cooling effect and, of course, Indian bread and rice.

1 1/8 c	red or green lentils	280ml
1 tbsp	butter	15ml
2	medium onions, chopped	2
3 1/2 tsp	curry powder	17ml
1/2 tsp	cumin powder	2ml
2 tsp	coriander powder	10ml
1/4–1/2 tsp	cayenne powder	1–2ml
	pepper and salt to taste	
2 c	chopped green cabbage (optional)	500ml
2 tbsp	lemon juice	30ml

☞ Cook the lentils in boiling water until tender, about 45 minutes for green and 15 minutes for red. Drain, saving 3/4 cup (185ml) of the liquid. Sauté the onion in the butter in a large frying pan, on low heat, until tender. Add the spices and sauté for a few minutes. Add the cabbage, if you're using it, and the cooked lentils, and sauté for 12 minutes. Add the liquid from the lentils, if needed, as the mixture cooks. Add the lemon juice and serve hot, or wrap into a pita with chopped green pepper and chopped celery.

Macaroni Casserole (North America)

Simple and more filling than plain macaroni casserole.

1 tsp	vegetable oil	5ml
1	medium onion, chopped	1
1	clove garlic, minced	1
19 fl oz	cooked kidney beans or use canned	540ml
4 c	cooked macaroni, whole wheat or tri-coloured	1 litre
1/8 tsp	salt	1/2ml
	pepper to taste	
10 oz	can tomato soup	284ml
1 tsp	dried oregano	5ml
1/2 tsp	garlic powder	2ml
3	slices whole wheat bread, buttered and torn into bite-size pieces	3

☞ Sauté the onion and garlic in the oil on low heat until tender. Combine with the rest of the ingredients, except the breadcrumbs, and place in a non-stick 12" x 9" (30cm x 22.5cm) casserole dish. Top with the breadcrumbs and bake, covered, at 350F (180C) for 30 minutes. Serve hot.

Bean and Vegetable Casserole (North America)

A complete meal that you can assemble in advance and bake at the last minute. Serve with a salad or green vegetable.

3	medium potatoes, thinly sliced	3	
3	medium carrots, thinly sliced	3	
1/2 c	cooked brown rice	125ml	
19 fl oz	cooked kidney beans or use canned	540ml	
1/2 c	sliced green beans (optional)	125ml	
1	medium onion, chopped	1	
	salt and pepper to taste		
4–6 tbsp	olive oil	60–90ml	
28 fl oz	tomatoes, cooked and chopped (see pg. 24) or canned tomatoes, broken apart	850ml	
2	slices buttered whole wheat bread, torn into bite-size pieces	2	

☞ In a 12" x 9" (30cm x 22.5cm) casserole dish, layer the vegetables (down to, and including, the onions) in the order they're listed. Season with salt and pepper to taste and pour the olive oil and the tomatoes over them. Top with the bread pieces, cover, and bake at 350F (180C) for 1/2 hour. Remove the cover and bake for another 30 minutes. Serve hot.

Chinese Lentil Casserole (Asia)

Unusual, but delicious. I know the crushed potato chips sound weird, but they go very well in this dish.

4 c	cooked green lentils	1 litre	
2 c	celery, sliced diagonally	500ml	
1 c	frozen peas	250ml	
	sea salt and pepper to taste		
1 tbsp	vegetable oil	15ml	
1	medium onion, chopped	1	
10 oz	can condensed cream of mushroom soup	284ml	
1 c	soy milk	250ml	
3 tbsp	soy sauce	45ml	
1/2 c	crushed potato chips	125ml	
approx. 1/2 tsp	paprika powder	approx. 2ml	

☞ Place the cooked lentils, then the celery, peas and salt and pepper to taste in a greased 12" x 9" (30cm x 22.5cm) casserole dish. Sauté the onion in the oil on low heat until tender. Mix together the onion, mushroom soup, soy milk and soy sauce and pour it over the mixture in the casserole dish. Top with the crushed potato chips and sprinkle with paprika. Cover and bake at 350F (180C) for 25 to 30 minutes. Serve hot.

Woodsy Lentil Loaf (North America)

Delicious, whether you eat it alone, with the sauce or with Dijon mustard.

2 1/2–3 c	cooked green lentils	625–750ml
1/4 c	cooking water reserved from the lentils	60ml
1 tbsp	butter	15ml
1 c	sliced mushrooms	250ml
2	medium onions, chopped	2
1	stalk celery, finely chopped	1
1 1/2 tbsp	dried thyme	22ml
1/4 tsp	dried winter savoury	1ml
1/4 c	wheat germ	60ml
1	egg, beaten, or use egg substitute (optional)	1
1 tsp	red wine vinegar	5ml
3–4 tbsp	tamari soy sauce	45–60ml
	dash of vegetarian Worcestershire sauce	
1 tbsp	dried parsley	15ml
1 tbsp	whole wheat flour	15ml
2 tbsp	sunflower or sesame seeds	30ml
	pepper and salt to taste	
	sesame seeds for garnish	

SAUCE ...

2 tbsp	butter	30ml
1	medium onion, chopped	1
1	clove garlic, minced	1
2 c	sliced mushrooms	500ml
1 c	sliced red cabbage (optional)	250ml
1/2–1 c	red wine	125–250ml
1 tbsp	whole wheat flour (optional)	15ml
	pepper to taste	

☛ Cook the lentils, using approx. 1 3/4 cups (435ml) dry lentils to 4 cups (1 litre) water. Bring to a boil and then simmer for about 50 minutes or until they're tender, adding more water if necessary. Meanwhile, sauté the onions and the mushrooms in the butter on low heat until tender. Combine with the rest of the ingredients, except the sesame seeds used for garnish, and mix well. Press into a greased 4.5" x 8.5" (11.25cm x 21.25cm) loaf pan. Sprinkle with the sesame seeds and bake, covered, for the first 20 minutes or so, at 375F (190C). Remove cover and bake for another 30 minutes, or until the loaf is set. Serve sliced like a loaf as it is, or with Dijon mustard, or with a mushroom sauce, or with the sauce that follows.

☛ Sauté the onion in the butter in a large frying pan on low heat until tender. Add the garlic, mushrooms and cabbage and sauté for a few minutes. Add the flour and toast it lightly, stirring. Slowly add the wine, stirring to prevent sticking, and allow it to thicken a little. Simmer gently until the cabbage is cooked. Add the pepper and serve hot, as is, over the lentil loaf, or over rice or pasta. Make sure the cabbage doesn't get mushy.

Spicy Beans (Portugal)

A great spicy dish from Portugal. Green beans are used in a lot of their dishes, so I included them here, too.

1–2 tbsp	butter	15–30ml
2	medium onions, chopped	2
3	cloves garlic, minced	3
1/2 c	finely chopped green beans	120ml
19 fl oz	cooked kidney beans or 1 can kidney beans, drained and rinsed	540ml
	pepper and salt to taste	
1 tsp	cumin powder	5ml
1/8 tsp	cayenne powder	1/2ml
1 c	chopped fresh tomatoes	250ml
2 tbsp	olive oil	30ml
	a little fresh chopped parsley for garnish	

☞ Sauté the onions in the butter until tender. Add the garlic and green beans and sauté for a few minutes. Add the rest of the ingredients, except the parsley, and simmer gently for 25 minutes. Garnish with the parsley and serve hot with rice and a salad.

Asian Adzuki Beans (Asia)

Simple, easy and delicious. Serve with stir-fried greens and mushrooms.

1/4 c	soy sauce	60ml
1	medium onion, chopped	1
3	cloves garlic, minced	3
1/2–1 tsp	black pepper	2–5ml
1	green pepper, chopped	1
3 c	cooked adzuki beans, plus 2 tbsp (30ml) reserved cooking liquid	750ml
1/2 tsp	ginger powder	2ml
1/2 tsp	garlic powder	2ml

☞ Cook the onion in the soy sauce, on low heat, stirring, until it is translucent. Add the garlic and green pepper and sauté for 2 minutes. Add the remaining ingredients and heat through for about 5 minutes. Add a little more soy sauce if it seems dry. Serve hot.

Falafel (Middle East)

A classic Middle Eastern dish. Serve with tabbouleh, hummus, baba ghanouj and pita bread for a great Middle Eastern feast. Add olives and rice, if you like, and grilled red pepper.

1 tbsp	butter	15ml
2	medium onions, chopped	2
19 fl oz	cooked or canned chickpeas, drained and well mashed	540ml
2	scallions, chopped (optional)	2
1 1/2 tsp	cumin, ground	7ml
2 tsp	coriander powder	10ml
1 tsp	dried parsley	5ml
1	egg, beaten	1
	sea salt and pepper to taste	
1/4–1/2 tsp	cayenne powder	1–2ml
	whole wheat flour	
	oil for frying	
	tahini, tomato, cucumber, sprouts, fresh chopped parsley, cayenne for garnish (optional)	

☞ Sauté the onions in the butter on low heat until tender. In a bowl, mix together the onions and the rest of the ingredients, except the flour, oil and garnishes. Form into balls, about 1 1/2" (4cm) in diameter, and roll lightly in the flour. Heat the oil in a frying pan on medium heat. Brown the falafel in the hot oil and drain on paper towels; or brush with oil and bake on a cookie sheet, at 375F (190C) for about 25 minutes, or until browned. Serve wrapped in a pita with tahini, cayenne and other garnishes, or serve over rice with a mushroom or onion sauce. Or eat plain, or topped with hummus or baba ghanouj.

Baleadas (Honduras)

This recipe is from Central America, a land of beans and rice. I had these all over Honduras, and they were so good that I ate them everywhere. They were often sold in the streets, at tiny temporary stands, by local women.

6	soft wheat burrito wrappers, heated	6
19oz	cooked pinto, or cooked black beans, or cooked red beans	540ml
	salt and pepper to taste	
2 tbsp	olive oil	30ml
1 tbsp	hot water	15ml
2 tbsp	hot sauce	30ml
	pickled onions, sliced	
	about 6 tbsp of grated parmesan cheese, or other sharp hard cheese	90ml
	hot sauce	

☞ Place the beans in a food processor and blend until smooth. Add the oil, 1 tbsp (15ml) hot water and 2 tbsp (30ml) hot sauce, blend well. Smooth some of the bean mixture, about 1/6, on 1/2 of a heated burrito wrapper. Repeat on all six wrappers. Add some pickled onions and hot sauce and about 1 tbsp (15ml) of grated cheese to each. Fold over and eat hot.

Baked Beans (U.S.A.)

This takes a while to make, but it's so incredible it's worth the bother. Serve with cornbread and greens.

1 tbsp	olive oil	15ml
2	small onions, chopped	2
1	large clove garlic, minced	1
4 c	sliced, sautéed mushrooms	1 litre
3 1/2 c	cooked navy beans, plus 1/2 cup (120ml) reserved cooking liquid	875ml
5 tbsp	soy sauce	75ml
1 1/2 tbsp	Dijon mustard	22ml
1	green pepper, finely chopped	1
	pepper to taste	
1/3 c	molasses, preferably the fancy Barbados kind	85ml
1 tbsp	olive oil	15ml
1 tbsp	red wine (optional)	15ml
1 tbsp	butter	15ml

☞ Cook 1 1/3 cups (335ml) dry navy beans in about 8 cups (2 litres) water. Bring to a boil and then simmer, partially covered, for about 3 hours, or until tender. Drain, reserving 1/2 cup (125ml) of the liquid. Sauté the onions in the 1 tbsp oil on low heat until tender. Add the garlic and sauté 1 minute. Add the mushrooms and sauté for a few minutes, or until browning. Mix together everything, including the reserved cooking water from the beans, and pour into a greased 11" x 8.5" (27.5cm x 21.25cm) baking dish. Cover and bake at 325F (170C) for about 50 minutes. Serve hot.

Refried Beans (Mexico)

Another classic that happens to be one of my favourites. Whenever I go out for Mexican food, I always order it. It's easy to make at home, too.

8 c	water	2 litres
2 c	pinto beans	500ml
1/4–1/2 tsp	chilli powder	1–2ml
2 tbsp	olive oil	30ml
1 c	grated old cheddar cheese	250ml
2 tbsp	yoghurt/sour cream	30ml
4	scallions, chopped	4
1/4–1/2 tsp	sea salt	1–2ml
	pepper to taste	

☞ Bring the water and beans to a boil, reduce heat and simmer, partially covered, for about 3 hours, or until the beans are tender. Drain, reserving 2 tbsp (30ml) of cooking liquid. Place all the ingredients, including the cooked beans, in a food processor or blender, and blend until smooth. Add the reserved cooking liquid only if it seems dry. Serve hot or cold, as is, or rolled into a burrito.

Cornmeal and Bean Pie (Mexico)

Spicy and filling. Serve with a light salad for contrast.

2 c	cornmeal	500ml
3/4 tsp	chilli powder	3ml
2 tbsp	dried oregano	30ml
1 tsp	baking powder	5ml
1/2 tsp	salt	2ml
1	small pepper squash, well cooked and mashed, or omit and use more soy milk	1
2	eggs, or egg substitute	2
1 c	grated old cheddar cheese	250ml
1/4 c	soy milk, adding more if it seems dry	60ml
2 tbsp	olive oil	30ml

☛ Mix together the dry ingredients first. Cut the squash in half and scoop out the seeds. Bake, flat side down, in the oven at 375F (190C) until tender, about 40 minutes. Scoop out the flesh and mash. Mix together with the dry ingredients and the remaining ingredients. Press 1/2 of the mixture into a greased 9" (23cm) diameter pie plate and press smooth.

FILLING ...1 tbsp	olive oil	15ml
2	medium onions, chopped	2
3	cloves garlic, minced	3
1 1/2 c	cooked kidney or pinto beans, or use canned, drained and rinsed	375ml
1	large fresh tomato, chopped	1
1/2	green pepper, chopped	1/2
1/2	red pepper, chopped (optional)	1/2
1	stalk celery, chopped (optional)	1
3 tsp	dried oregano	15ml
1/2 tsp	chilli powder, or less if you prefer it milder	2ml
	olive oil	
	dried oregano	
1 c	grated old cheddar cheese	250ml

☛ Sauté the onion in the oil on low heat until tender. Add the garlic and the vegetables and sauté for 5 minutes. Drain any liquid. Add the 3 tsp (15ml) oregano and the chilli powder. Spread the filling over the piecrust and top with the other half of the cornmeal mixture. Sprinkle with olive oil, oregano and grated cheese. Bake at 350F (180C) for 30 to 45 minutes. Serve hot.

Lentils with Curry and Fennel (India)

Cauliflower makes a nice accompaniment to this, steamed and topped with a little flax seed oil and lemon juice. This dish is not too spicy.

2 c	red lentils	500ml	☛ Cook the lentils in 3 cups (750ml) of boiling water until tender, about 15 minutes. Drain. Meanwhile, sauté the onion in the 1 tbsp of butter on low heat until tender. Add the garlic and carrots (or sweet potato) and sauté for a few minutes. Add the spices and sauté 2 minutes. Add the remaining ingredients, including the cooked and drained lentils, and simmer on low heat for 10 minutes, or until the carrots are cooked. Serve hot with rice and Indian bread.
1 tbsp	butter	15ml	
1	onion, chopped	1	
4	cloves garlic, minced	4	
2	diced carrots	2	
	or		
1 c	diced sweet potato	250ml	
2 tsp	curry powder	10ml	
1/4 tsp	salt	1ml	
1/4 tsp	fennel seed, crushed a little	1ml	
1/4 tsp	garlic powder	1ml	
1 tbsp	butter	15ml	
1/4–1/2 c	vegetable stock or cubed vegetarian chicken broth	60–125ml	
1 tbsp	olive oil	15ml	

Rich Bean Bake (France)

A rich tasting bean dish with a bit of zing. If you like, add 1/4–1/2 cup (60–125ml) freshly chopped green beans.

2 1/2 c	cooked red kidney beans, or use canned, drained and rinsed	625ml	☛ Layer the vegetables in an 8" x 8" (20cm x 20cm) casserole dish. Mix together the other ingredients and pour over the vegetables. Cover and bake at 325F (170C) for about 1 hour. Serve hot.
1	medium purple onion, chopped finely	1	
1	red pepper, chopped	1	
1	fresh tomato, chopped	1	
1 c	red wine	250ml	
1 1/2 tsp	horseradish	7ml	
2 tsp	brown sugar	10ml	
1 tbsp	olive oil or butter	15ml	
	pepper to taste		
1 c	strong vegetable broth	250ml	

Spicy Chickpeas (India)

Tamarind tastes a bit like lemon and is available at Indian food stores. It's what gives this dish its rich colour.

2 tbsp	ghee or butter	30ml
2	medium onions, chopped	2
4	cloves garlic, minced	4
1 1/2 c	fresh tomatoes, cooked chopped (see pg. 24) or use canned tomatoes and liquid, chopped	375ml
	sea salt and pepper to taste	
	dash of cayenne powder	
1/2 tsp	ginger powder	2ml
3	dried chilli peppers, chopped	3
2 tsp	tamarind concentrate dissolved in 1 cup (250ml) hot water	10ml
19 fl oz	cooked chickpeas, or use canned, drained and rinsed	540ml
1	medium carrot, cut in matchsticks	1
1 1/2 tbsp	lemon juice	22ml
1 inch	segment of cucumber, cut in matchsticks (optional)	2.5cm

☛ Sauté the onions in the ghee on low heat until tender. Add the garlic and sauté 1 minute. Add the tomatoes, spices, chillies and tamarind and cook for 5 minutes. Blend in a food processor or blender and return to the pan on medium heat. Add the chickpeas and cook for 15 minutes, stirring. Add the remaining ingredients and heat through. Serve hot.

Split Peas with Onions (Germany)

Oniony and good. I like this one quite lemony, but you can tone it down if you don't like lemon as much as I do. It's nice served with roast potatoes and cauliflower soup.

1 1/2 c	yellow split peas	375ml
2–4 tbsp	butter	30–60ml
4	medium onions, sliced in rings	4
2 c	sliced mushrooms (optional)	500ml
4 tbsp	olive oil	60ml
6 tbsp	lemon juice	90ml
	salt and pepper to taste	

☛ Cook the split peas in boiling water until tender, about 45 minutes. Drain well. Sauté the onions in the butter on low heat until tender. If you're using the mushrooms, sauté them as well. Add the cooked split peas to the onions. Add the remaining ingredients and heat through. Serve hot.

Spicy Caribbean Chilli (Caribbean)

Spicy, filling and delicious. It makes a nice change from other chillies.

1/4 c	texturized vegetable protein (T.V.P.)	60ml
1/4 c	bulgur	60ml
2 tbsp	butter	30ml
2	medium onions, chopped	2
3	cloves garlic, minced	3
1 c	diced pepper squash, peeled	250ml
1	small carrot, diced (optional)	1
19 fl oz	cooked red kidney beans, or use canned, drained and rinsed	540ml
2 1/2 c	tomatoes, cooked and chopped (see pg. 24) or use canned tomatoes, chopped	625ml
3 tsp	coriander powder	15ml
1/2–1 tsp	cayenne powder	2–5ml
	pepper and salt to taste	
1 tbsp	olive oil	15ml
	fresh cilantro, chopped, for garnish (optional)	

☛ Put the T.V.P. and the bulgur in a bowl and cover with 5 cups (1.25 litres) of water. Cover and allow to stand for 20 minutes. Drain. Meanwhile, sauté the onion in the butter on low heat until tender. Add the garlic and sauté 2 minutes. Add the squash and the carrot and sauté for a few minutes. Add the beans, tomatoes, spices and olive oil and cook on low heat, stirring, for about 10 minutes. Add the drained bulgur mixture to the chilli. Cook for 10 more minutes. Serve hot, garnished with the cilantro, if you're using it.

Mushroom Lentil Loaf (North America)

Good for company or just an ordinary night.

2 3/4 c	cooked green lentils	685ml
1/4 c	reserved lentil cooking water	60ml
1/4 tsp	salt	1ml
	pepper to taste	
1	stalk celery, finely chopped	1
1	large onion, chopped	1
1 tsp	olive oil	5ml
3 tbsp	soy sauce	45ml
10 oz	can condensed mushroom soup	284ml
10 oz	can mushrooms, drained and rinsed	284ml
2 tbsp	wheat germ	30ml
1 tbsp	powdered onion soup mix mixed with 4 tbsp (60ml) water	15ml
2 tbsp	texturized vegetable protein (T.V.P.)	30ml
1	egg, beaten	1
	sesame seeds for topping	

☛ Sauté the onion in the oil on low heat until tender. Cook 1 1/2 cups (375ml) of green lentils in 4 cups (1 litre) of boiling water until tender, about 50 minutes. Drain, reserving 1/4 of the liquid. Mix together all the ingredients, except the sesame seeds, and pour into a greased 4.5" x 8.5" (11.25cm x 21.25cm) loaf pan. Sprinkle with the sesame seeds and bake, covered, for 30 minutes at 350F (180C). Uncover and bake for 40 minutes or until the liquid evaporates. Serve hot or cold, cut in slices.

Lentil Burgers (Eastern Europe)

Tasty and filling burgers from Eastern Europe that I like smothered with Dijon mustard and lots of pickles.

1 tbsp	oil	15ml
2	small onions, chopped	2
2 c	cooked brown lentils	500ml
1/2 c	cooking liquid reserved from the lentils	125ml
2 tbsp	whole wheat flour	30ml
1/2 c	texturized vegetable protein (T.V.P.) or tofu, or mashed potatoes	125ml
2	eggs, beaten	2
1/8 tsp	each, salt and pepper	1/2ml
1 tsp	onion powder	5ml
2 tbsp	vegetable broth	30ml
1 1/2 tsp	paprika powder	7ml
1 tsp	Dijon mustard	5ml
	chopped celery and lightly fried mushrooms (optional)	
	matzoh meal or flour	
	butter or oil for frying	

☞ Sauté the onion in the oil on low heat until tender. In a bowl, mix the onion together with the rest of the ingredients, except the matzoh meal and the butter, and allow to stand for 10 minutes. Then shape into patties and coat in the matzoh meal or flour. Next, either fry in butter in a frying pan or brush with oil and bake on a cookie sheet at 350F (180C) for 20 minutes or so—burgers should be set. Serve hot as a burger with pickles and Dijon, or smothered in gravy.

Main Dishes and Accompaniments

Note

In all the stir-fries, if you prefer, you can use a little bit of stock instead of oil.

Szechwan Stir-Fry (Asia)

Spicy, crunchy and delicious. Don't let the vegetables get mushy.

3/4 oz	package of hot and spicy Szechwan Asian seasoning mix	20g
1 tsp	vinegar	5ml
3 tbsp	soy sauce	45ml
2 tbsp	water	30ml
	or	
5–6 tbsp	Szechwan sauce	75–90ml
1 tbsp	sesame oil	15ml
1	medium onion, chopped	1
1	green pepper, chopped	1
10	mushrooms, chopped	10
1/2 c	green beans, chopped	125ml
1/4 c	mung bean sprouts	60ml
1 c	chopped broccoli florets	250ml
1 c	chopped cauliflower florets	250ml
1 1/2 c	snow peas	375ml
1/8–1/4 c	peanuts	30–60ml
2 tbsp	walnuts (optional)	30ml
	sea salt and pepper to taste	
	cooked rice, or rice noodles	

☛ Mix together the packaged seasoning mix, vinegar, soy sauce and water, or use the bottled sauce alone. Meanwhile, in a wok or other suitable pan, sauté, on low-medium heat, the onion in the oil until tender. Turn the heat up to medium-high. Add the green pepper, mushrooms and beans and sauté until tender-crisp. Add the remaining ingredients, including the Szechwan sauce, and sauté 3 minutes. Do not let the vegetables get mushy. Serve hot over cooked rice or noodles.

Zucchini and Sesame Stir-Fry (Asia)

Sweet and smoky tasting vegetables over pasta. Delicious.

1 tbsp	olive oil	15ml
1 tbsp	sesame oil	15ml
2 tbsp	soy sauce	30ml
1 tbsp	honey	15ml
	pepper to taste	
2	zucchini, sliced thinly	2
1	stalk broccoli, chopped	1
1	tomato, chopped	1
1	green pepper, chopped	1
2	scallions, chopped	2
1/2 c	brown sesame seeds	125ml
1/4 c	sliced almonds	60ml
	cooked pasta	

☞ Place all the ingredients in a wok on medium-high heat and stir-fry until the vegetables are tender-crisp, about 3 to 5 minutes. Serve hot over pasta.

Moroccan Fried Eggplant (Morocco)

I first had this in a Moroccan restaurant and liked it so much I tried to duplicate it at home. It worked and I often serve it as an appetizer.

1	eggplant, sliced in 3/4-inch (1 1/2cm) rounds	1
3–4 tbsp	butter	45–60ml
4	cloves garlic, minced	4
1 tbsp	chopped fresh parsley	15ml
3 tbsp	lemon juice	45ml
	salt to taste	

☞ Slice the eggplant and leave it in salted water for 2 hours. Drain and rinse. This will remove all the bitter juices. Cook the eggplant and garlic in a frying pan in the butter, on low heat, until the eggplant is tender and golden. Add the remaining ingredients, heat through and serve hot. Alternatively, if you want to cut down on the fat, grill the eggplant on a barbecue or in the oven on a grill, brushing each slice with a little olive oil and garlic instead of the butter. When the eggplant is tender, sprinkle the remaining ingredients on top. Heat through and serve hot.

Cashew Stir-Fry (Asia)

Another healthy and delicious stir-fry. As with all stir-fries, the trick is to not let the vegetables get mushy.

1 tbsp	sesame oil	15ml
1 tbsp	olive oil	15ml
1	medium onion, chopped	1
1	green pepper, chopped	1
1	red pepper, chopped	1
1 c	mushrooms, sliced	250ml
1	can of drained and rinsed water chestnuts (optional)	1
1	scallion, chopped	1
1	stalk celery, chopped	1
1	stalk broccoli, chopped	1
1/4 c	soy sauce	60ml
1 tsp	garlic powder	5ml
1 tsp	brown sugar	5ml
1/4 tsp	cayenne powder	1ml
1/8 tsp	ginger powder, or grated fresh ginger	1/2ml
1 tsp	cornstarch	5ml
	pepper and sea salt to taste	
1/4 c	cashews	60ml
2 tbsp	pecans	30ml
1/4 c	sesame seeds	60ml
	cooked brown rice	

☞ Put the oils and the onion in a wok on low-medium heat and sauté until tender. Turn the heat up to medium-high. Add the other vegetables and sauté for a few minutes, until tender-crisp but not mushy. Mix together the seasonings and add to the wok. Add the nuts and seeds and sauté for 1 to 2 minutes. Serve hot over rice.

Potatoes with Herbs (Eastern Europe)

A simple way of serving potatoes that's a little different.

5–6	red mini new potatoes	5–6
	sea salt and pepper to taste	
3 tbsp	fresh or 3 tsp (15ml) dried tarragon, or basil, or winter savoury, or oregano (used dried), or other herb	45ml
1–2 tbsp	olive oil	15–30ml
1 tbsp	red wine vinegar	15ml

☞ Cook the potatoes in boiling water, with skins on, until tender. Drain, cut in halves or quarters and place back in the pot. Add the rest of the ingredients and sauté briefly. Serve hot or cold.

Japanese Nuts (Asia)

This is one of the first vegetarian dishes I invented, and it's still one of my husband's favourites.

1/4–1/2 c	strong soy sauce	60–125ml
3 tsp	brown sugar	15ml
1/2 tsp	dry mustard powder	2ml
	pepper to taste	
1 tbsp	oil	15ml
1	medium onion, chopped	1
1/2 c	peanuts	125ml
1	green pepper, chopped	1
12	mushrooms, sliced	12
1/2 tsp	garlic salt or powder	2ml
2	cloves garlic, crushed	2
14 oz	can sliced pineapple, and 1/2 the juice	435ml
1/2 c	mung bean sprouts	125ml
	cooked rice	

☞ Mix together the soy sauce, sugar, dry mustard and pepper. In a wok, on low-medium heat, stir-fry the onion in the oil until tender. Turn the heat up to medium-high. Add the peanuts, green pepper and mushrooms and stir-fry for 5 minutes. Add the garlic salt or powder, garlic, pineapple and juice and stir-fry for 1 minute. Add the bean sprouts and the sauce and stir-fry for 3 minutes. Serve hot over a small bed of rice.

Zesty Honey Glazed Tempe, or Tofu (Asia)

A sauce with a zing to it.

1	package of either tempe or firm tofu, cubed	1
3–4 tbsp	light vegetable oil	45–60ml
1/8 tsp	salt	1/2ml
1/4 tsp	vegetarian poultry seasoning	1ml
1/2 c	honey	125ml
2 1/2 tsp	yellow mustard	12ml
1/2	green or red pepper, cubed (optional)	1/2
	a few lychee nuts (optional)	
	a few slices of pineapple (optional)	
2 tbsp	pineapple juice (optional)	30ml

☞ Fry the tofu or the tempe in the light oil on medium-high heat until browned. Place in an ovenproof dish. Mix the other ingredients together and pour over the cubes of tofu or tempe, coating the cubes well. Bake, covered, at 375F (190C) for 30 minutes, basting every 5 minutes with the sauce. Serve hot.

Tofu Japanese Style (Asia)

Flavourful and healthy.

1 c	firm tofu, cubed	250ml
	a little oil for frying	
1	large onion, sliced in rings	1
2	green peppers, chopped, or one red and one green	2
2 c	whole button mushrooms (optional)	500ml
	pepper to taste	
1/4 c	soy sauce	60ml
1 tsp	garlic powder, or 1/2 tsp (2ml) garlic salt	5ml
2 tsp	brown sugar	10ml
1	can water chestnuts, drained and rinsed	1
3 tbsp	soy sauce	45ml
3	dashes garlic powder	3
	dash of brown sugar	
1 c	pineapple spears (optional)	250ml
1 c	celery, sliced diagonally	250ml
2 c	cooked Chinese noodles, or chow mein noodles	500ml
	peanuts, almonds, sesame seeds (optional)	
	cooked rice (optional)	

☞ Cube the tofu and fry in the oil, on medium-high heat, until golden. Remove the tofu, and sauté the onion until tender. Add the peppers, mushrooms, pepper, soy sauce, garlic powder and sugar and stir-fry for about 7 minutes. Marinate the water chestnuts in the 3 tbsp (45ml) soy sauce, garlic powder and brown sugar. Add the pineapple, celery, noodles and chestnuts with marinade to the pan and cook for about 3 minutes. Add the nuts and seeds, if you're using them, and serve hot over rice if desired.

Welsh Rarebit (Wales)

Another classic with a twist. Good for lunch or dinner.

4	slices whole wheat bread	4
1 1/4 c	grated aged cheddar cheese	300ml
1/4 c	grated mozzarella cheese	60ml
4 tbsp	milk	60ml
1/4 tsp	cayenne powder	1ml
	pepper and salt to taste	
	dash of mustard powder	
1	chopped scallion (optional)	1
1 c	sliced mushrooms sautéed in butter or oil (optional)	250ml

☞ Toast the bread. Meanwhile, place everything else in a pot on low heat and stir until it's melted and smooth. Arrange the toast on baking sheets and pour the sauce over it. Bake for 5 minutes at 325F (170C), or until the cheese is bubbling. Serve hot.

gg Vegetable Stir-Fry (Asia)

A filling egg dish that is spicy and full of crunchy veggies.

2 tbsp	oil	30ml
2	medium onions, chopped	2
1	red pepper, chopped	1
8	mushrooms, chopped	8
1	scallion, chopped	1
1/2 c	chopped broccoli	125ml
1/8 tsp	pepper	1/2ml
2	eggs, beaten	2
1 c	chopped green cabbage	250ml
1/4 c	soy sauce	60ml
	pepper and sea salt to taste	
1/8 tsp	cayenne powder	1/2ml
1 tsp	cornstarch	5ml

☞ Sauté the onions in the oil, on low-medium heat, until tender. Turn heat up to medium. Add the red pepper, mushrooms, scallion, broccoli, pepper and eggs and stir-fry until the eggs fall apart. Add the cabbage. Mix together the soy sauce, pepper, sea salt, cayenne and cornstarch. Add to the pan. Heat until it thickens and mix with the vegetables to coat them. Serve hot over rice or pasta, or on its own.

Spicy Indian Roll-Ups (India)

A delicious, spicy way of eating potatoes and peas.

2 tbsp	olive oil	30ml
1	medium onion, chopped	1
2	potatoes, cubed	2
1	tomato, cubed	1
1 tsp	black mustard seed	5ml
1/2 tsp	cumin powder	2ml
1/2 tsp	coriander powder	2ml
1/4 tsp	turmeric powder	1ml
1/4 tsp	ginger powder	1ml
1/4 tsp	cayenne powder	1ml
1 c	frozen peas	250ml
1/4	cauliflower, finely chopped (optional)	1/4
	thin bread, like pita or Azim bread, for rolling (optional)	

☞ Sauté the onion in the oil on low heat until tender. Add the potatoes, tomato and spices and sauté until the potatoes are tender, adding a little water to prevent sticking. Add the peas and the cauliflower and cook 2 minutes. Serve hot, or wrap in the bread, either hot or cold, as a sandwich.

Baked Squash Gratin (Caribbean)

This is one of my mother's favourites. It sold her on squash.

1	peppercorn or acorn squash, cut in half, with the seeds removed	1
2	large potatoes, peeled and cooked in boiling water until tender	2
1	medium onion, chopped and sautéed in 1 tbsp oil until tender	1
2 tbsp	butter	30ml
	salt and pepper to taste	
1	egg, beaten	
3/4 c	grated cheddar cheese	185ml
1/2 c	additional cheddar cheese for topping	125ml

☛ Bake the squash halves on a cookie sheet with the insides down, in an oven at 375F (190C) for about 40 to 45 minutes, or until tender. Meanwhile, cook the potatoes in boiling water until tender. Drain and mash them. Sauté the onion in the oil until tender. When the squash is done, remove it from the skin and mash well. Combine with the mashed potatoes. Add the butter, salt and pepper to taste, onion, egg and 1/2 the cheese. Mix well. Spread 1/2 the mixture in a greased loaf pan. Layer the other half of the cheese, the rest of the mixture, and top with the additional cheese. Bake at 350F (180C) until golden. Serve hot.

Plum Stir-Fry (Asia)

The tangy zip of the plum sauce adds a nice fruity flavour.

1 tbsp	light vegetable oil	15ml
1	medium onion, in rings	1
2	cloves garlic, minced	2
1	green pepper, sliced	1
1 c	mushrooms, sliced	250ml
1/2 c	chopped broccoli	125ml
1/2 c	chopped cauliflower	125ml
1 c	snow peas	250ml
1/4–1/2 c	bottled plum sauce	60–125ml

☛ Put the oil and the onion in a wok on low-medium heat and sauté until the onion is tender. Turn the heat up to medium-high. Add the garlic, green pepper and mushrooms and sauté for 4 minutes. Add the broccoli and the cauliflower and sauté 2 minutes. Add the snow peas and sauté 1 minute. Add the sauce and heat through. Serve hot over cooked rice or other grain.

Potatoes and Onion (France)

A layered potato dish with added zing. You can assemble it in advance and bake when ready. Serve with a salad and steamed greens and perhaps some lentil soup.

4 tbsp	butter	60ml
2	large onions, finely sliced	2
3	large potatoes, finely sliced	3
1	yam, finely sliced (optional)	1
1/2–3/4 c	grated cheddar cheese	125–185ml
	pepper and salt to taste	
4	scallions, chopped	4

☛ Sauté the onions in 2 tbsp (30ml) of the butter on low heat until tender. In a greased casserole dish, layer 1/2 of the potatoes and yam, if you are using it, 1 tbsp (15ml) of butter, the sautéed onions, 1/2 of the cheese, the salt and pepper to taste, 1/2 of the scallions, the other half of the potatoes, 1 tbsp (15ml) of butter, the rest of the cheese and scallions. Cover and bake at 375F (190C) for 40 minutes, until tender. Uncover during last 10 minutes of cooking and bake until golden. Serve hot.

Cheesy Bake (North America)

A well-flavoured, filling dish. Serve with a salad and maybe a little soup, and lots of steamed vegetables.

1 tbsp	butter	15ml
1	medium onion, chopped	1
1 c	sliced mushrooms	250ml
1/2	red pepper, chopped	1/2
1/2	green pepper, chopped	1/2
1	clove garlic, minced	1
	salt and pepper to taste	
2 tsp	dried oregano	10ml
2 c	bread crumbs	500 ml
1/4 c	wheat germ	60ml
1 c	cheddar cheese, grated	250ml
2	eggs, beaten	2
1/2 tsp	vegetarian Worcestershire sauce	2ml
1/8 tsp	cayenne powder	1/2ml
1/4 tsp	mustard powder	1ml
2 tbsp	freshly grated Parmesan cheese	30ml
1 c	milk or soy milk	250ml

☛ Sauté the onion in the butter on low heat until tender. Add the mushrooms and peppers and sauté for a few minutes, until soft. Add the garlic and sauté until soft. Add seasonings, oregano, bread crumbs and wheat germ. Mix well. Place half the mixture in a 9" (23cm) diameter pie plate, then layer with 1/2 the cheddar cheese, the other half of the mixture and the other half of the cheese. Mix together the remaining ingredients and pour over the mixture. Bake at 350F (180C) for about 35 to 45 minutes, or until a toothpick comes out cleanly. Serve hot.

Potato, Cauliflower and Pea Curry (India)

This is one of my favourite Indian dishes. The peas pop in your mouth and the cauliflower crunches.

1 tbsp	butter	15ml
2	medium onions, chopped	2
1	clove garlic, minced	1
1/4 tsp	ginger powder	1ml
1/2 tsp	cumin powder	2ml
1/2 tsp	turmeric powder	2ml
1/4 tsp	cayenne powder	1ml
1 1/2 tsp	coriander powder	7ml
3 tsp	black mustard seeds	15ml
	sea salt to taste	
1/4 tsp	cinnamon powder	1ml
2	potatoes, cut in cubes	2
2–4 tbsp	water	30–60ml
1 c	chopped cauliflower	250ml
4	mushrooms, sliced	4
1–2	tomatoes, chopped	1–2
1 c	peas	250ml
1 tsp	chopped fresh parsley	5ml
1–2 tbsp	lemon juice (optional)	15–30ml

☛ Sauté the onions in the butter, on low heat, until tender. Add the garlic and the spices and cook for 2 minutes. Add the potato and the water and cook, stirring, for 5 to 10 minutes, or until the potatoes are tender. Add the cauliflower, mushrooms and tomatoes and cook for 2 minutes. Add the peas and cook for 2 minutes. Add the parsley. Heat and serve with the lemon juice, if desired.

Mushroom Spinach Side Dish (Asia)

This is one of the ways that I actually like cooked spinach. You can hardly taste it and it's easy, too.

1 tbsp	butter or olive oil	15ml
1	medium onion, chopped	1
10–12	mushrooms, sliced	10–12
2 tbsp	soy sauce	30ml
1/8 tsp	pepper	1/2ml
2 tbsp	water	30ml
1 tsp	powdered onion stock: put in a cup, pour 2 tbsp (30ml) boiling water over it and dissolve. Cover.	5ml
1 1/2 c	fresh spinach	375ml

☛ Sauté the onion in the oil on low heat until tender. Add the mushrooms and cook for a few minutes. Add the soy sauce, pepper, water, stock mixture and spinach and simmer for 3 to 4 minutes on low heat, covered. Serve hot.

Eggplant Parmesan (Italy)

A classic, and I think the very best eggplant Parmesan ever. Serve with rice and a big salad.

1	eggplant cut into 3/4" (2cm) rounds	1
1 c	whole wheat flour	250ml
	pepper to taste	
1/8 tsp	salt	1/2ml
1/2 tsp	garlic powder	2ml
2	eggs, beaten	2
	oil for frying	
1	medium onion, chopped	1
1 tbsp	oil	15ml
1	green pepper, chopped	1
3	cloves garlic, minced	3
1 3/4 c	mushrooms, sliced	420ml
1	stalk celery, chopped finely	1
3 c	Italian-flavoured spaghetti sauce (see pg. 24), or use canned	720ml
1 1/2 c	grated mozzarella cheese	375ml
1/4 c	grated Parmesan cheese	60ml

☛ Slice the eggplant and leave in a bowl of warm salted water for 2 hours. Drain and rinse. Mix together the flour, pepper, salt and garlic powder. Dip the eggplant slices into the beaten egg and then into the dry mixture and fry in oil in a pan on medium high heat until golden on both sides. Set aside. Sauté the onion in the 1 tbsp (15ml) oil, on low heat, stirring, until tender. Add the green pepper, garlic, mushrooms and celery and sauté 5 minutes. Add the spaghetti sauce and sauté 2 minutes. In an oblong 12" x 9" (30cm x 22.5cm) baking dish, place a little of the sauce mixture, then a layer of eggplant, the rest of the sauce, mozzarella cheese and Parmesan cheese. Cover and bake at 350F (180C) for 45 minutes, or until the eggplant is tender. Serve hot.

Salsa Potatoes and Corn (Mexico)

Great for picnics and parties.

2 tbsp	olive oil	30ml
	a little water	
2	potatoes, cubed	2
3 tbsp	lemon juice	45ml
1/4 c	salsa, mild or hot (see pg. 21), or use bottled	60ml
1 c	frozen corn	250ml
	sea salt and pepper to taste	

☛ Sauté the potatoes in the oil on low heat, stirring, until tender, adding a little water to prevent sticking. Add the remaining ingredients and heat through. Serve hot.

Ratatouille (Italy)

I first had this dish in Greece. When I ordered it I didn't even know what Ratatouille was! But, of course, it's a well-known dish. I think this version is especially good.

1	large eggplant: chop in bite-size pieces and left in warm, salted water for 2 hours, drained and rinsed	1
3 tbsp	olive oil	45ml
1	medium onion, chopped	1
5	cloves garlic, minced	5
1	red pepper, chopped	1
3	tomatoes, chopped	3
1	zucchini, thinly sliced	1
	salt and pepper to taste	
2 tbsp	chopped fresh basil	30ml
1 tbsp	olive oil	15ml

☛ Sauté the onion in the 3 tbsp (45ml) of oil on low heat until tender. Add the garlic and the eggplant and sauté for 5 minutes. Add the red pepper and tomatoes and sauté for 5 minutes. Add the zucchini, salt and pepper to taste, basil and oil and sauté for 5 minutes. Serve hot or cold.

Caponata (Italy)

Caponata is served all over Sicily. It's delicious hot or cold, as a salad or a main dish. It's good for picnics too.

1	eggplant, cubed	1
3 tbsp	olive oil	45ml
1	medium onion, chopped	1
4	cloves garlic, minced	4
1 1/2 c	mushrooms	375ml
2 1/2 c	tomatoes, chopped	625ml
1	red pepper, chopped	1
2	zucchini, chopped	2
2 tbsp	chopped fresh basil	30ml
1 tbsp	lemon juice	15ml
1 tbsp	red wine vinegar	15ml
2 tbsp	olive oil	30ml
	pinch of capers (optional)	

☛ Soak the eggplant in warm, salted water for 2 hours, drain and rinse. Meanwhile, sauté the onion in 3 tbsp (45ml) olive oil until tender. Add the garlic and eggplant and sauté for 5 minutes. Add the mushrooms, tomatoes, red pepper and sauté for 7 minutes. Add the zucchini and sauté for 3 to 5 minutes. Add the remaining ingredients and heat through. Serve hot or cold.

Stuffed Eggplant, Greek Style (Greece)

A Greek classic served in variations all over the Mediterranean. The feta cheese is traditional, but if you don't like feta, you can leave it out or use cheddar cheese.

1	eggplant, cut in half, lengthwise, and left in warm, salted water for 2 hours, drained and rinsed	1
2	large onions, chopped	2
2 tbsp	olive oil	30ml
4	cloves garlic, minced	4
1 1/2	tomatoes, chopped	1 1/2
	pepper and sea salt to taste	
1 tbsp	dried oregano	15ml
1 tbsp	dried parsley	15ml
1/2 tsp	sugar	2ml
1 c	cooked brown rice	250ml
1 c	grated cheese, either cheddar or feta (optional)	250ml
1/4 c	olive oil	60ml
	serve with sliced tomatoes, peppers and olives (optional)	

Using a spoon, scoop out the flesh of the eggplant after it has been soaked, being careful not to tear the outer skin. Cut the flesh into small pieces and discard about 1/2 of the insides.

Put the skins open side down on a baking sheet in the oven and bake at 400F (200C) for 20 minutes. Rinse and drain the baked skins, being careful not to tear them. Meanwhile, sauté the onions in oil on low heat until tender. Add the garlic and the eggplant pieces and cook for about 10 minutes, stirring. Add tomatoes, seasoning, herbs, cooked rice and sugar and cook for 5 minutes. Mix in the cheese. Fill the baked skins with the mixture and drizzle with the olive oil. Place in an ovenproof dish and add a little water to the bottom. Cover and bake for about 30 minutes, at 400F (200C), or until tender. Serve hot or cold.

Greek Cauliflower (Greece)

Use really fresh ingredients. It's the secret to good Greek cooking.

1/4 c	olive oil	60ml
4	medium onions, chopped	4
4	cloves garlic, minced	4
4	tomatoes, chopped	4
1	small cauliflower, broken in florets	1
	salt and pepper to taste	
2 tbsp	lemon juice	30ml
1/4 c	chopped fresh parsley	60ml

Heat the olive oil in a pan on low heat, add the onions and sauté until tender. Add the garlic and tomatoes and sauté for 2 minutes. Add the cauliflower and seasoning and sauté for 3 to 5 minutes, or until tender-crisp. Add the lemon juice and the parsley and heat through. Serve hot or cold.

Curried Eggplant and Potato (India)

This one is spicy, but not too hot. Serve it with other Indian dishes for a full meal.

1/2	small eggplant, sliced, soaked for 1 hour in warm, salted water, drained and rinsed, then cubed	1/2
2–3 tbsp	butter	30–45ml
1	medium onion, chopped	1
1–2	small potatoes, cubed	1–2
2 tbsp	black mustard seed	30ml
1/4 tsp	ginger powder	1ml
1/4 tsp	cinnamon powder	1ml
1/4 tsp	cayenne powder	1ml
1 tsp	cumin powder	5ml
1 tsp	coriander powder	5ml
2	cloves garlic, minced	2
1–2	tomatoes, cubed	1–2
1/2 tsp	powdered tandoori masala, or other masala (optional)	2ml
1–2 tbsp	lemon juice	15–30ml
	a little water	
	salt to taste	

☞ Sauté the onion in the butter on low heat until tender. Add the eggplant and the potatoes and sauté, stirring often, adding a little water if necessary to prevent sticking. When the potato is soft, add the spices, except the masala, the garlic and tomatoes and sauté for about 5 minutes. Add the remaining ingredients, heat and serve hot.

Stuffed Tomatoes (Portugal)

A variation on stuffed tomatoes. Use a sharp Portuguese cheese if you can get it, otherwise use cheddar or mozzarella, or a little of each.

2	large tomatoes	2
	pepper and sea salt to taste	
1/2 c	very finely chopped green beans, cooked 2 minutes in a steamer	125ml
1/2 c	bread crumbs	125ml
3/4 c	grated cheese	180ml
2	cloves garlic, minced	2
1 tbsp	dried parsley	15ml
	olive oil	

☞ Take the top off the tomatoes and set aside. Scoop out and chop the flesh of the tomatoes. Mix in a bowl with everything but the olive oil. Stuff the tomato skins with the mixture and place in a casserole dish. Put the tops back on the tomatoes and drizzle with olive oil. Cover and bake at 350F (180C) for 30 to 40 minutes, or until tender. Serve hot.

Cabbage Rolls (Eastern Europe)

A filling vegetarian version of a classic that tastes and smells wonderful, too.

10	outer leaves of a green cabbage	10
2–3 tbsp	olive oil	30–45ml
3	medium onions, chopped	3
5	cloves garlic, minced	5
19 fl oz	cooked kidney beans, or use canned, drained and rinsed	540ml
2 c	cooked barley, brown rice or other grain	500ml
1/4 tsp	salt	1ml
	lots of pepper	
1/4 c	vegetable stock	60ml
2 1/2 tsp	dried oregano	12ml
1 tsp	garlic powder	5ml
1 tsp	onion powder	5ml
4 1/2 c	fresh tomatoes, cooked and chopped (see pg. 24), or use canned, broken apart with the juice,	1120ml
2 tbsp	olive oil	30ml

☛ Place the cabbage in boiling water for a few minutes, to help separate the outer leaves. Remove the outer 10 leaves, being careful not to tear them.

☛ Meanwhile, sauté the onions in the oil, on low heat, until they are soft, add the garlic and sauté for 2 minutes. Add the remaining ingredients, except the cabbage leaves, tomatoes and olive oil, and cook for 10 minutes. Trim the tough part (the thicker part near the bottom) from the 10 cabbage leaves. Then place some of the filling in each of the leaves and roll into a tight package, tucking in the sides as you roll them so the filling doesn't fall out. Secure with toothpicks. Place the cabbage rolls in a casserole dish and pour on the tomatoes and juice and the olive oil. Add a good grinding of pepper and cover. Bake at 375F (190C) for about 1 hour or until the cabbage rolls are tender. Serve hot.

Doubled Stuffed Peppers (Peru)

Here is a recipe I picked up on a recent trip to Peru. While you can use any bell pepper, I prefer the spicy ones used there: they give the dish zing. I first had these peppers in a busy, colourful market. They were absolutely delicious and have tantalized me ever since.

1	cup finely chopped green beans	250ml
10	olives, chopped, pits removed	10
1	carrot, peeled, diced small	1
1/4 c	raisins	60ml
1 1/2 c	well-flavoured gravy. See below.	375ml
3	potatoes, peeled, finely chopped	3
2	medium-sized hot peppers shaped like bell peppers, or use bell peppers: cut a small hole in the top and remove insides	2

⇨

☛ Chop all the vegetables, except the peppers, and mix with fruit and the gravy. Heat in a frying pan, on medium-low heat, covered, for 5-7 minutes in a little oil, stirring. Mix with cheese if you are using it. Stuff the peppers, through the small whole in the top, with the mixture.

⇨

1/2 c	grated mozzarella cheese (optional)	375ml
2	eggs, scrambled	2
	vegetable oil	
	cornmeal	
	pepper, salt to taste	

Dip each stuffed pepper in the eggs, which have been scrambled, and coat in the cornmeal, salt and pepper. Fry in hot oil until crispy. Serve hot.

☛ For gravy: Use 1 1/2 tbsp (22.5ml) flour, 1 1/2 tbsp (22.5ml) butter, 1 1/2 cups (375ml) strong mushroom or onion stock. Toast flour on the stove, on medium low heat, in the butter and add the stock and mix until thick and smooth.

Greek Stuffed Tomatoes and Peppers (Greece)

Yemista (stuffed vegetables) is served everywhere in Greece and it's one of my favourite Greek dishes. I recommend adding the potatoes. They come out deliciously roasted. Serve with a Greek salad, some good bread and retsina. And, of course, don't forget the olives.

2	large onions, chopped	2
1 tbsp	olive oil	15ml
2	green peppers	2
4	tomatoes	4
1 tsp	dried dill	5ml
1/2 c	bread crumbs or cooked rice	125ml
	pinch of dried mint (optional)	
2 tsp	dried oregano	10ml
1 tbsp	dried parsley	15ml
2 c	cooked rice	500ml
	salt and pepper to taste	
1/2 tsp	sugar	2ml
4 tbsp	olive oil	60ml
2-3	potatoes, sliced	2-3
4-6 tbsp	olive oil for drizzling	60-90ml
1-2 tbsp	water, or tomato juice (optional)	15-30ml

☛ Sauté the onions in the 1 tbsp (15ml) of olive oil until they are tender. Meanwhile, cut the green peppers in half, lengthwise, and scoop out the insides, discarding the pulp and the tops. (You can make this dish with just the tomatoes, if you prefer.) Cut the tomato tops off and set aside. Scoop out the insides, place them in a large bowl and chop.

Add the remaining ingredients, including the 4 tbsp (60ml) of olive oil (but not the 4-6 tbsp/60-90ml of olive oil for drizzling), to the bowl. Do not add the water and the potatoes. Mix well. Stuff the tomato and pepper skins with the mixture. Extra filling can be heated and eaten separately.

Place the tomatoes and peppers, stuffed side up, in a casserole dish. Cover the tomatoes with their tops. Insert the potato slices between the tomatoes and peppers, and drizzle everything with the 4-6 tbsp (60-90ml) of olive oil. Cover and bake at 350F (180C) for 50 minutes, or until tender. If desired, add 1-2 tbsp (15-30ml) of water or tomato juice. (I usually don't.) Uncover during the last 10 minutes of cooking time. Serve hot.

Baked Greek Vegetables (Greece)

This can be prepared in advance and popped in the oven when it's time to cook it. Serve it the Greek way with some good bread, a salad, olives, and retsina.

1	eggplant, sliced and soaked in warm, salted water for 1 hour, drained and rinsed	1
2	medium zucchini, sliced in rounds	2
3	large tomatoes, sliced	3
3 c	mushrooms, cut in half	750ml
2	potatoes, sliced	2
4	cloves garlic, minced	4
2	medium onions, sliced in rings and lightly fried in 1 tbsp (15ml) of olive oil	2
1	carrot, sliced in rounds	1
1/2 c	tomato juice	125ml
1/4–1/2 c	olive oil	60–125ml
	plenty of pepper	
	sea salt to taste	
3 tsp	dried oregano	15ml
	serve hot with feta cheese or other grated cheese (optional)	

☞ In an ovenproof casserole dish, layer the vegetables in the order given. Make sure that the eggplant has been soaked and the onions have been sautéed first. Add the remaining ingredients and cover. Bake at 350F (180C) for 1 hour, or until the vegetables are tender. Uncover during the last 15 minutes. Serve hot.

Potatoes in Yoghurt and Cheese (North America)

This is a rather mild dish, perfect if you're not up to eating anything spicy or you have a fussy eater in the house who likes potatoes.

4	large potatoes, peeled and thinly sliced	4
1 1/2 c	sliced cauliflower (optional)	375ml
1/4 c	wheat germ	60ml
	Parmesan cheese, grated	
1 tbsp	butter	15ml

SAUCE ...

1 tbsp	butter	15ml
2	medium onions, chopped	2
1 c	yoghurt	250ml
1/4–1/2 tsp	pepper	1–2ml
	sea salt to taste	
3/4 c	mozzarella cheese, grated	180ml

☞ Sauté the onions in the 1 tbsp (15ml) of butter, on low heat, until tender. Mix in the rest of the ingredients.

Butter a casserole dish. Layer half the potatoes, half the sauce, the remaining potatoes and the rest of the sauce. If you use the cauliflower, add it with the second layer of potatoes. Sprinkle with wheat germ and grated Parmesan and dot with the butter. Cover and bake at 325F (170C) for 1 hour. Serve hot.

Stuffed Squash (Caribbean)

Squash is delicious with the addition of onions and butter. This is a favourite at our house.

1	pepper squash, split in half lengthwise	1
2 tbsp	butter	30ml
2	medium onions, chopped	2
3	cloves garlic, minced	3
	pepper and sea salt to taste	
1	egg, well beaten (optional)	1
1/2 c	grated cheese, any kind (optional)	125ml
2 tbsp	butter	30ml

☛ Remove the seeds from the squash and turn the squash face down on a baking sheet. Bake for 30 to 40 minutes at 375F (190C). Remove and allow to cool. Scoop out the pulp and save. Meanwhile, sauté the onions in the 2 tbsp (30ml) butter until they are tender. Add the garlic and sauté 2 minutes. Add the squash pulp and sauté 3 minutes. Remove from the heat. Add the pepper and salt, egg, cheese and butter and mix well. Place the mixture inside the squash skins and bake at 350F (180C) for 25 minutes. Serve hot.

Stuffed Squash (North America)

These look really impressive and rather festive when you serve each person a brightly coloured half squash. They are incredibly filling.

1	pepper squash, split in half lengthwise	1
2 tbsp	olive oil	30ml
2	medium onions, chopped	2
4	cloves garlic, minced	4
1	tomato, chopped finely	1
1 tsp	dried tarragon, or other herb such as dried oregano, or dried basil (optional)	5ml
	salt and pepper to taste	
1 1/2 c	cooked brown rice	375ml
2 tbsp	butter	30ml

☛ Cut the squash in half lengthwise, discarding the seeds. Bake the squash halves at 350F (180C), face down on a cookie sheet for 40 minutes, or until tender. Scoop out the pulp and chop finely. In the meantime, sauté the onions in the oil, on low heat, stirring, until tender. Add the garlic and sauté for a few minutes. Add the tomato, squash pulp, herb and salt and pepper to taste and sauté for a few minutes. Add the remaining ingredients and heat through. Mix well and mound in the squash halves. Bake at 350F (180C) for 25 minutes and serve hot.

Greek Stuffed Zucchini (Greece)

These are often called zucchini shoes and they're found in many of the restaurants in Greece. Serve with a salad and some roasted potatoes or rice.

2	zucchini, cut in half lengthwise: scoop out pulp and chop finely	2
2 tbsp	olive oil	30ml
2	small onions, chopped	2
	salt and pepper to taste	
1 tbsp	butter	15ml
1 c	diced feta cheese	250ml
1 1/2 tsp	dried oregano	7ml
1 tbsp	dried parsley	15ml
2 tbsp	olive oil	30ml

☛ Sauté the onion in the 2 tbsp (30ml) of olive oil on low heat until tender. Add the zucchini pulp and sauté 1 minute. Place the zucchini skins in a casserole dish, open side up, sprinkle with salt and pepper to taste and brush with butter. Mix together the onion mixture, the feta cheese, oregano, parsley and olive oil. Fill skins with the mixture. Make the sauce.

SAUCE ...

2 tbsp	butter	30ml
2 tbsp	flour	30ml
1 c	milk	250ml
1/2 c	grated mozzarella cheese	125ml
1	egg, beaten	1

☛ In a heavy pot on low heat, melt the butter. Add the flour and toast it, stirring. Slowly add the milk, blending until smooth and thick. Add the cheese and remove from heat. Stir in the beaten egg. Pour the sauce over the zucchini and bake, covered, at 350F (180C) for 50 minutes, until tender. Serve hot.

Fried Zucchini (Middle East)

The zucchini takes on a slightly smoky taste. Make sure you only cook it a little—it should still be crunchy when you serve it.

1 tbsp	olive oil	15ml
2	zucchini, sliced thinly in rounds	2
1/2 tsp	sesame oil	2ml
	salt and pepper to taste	
1/4 c	grated Parmesan cheese	60ml
	a little chopped fresh parsley	

☛ Sauté the zucchini in the olive oil on medium heat for 1 minute. Add the remaining ingredients, except the cheese and parsley, and sauté for 2 minutes. Add the cheese and parsley and serve hot.

Savoury Potatoes (North America)

These are easy and taste terrific.

2 tbsp	olive oil	30ml
1	medium onion, chopped	1
6	cloves garlic, minced	6
3 c	new red potatoes, with skins on, cut in quarters	750ml
	sea salt and pepper to taste	
3 tbsp	fresh summer savoury or 3 tsp (15ml) dried	45ml
1 tbsp	fresh winter savoury or 1 tsp (5ml) dried	15ml
1 c	vegetable broth	250ml
1 tbsp	red wine vinegar	15ml

☛ Put the oil and the onion in a pan and sauté, on low heat, stirring, until tender. Add the garlic and sauté 2 minutes. Add the potatoes, dried herbs, if you're using them (summer savoury and winter savoury), salt and pepper to taste and sauté for a few minutes, stirring to prevent sticking. Add the vegetable broth and simmer gently, covered, for 30 minutes, or until the potatoes are tender. Add the vinegar and fresh herbs, if you're using them, and cook 3 minutes, with the lid off. Serve hot.

Mashed Potatoes Topped with Fried Onions (Eastern Europe)

A variation on mashed potatoes. If you like onions you'll love this dish.

5	large potatoes, peeled and cut into chunks	5
	salt and pepper to taste	
1/4 tsp	paprika powder	1ml
1/4 tsp	onion powder	1ml
1/4–1/2 c	soy milk	60–125ml
2–3 tbsp	butter	30–45ml
1/2–1 c	grated cheddar cheese (optional)	125–250ml
2 tbsp	butter	30ml
4	medium onions, sliced in rings	4
2 1/2 c	sliced mushrooms	625ml

☛ Cook the potatoes in boiling water until tender. Drain and mash very well. Add the salt and pepper to taste, paprika, onion powder, soy milk and the 2–3 tbsp (30–45ml) butter, and cheese, if you're using it. Mix very well. Meanwhile, sauté the onions in the 2 tbsp (30ml) of butter, on low heat, stirring, until very tender–about 25 to 35 minutes. Add the mushrooms and sauté 5 minutes, or until browned and tender. Serve the potatoes hot, topped with the onion-mushroom mixture.

Stuffed Eggplant (Yugoslavia)

A variation on Greek stuffed eggplant. I first had this one in a house in Macedonia (former Yugoslavia), and it was delicious. They don't use cheddar but I think using extra old cheddar heightens the flavour.

2	small eggplants, cut in half lengthwise	2
1 tbsp	oil	15ml
1	medium onion, finely chopped	1
2 c	finely sliced mushrooms	500ml
1 tbsp	dried parsley	15ml
	sea salt and pepper to taste	
2 tbsp	olive oil	30ml
1	large tomato, chopped	1
1 1/2 tsp	dried oregano	7ml
1	egg, well beaten	1
1 c	grated cheddar cheese, or whatever cheese you prefer	250ml
1 c	chopped tomatoes	250ml
4 tbsp	olive oil	60ml
	pepper to taste	

☛ Place the eggplant in salted water for one hour, drain and rinse. Scoop out the flesh and mash it in a bowl, saving the skins. Meanwhile, sauté the onions and the mushrooms in 1 tbsp (15ml) of oil until tender. Mix together the eggplant pulp, onions, mushrooms, parsley, salt and pepper to taste, 2 tbsp (30ml) of olive oil, the large tomato, oregano, egg and cheese. Place the skins in a buttered casserole dish and mound with the mixture. Pour the cup (250ml) of tomatoes, 4 tbsp (60ml) of olive oil and pepper over the eggplant, allowing it to spill into the casserole dish. Bake at 375F (190C) for about 40 minutes, or until tender. Serve hot.

Avocados Stuffed With Quinoa, Corn and Tomato (South America)

Another great recipe using quinoa. Tangy and delicious and rather festive too.

1 tbsp	olive oil	15ml
1	onion, finely chopped	1
1	large ripe tomato, chopped	1
2	avocados	2
1 c	cooked quinoa, or use cooked amaranth	250ml
2 tbsp	fresh lime juice	30ml
	dash of cayenne pepper	
2 tbsp	cooked corn	30ml
	salt to taste	

☛ In a frying pan, sauté on medium-low heat the onion, in the oil, until translucent. Carefully cut the avocados in half lengthwise. Using a sharp knife remove the pit and pulp, keeping the shells intact. Discard the pits. Chop up the flesh and mix with the other ingredients including the cooked onion. Place some filling in the avocado shells and serve.

Masala Potatoes (India)

A traditional dish served all over India. Its spiciness can be controlled by the amount of hot peppers used.

3 tbsp	oil	45ml
1 1/2 tsp	black mustard seed	7ml
2–3	onions, chopped	2–3
2	large potatoes, peeled and cubed	2
1	jalapeño pepper, chopped	1
	or	
2–3	dried chilli peppers plus 1/4 green pepper, chopped	2–3
1/2–1 c	water	125–250ml
1/4 tsp	salt	1ml
	pepper to taste	
1/4 tsp	turmeric powder	1ml
1/2 tsp	each, cumin and coriander powder	2ml
	dash of cayenne powder	
1/4 tsp	ginger powder	1ml
1 tbsp	sweet pickle relish (optional)	15ml
2–3 tbsp	lemon juice	30–45ml
	chopped fresh coriander leaves (optional)	

☛ Pour the oil into a skillet on medium heat and heat the mustard seed, covering the pan and allowing the seeds to pop. Add the onions and sauté until tender. Add the potatoes and peppers and sauté for a few minutes. Add the water, salt, pepper, turmeric, cumin, coriander, cayenne, ginger and pickle relish, if you're using it, and cook for 10–20 minutes, or until tender, stirring and checking to make sure it's not sticking. Add water if necessary. Add the lemon juice and the coriander leaves and serve. It can also be used to stuff Indian bread.

Mini Cheese Potatoes (North America)

These are served often in our house. They're quick, easy and tasty. I recommend using new potatoes; they taste much better.

1 1/2 c	new potatoes, with skin on, cut in quarters	375ml
1 tbsp	butter	15ml
1/2 tsp	pepper	2ml
	sea salt to taste	
1/4–1/2 c	grated Parmesan or cheddar cheese, or both	60–125ml

☛ Cook the new potatoes in boiling water until they are tender. Place the cooked potatoes in a casserole dish and cover with the remaining ingredients. Bake at 350F (180C) for 15 minutes and serve hot.

Mashed Potatoes (North America)

This recipe makes excellent, creamy, no lumps potatoes that are well flavoured. Try the variations–they're all good.

8	large potatoes, peeled and cut into chunks	8
	sea salt to taste	
	pepper to taste	
1 tbsp	butter or flax seed oil	15ml
1/4–1/2 c	soy milk and whip well	60–125ml
	or	
1 1/2 tbsp	soy sauce	22ml
1/4–1/2 c	vegetable or cubed vegetarian chicken-flavoured or cubed vegetarian beef-flavoured stock	60–125ml

☛ Cook the potatoes in boiling water until tender, drain and mash very well. Add salt, pepper and butter. Whip with a whisk or fork. Then add either,

☛ Whip well. Top with fried mushrooms or fried onions, or both, if desired. Or mash with 1 clove of finely chopped garlic, well cooked. Or serve as is, hot.

Baked Squash (North America)

Simple and perhaps the best way of eating squash.

1	peppercorn, or other squash, cut in half lengthwise, with seeds discarded	1
1 tbsp	butter	15ml
1 1/2 tsp	sucanat or brown sugar	7ml

☛ Place the squash on a baking sheet, flat side down, and bake at 375F (190C) for about 30 to 45 minutes. Prick the flesh with a fork and spread with butter. Sprinkle with sucanat, or sugar, and bake flat side up for 5 minutes, or until tender. Mash the flesh with a fork and serve hot.

Spicy Squash (Mexico)

Spicy and delicious.

2–3 tbsp	butter	30–45ml
1	very large onion, chopped, or two medium onions, chopped	1
1	pepper squash, or other, peeled and cubed	1
1/4–1/2 tsp	cayenne powder	1–2ml
	sea salt to taste and lots of pepper	
5–6 tbsp	water	75–90ml

☛ Cook the onion in half of the butter, on low heat, stirring, until very tender. Add the squash, the rest of the butter, and the spices and cook, stirring. Cover and add the water if it begins to stick. Cook until very tender, about 20 minutes, and serve hot.

Zippy Mushrooms (North America)

Incredible! The aroma and taste of this dish are wonderful—rich and wine-flavoured. If you like, you can serve it over rice or noodles.

2 tbsp	butter	30ml
1	medium onion, chopped	1
2	cloves garlic, minced	2
1	red pepper, chopped	1
1	green pepper, chopped (optional)	1
1	stalk celery, chopped (optional)	1
5 c	button mushrooms, whole or half	1250ml
	lots of black pepper	
1/4 c	extra firm tofu cubes (optional)	60ml

☛ Sauté the onion in the butter on low heat until tender. Add the garlic and sauté for 2 to 3 minutes. Add the remaining ingredients and sauté for 3 to 4 minutes. Make the sauce.

SAUCE ...			
	1 1/2 tbsp	vegetarian Worcestershire sauce	22ml
	2 tbsp	soy sauce	30ml
	2 tsp	Dijon mustard	10ml
	1 c	red wine, or white if you don't have red	250ml
	4 tbsp	brown sugar	60ml
		dash of cayenne powder	

☛ Mix ingredients together well and add to the pan of vegetables. Cook on low heat, partially covered, for 30 minutes, stirring now and then. Serve hot.

Tamarind with Bok Choy and Mushrooms (India)

A delicious way of hiding the sometimes bitter taste of the bok choy. The mushrooms turn dark, fragrant and irresistible.

4	cloves garlic, minced	4
1 tsp	tamarind paste dissolved in 1/2 cup (125ml) hot water	5ml
2 c	button mushrooms, or other, whole or halved	500ml
1/8 tsp	cayenne powder	1/2ml
1/4 tsp	ginger powder	1ml
	lots of pepper	
4 c	roughly chopped bok choy or other green	1 litre

☛ In a saucepan, put the garlic and the tamarind-water mixture. Bring to a boil and add the mushrooms and then simmer for 10 minutes, covered, stirring now and then. Add the spices and sauté for 5 minutes. When the sauce is thick, add the bok choy and cook, stirring, 2 minutes. Serve hot.

Cheese Vegetable Pie (Switzerland)

This one tastes fantastic, and it's great for company, too. Serve with salad, soup and some steamed vegetables.

2–3	large potatoes, chopped	2–3
2 tbsp	butter	30ml
1/4 tsp	salt	1ml
	pepper to taste	
1/4 c	soy milk or vegetable stock	60ml
1–2 tbsp	grated Parmesan cheese	15–30ml
2 tbsp	butter	30ml
2	medium onions, chopped	2
4	cloves garlic, minced	4
2	tomatoes, chopped	2
1	zucchini, chopped	1
1/4 c	sliced fresh mushrooms	60ml
	a little salt	
	pepper to taste	
	dash of paprika powder	
1/2	stalk celery, chopped	1/2
1 c	chopped fresh spinach (optional)	250ml
3	eggs, beaten	3
1/4 c	soy milk	60ml
1 tbsp	grated Parmesan cheese	15ml
1 3/4 c	grated Swiss cheese	435ml
	grated Parmesan cheese for topping	
	wheat germ for topping	

☛ Cook the potatoes in boiling water until tender. Drain and mash well with the butter, salt, pepper, soy milk or stock. Press the potatoes into the bottom and sides of a greased 9" (23cm) diameter pie plate to form a piecrust. Dust with 1–2 tbsp (15–30ml) grated Parmesan cheese. Meanwhile, sauté the onions in the butter, on low heat, until tender. Add the garlic and sauté 2 to 3 minutes. Add the tomatoes, zucchini, mushrooms, salt, pepper, paprika and celery and cook, stirring, until the liquid has evaporated from the vegetables. Add the spinach, if you're using it, and wilt. Drain any extra liquid. In a large bowl, beat together eggs, soy milk and 1 tbsp (15ml) Parmesan cheese. Add the vegetable mixture and mix well. Pour half of the mixture over the potatoes, then add 3/4 cup (185ml) of Swiss cheese, the other half of the mixture, and 1 cup (250ml) of Swiss cheese. Sprinkle liberally with Parmesan cheese and wheat germ. Bake at 350F (180C) for 30 minutes to 1 hour, or until a toothpick comes out clean. Let sit a couple of minutes before cutting into wedges. Serve hot.

Vegetable Curry (India)

A dish well known all over India. Use whatever vegetables you have about, or whatever needs using up.

1–2 tbsp	ghee or butter	15–30ml
1	medium onion, chopped	1
1 tbsp	black mustard seed	15ml
3	cloves garlic, minced	3
4 tsp	coriander powder	20ml
1 tsp	cumin powder	5ml
1	dried bay leaf	1
1/4 tsp	turmeric powder (optional)	1ml
1/4 tsp	cayenne powder	1ml
	sea salt and pepper to taste	
1–2	potatoes, chopped	1–2
2	carrots, chopped	2
4	tomatoes, chopped	4
	or	
19 fl oz	can of tomatoes, drained and chopped, reserving the liquid	540ml
1/2 c	chopped green beans	125ml
1/2 c	chickpeas, cooked (optional)	125ml
1/2 c	mushrooms	125ml
1 c	of water or tomato juice	250ml
1/2 c	peas	125ml
1 c	chopped cauliflower	250ml

☞ Sauté the onion in the ghee, on low heat, stirring, until it is tender. Add the garlic, mustard seed and spices and sauté for 2 to 3 minutes. Add the potatoes, carrots, tomatoes, green beans, chickpeas and mushrooms and sauté for 2 to 3 minutes. Add water or tomato juice and cook, stirring, for 20 to 25 minutes. Add the peas and the cauliflower and cook 4 to 5 minutes. Remove the bay leaf. Serve hot.

Other possible vegetables you can use are red or green pepper, corn, eggplant, zucchini, or whatever else you have on hand. Just make sure to use the harder, longer-cooking vegetables at the beginning of the cooking time and the softer, shorter-cooking ones near the end.

Curried Cauliflower (India)

This is one of my favourite Indian dishes. Don't let the cauliflower get mushy. Serve as an accompaniment to other Indian dishes.

2 tbsp	butter or ghee	30ml
3 tsp	black mustard seed	15ml
2 tsp	coriander powder	10ml
1 tsp	cumin powder	5ml
1/4 tsp	turmeric powder	1ml
1/4 tsp	sea salt	1ml
	pepper to taste	
	dash of cayenne powder	
2	cloves garlic, minced	2
2–3	tomatoes, diced	2–3
	or	
5–6	canned tomatoes, diced, plus 3 tbsp (45ml) liquid	5–6
2 c	chopped cauliflower	500ml
1 c	chopped snow peas or peas (optional)	250ml
2 tbsp	water or tomato juice	30ml
2 tbsp	lemon juice	30ml

☛ Warm the ghee in a pan on low heat. Add the mustard seeds and allow them to pop. Then add the spices and the garlic and sauté for 2 minutes, stirring. Add the tomatoes and cook 4 to 5 minutes, stirring. Add the cauliflower and peas, if you're using them, and the water or tomato juice and cook 3 minutes. Add the lemon juice, heat and serve hot.

Sweet Curry (India)

An unusual dish by North American standards, but sweet and spicy work well together in Indian cuisine. Use mango juice if you have it.

1–2 tbsp	ghee or butter	15–30ml
2	cloves garlic, minced	2
2 tsp	coriander powder	10ml
1 tsp	cumin powder	5ml
1/8 tsp	ginger powder	1/2ml
	pepper and sea salt to taste	
1/4 tsp	cinnamon powder	1ml
	dash of cayenne powder	
2 c	grated carrots	500ml
1/4 c	raisins	60ml
1/4 c	currants	60ml
1/2	banana, sliced in rounds	1/2
1/4 c	orange or mango juice	60ml

☛ Sauté the garlic in the ghee, on low heat, stirring, for 2 to 3 minutes, but make sure you don't brown the garlic. Add the spices and carrots and sauté for 2 to 3 minutes, stirring. Add the raisins and currants and sauté for 3 minutes, stirring. Add the banana and the juice and heat. Serve hot or cold.

Spicy Tofu (Mexico)

A great way to spice up tofu.

1/2-3/4 c	cubed extra firm tofu	125-185ml
1 tbsp	oil	15ml
3	cloves garlic, minced	3
1 c	chopped green beans	250ml
1 c	chopped green or red pepper	250ml
1 c	sliced mushrooms	250ml
1 1/4 c	chopped skinned tomatoes, or use canned with liquid	300ml
1/8-1/4 tsp	cayenne powder	1/2-1ml
	pepper and sea salt to taste	
1 1/2 tsp	dried oregano	7ml
1/4	jalapeno pepper, chopped finely	1/4
1 c	corn, fresh or frozen	250ml
	grated cheddar or Monterey Jack cheese (optional)	

☛ In a frying pan or wok, sauté the tofu in the oil until the tofu is a little browned. Add the garlic and green beans and sauté 3 minutes. Add the green or red pepper and mushrooms and sauté 3 minutes. Add the tomatoes, spices and herbs and jalapeño pepper and cook 5 to 10 minutes. Add the corn and the cheese, if you're using it, and heat through. Serve hot with a green salad.

Rich Peasant Casserole (Mediterranean)

The olive oil bakes right into the vegetables, giving everything an incredible flavour.

6	large potatoes, peeled and sliced thinly	6
4	medium onions, thinly sliced	4
1 c	chopped green beans	250ml
1 c	chopped carrots	250ml
10 oz	can of mushrooms, drained (optional)	284 ml
1/4-1/2 c	olive oil	60-125ml
1/4 c	green lentils	60ml
	sea salt to taste	
1 1/2 tbsp	dried oregano	22ml
	lots of black pepper	
28 oz	can tomatoes, chopped with liquid	840ml
	or	
2 1/2 c	chopped fresh tomatoes plus 1 cup (250ml) tomato juice	625ml
5	large cloves garlic, minced	5
1 tsp	dried basil	5ml
	lemon juice	

☛ In a greased 12" x 9" (30cm x 22.5cm) casserole dish, layer half the potatoes and onions, the beans, carrots and mushrooms, and the remaining onions and potatoes. Mix the remaining ingredient together, except the lemon juice, and pour over the vegetables. Add 1 1/4 cups (310ml) of water. Cover and bake at 350F (180C) for 2 hours, or until the vegetables are tender. If needed, add more water as it cooks. Serve hot, drizzled with a little lemon juice if desired.

Almond Vegetable Bake (Asia)

A bit like chow mein.

1 c	chopped fresh green beans, 1-inch (2.5cm) pieces	250ml
1 c	celery, sliced diagonally	250ml
1 c	mung bean sprouts	250ml
1/2 c	cut up broccoli (optional)	125ml
2 c	sliced mushrooms	500ml
1 c	chopped fresh green beans, in 1-inch (2.5cm) pieces	250ml
10 oz	can condensed cream of celery soup	284 ml
3 tbsp	soy sauce	45ml
	pepper to taste	
1 tbsp	soy milk	15ml
1/8 tsp	ginger powder (optional)	1/2ml
1/4 c	thinly sliced almonds, soaked in 1 tbsp soy sauce	60ml

☞ Layer the vegetables, in the order they are given, in a greased casserole dish. In a bowl, mix together the soup, 3 tbsp (45ml) of soy sauce, pepper, soy milk, and ginger, if you're using it. Pour over the vegetables. Bake covered at 350F (180C) for 20 minutes and then uncovered for 10 to 25 minutes, or until the vegetables are tender. Add the soaked almonds during the last three minutes. Serve hot.

Potato Cheese Baked Kugel (North America)

A great side dish, or on its own with a salad and steamed vegetables.

1 tbsp	butter	15ml
2	medium onions, chopped	2
6	mushrooms, sliced	6
1	red pepper, chopped or	1
2 c	grated carrots, or both	500ml
1/4 tsp	pepper	1ml
1 tsp	salt	5ml
1/4 tsp	cayenne powder	1ml
3	large potatoes, grated	3
3/4 c	grated mozzarella cheese	185ml
2	eggs, beaten	2
1/2 c	milk or soy milk	125ml
1/4 tsp	pepper, or less	1ml
	Parmesan cheese, grated	

☞ Sauté the onions in the butter on low heat until translucent. Add the mushrooms and red pepper (and/or carrots), pepper, salt and cayenne and sauté for a few minutes. Then mix in the rest of the ingredients, except the Parmesan cheese, and pour into a greased, square 8" x 8" (20cm x 20cm) casserole dish. Sprinkle with Parmesan cheese. Cover and bake at 350F (180C) for 1 hour. Uncover and brown during the last 10 minutes. Serve hot.

Broccoli Cauliflower au Gratin (North America)

Another great dish for company. Looks, smells and tastes terrific. Serve with chickpea loaf and salad or pasta.

1 tsp	olive oil	5ml
1	medium onion, chopped	1
1 1/2 c	chopped broccoli	375ml
2 c	chopped cauliflower	500ml
2 tbsp	whole wheat flour	30ml
1 tbsp	butter	15ml
	pepper and salt to taste	
3 tbsp	wheat germ	45ml
1 c	Swiss cheese or mozzarella	250ml
1 c	milk	250ml
1	egg, beaten	1
1/4 c	grated Parmesan cheese	60ml

☛ Sauté the onion in the oil on low heat until tender. Then mix together well the broccoli, cauliflower, onion, flour, butter, salt and pepper to taste and pour 1/2 of it into a greased 11" x 8.5" (27.5cm x 21.25cm) casserole dish. Sprinkle with half of the wheat germ and half of the Swiss or mozzarella cheese. Add the other half of the mixture, then the rest of the wheat germ and Swiss or mozzarella cheese, the milk, egg and Parmesan cheese. Cover and bake at 350F (180C) for 40 to 50 minutes. Uncover during the last 15 minutes and allow to turn golden. Serve hot.

Vegetable Egg Frittata (France)

A simple dish to throw together when you have little else in the house. Serve with crusty bread, salad, cheese and red wine.

2 tbsp	butter	30ml
4	large onions, chopped	4
3	cloves garlic, minced	3
4	fresh tomatoes, chopped	4
1/2	red and 1/2 yellow pepper, chopped	1/2
	salt and pepper to taste	
3	eggs, beaten	3
	freshly ground pepper	
	freshly grated Parmesan cheese	

☛ Sauté the onions in the butter on low heat until tender. Add the garlic and sauté 1 minute. Add the tomatoes, red and yellow pepper, salt and pepper to taste and cook for 7 minutes, stirring. Add the eggs and stir until cooked. Serve hot with a good grinding of pepper and freshly grated Parmesan cheese.

Spicy Cauliflower, Onion and Mushroom Balls in a Chickpea Mixture (India)

These spicy fritters are very popular at Indian restaurants and at my house, too. They make good finger food at parties. Instead of onion powder, they use asafoetida. So go ahead if you can get it.

3/4 c	chickpea flour	185ml
1 1/2 tsp	coriander powder	7ml
1 tsp	cumin powder	5ml
1/4 tsp	onion powder	1ml
	pepper to taste	
	salt to taste	
1/4 tsp	cayenne powder	1ml
	dash of paprika powder	
1 tbsp	olive oil	15ml
approx. 1/2 c	water	125ml
1/2–3/4 c	cauliflower, cut into large bite-size pieces	125–185ml
1/4 c	finely chopped mushrooms	60ml
2 tbsp	finely chopped onion	30ml
	oil for frying	
	chutney or lemon juice (optional)	

☞ In a bowl, mix together the flour, spices, olive oil and water to make a dough that will cling to the veggies. Drop veggies into the dough and coat well. Use a slotted spoon to pick up some of the vegetable mixture and drop into the hot oil. Fry each spoonful in hot oil until crispy and golden. Drain and serve with chutney or lemon juice or by itself.

Linda's Tofu Dog Sloppy Joes (North America)

A vegetarian version.

2 tbsp	olive oil	30ml
2	medium onions, chopped	2
3–4	tofu dogs, cut up in 1/2" (1cm) pieces	3–4
14 oz	can baked beans	398ml
5 1/2 oz	can tomato paste plus 1 can water	156ml
4 tbsp	hot taco sauce	60ml
	pinch of red chilli flakes	
	pepper to taste	
1 tsp	dried oregano	5ml
	buns	

☞ Sauté the onions in the oil on low heat until tender. Add the tofu dogs and sauté for a few minutes. Add the remaining ingredients and cook for 10 minutes. Serve hot over warmed buns.

Mashed Potatoes and Vegetable Bake (France)

A hearty, complete casserole that takes a bit of time to assemble, but then you can just pop it in the oven and let it bake. Serve with a salad.

4	large potatoes, peeled and cut in quarters	4
2 tbsp	milk	30ml
1 tbsp	butter	15ml
	salt and pepper to taste	
1/4 c	vegetable stock or cubed vegetarian chicken stock	60ml
2 c	chopped cauliflower	500ml
1 c	chopped green beans, steamed first (optional)	250ml
1 tbsp	olive oil	15ml
3 c	sliced mushrooms	750ml
	freshly grated Parmesan cheese	

☛ Cook the potatoes in boiling water until tender, about 15 to 20 minutes. Drain and add the milk, butter, salt, pepper and stock. Mash well. Steam the cauliflower and the beans for 3 to 4 minutes, if you're using them. Sauté the mushrooms in 1 tbsp (15ml) olive oil until tender. Layer in an 11" x 8.5" (27.5cm x 21.25cm) ovenproof dish as follows: potatoes, mushrooms, cauliflower and beans, if you're using them. Sprinkle with grated Parmesan cheese and repeat the layers. Make the cheese sauce.

CHEESE SAUCE ...

3 tbsp	butter	45ml
3 tbsp	whole wheat flour	45ml
1 1/2 c	milk	375ml
3/4 c	grated cheddar cheese	185ml
1/4 c	grated mozzarella cheese	60ml
1/2 tsp	mustard powder	2ml
	pepper and salt to taste	
	a little freshly chopped parsley	

☛ Heat the butter in a heavy saucepan until melted. Add the flour and toast it lightly, stirring. Slowly add the milk, stirring to prevent lumps. Add the remaining ingredients, except the parsley, and mix until smooth. Pour over the vegetables and bake, covered, at 375F (190C) for 35 minutes. Garnish with parsley and serve hot.

Roast Potatoes (North America)

A great accompaniment to just about everything.

2–3	potatoes, cut into pieces, skin on or off	2–3
1 c	vegetarian beef broth (cubed)	250ml
3 tbsp	olive oil	45ml
1	clove garlic, minced	1
	salt and pepper to taste	

☛ Place ingredients in a casserole dish, cover and bake at 375F (190C) for about 30 to 40 minutes, or until tender. Serve hot.

Mexican Fondue (Mexico)

This one's fun to do, especially if you use a fondue set and let everyone dip their vegetables and bread into the bubbling pot themselves.

19 fl oz	tomato sauce (see pg. 24), or uoo oonnod	540ml
1/2 c	grated cheddar cheese	125ml
1/2 c	grated Monterey Jack cheese	125ml
1	green chilli—leave the seeds in if you like it extra hot	1
1/8 tsp	chilli powder	1/2ml
1	clove garlic, cut in 1/2	1
1/4 tsp	garlic powder	1ml
1/4 tsp	onion powder	1ml
	cut vegetables (Use raw vegetables such as mushrooms, green, yellow or red pepper and cherry tomatoes, zucchini and green beans, or steam the following vegetables ahead of time: squash cubes, eggplant cubes, or anything you like.)	
	cubed bread	

☛ Mix together all the ingredients, except the vegetables and the bread, and heat in the fondue pot until hot and bubbly. Dip in the vegetables and the bread and eat hot. Light some candles and make a night of it.

Potato Casserole (France)

A simple, rich-tasting recipe, either as an accompaniment or a main dish. A good one for fussy eaters if they like potatoes and cheese.

4	large potatoes, peeled	4
1/4 c	vegetable stock	60ml
	salt and pepper to taste	
	dash of cayenne powder (optional)	
2 tbsp	butter	30ml
4 tbsp	freshly grated Parmesan cheese	60ml
2	eggs, beaten	2
3/4 c	milk or soy milk	185ml
1/2 tsp	mustard powder	2ml
2 c	grated cheese: half mozzarella, half cheddar	500ml
1/4 c	Parmesan cheese	60ml
	wheat germ	
	salt and pepper to taste	

☛ Cut the potatoes into chunks and cook in boiling water until tender. Mash well. Add the stock, salt and pepper to taste, cayenne, butter and 4 tbsp (60ml) Parmesan cheese. Mix well. Add the remaining ingredients, except the 1/4 cup (60ml) Parmesan cheese and the wheat germ, and mix well. Pour into a greased 8" x 8" (20cm x 20cm) ovenproof dish. Top with the Parmesan cheese, a little wheat germ, and salt and pepper to taste. Bake until golden at 350F (180C) for about 40 minutes. Serve hot.

Vegetarian Moussaka (Greece)

A vegetarian version of a classic. I ate moussaka all over Greece before I was a vegetarian, and I was determined to find a good vegetarian version. This tastes surprisingly like the original.

1	eggplant, sliced in 3/4" (2cm) rounds	1
	olive oil for frying	
1 tsp	olive oil	5ml
1	medium onion, chopped	1
3	cloves garlic, minced	3
1	stalk celery, chopped	1
3/4 c	mushrooms, sliced	185ml
1/2	green pepper, chopped	1/2
1	zucchini, sliced thinly in rounds	1
3	fresh tomatoes, chopped	3
1	medium carrot, chopped	1
1 1/2 c	cooked green lentils (optional)	375ml
	pepper to taste	
1	dried bay leaf	1
1 tsp	cinnamon powder (optional)	5ml

☛ Slice the eggplant and leave it in salted water for 1 hour. Drain and rinse well. Dry well on paper towels. Cook the eggplant in hot oil until browned on both sides. Set aside. Sauté the onion in the 1 tsp oil on low heat until tender. Add the garlic and sauté for 1 minute. Add the other vegetables, the lentils if you're using them, and the seasonings and sauté for 7 minutes. Drain excess liquid. Make the sauce.

SAUCE ...

2 tbsp	butter	30ml
4 tbsp	flour	60ml
1 1/2 c	milk	375ml
1/2 c	grated cheddar cheese	125ml
1/8 tsp	cayenne powder	1/2ml
1	egg, beaten	1
	Parmesan cheese, grated	

☛ Heat the butter in a heavy saucepan. Add the flour and toast it lightly, stirring. Add the milk slowly, stirring to avoid lumps. Add the cheese, and cayenne, and allow the cheese to melt. When it's smooth, add the egg and allow to thicken. Sprinkle with Parmesan cheese and remove from the heat. In a 12" x 9" (30cm x 22.5cm) oblong ovenproof dish, layer the eggplant, vegetable mixture, and sauce. Sprinkle with more Parmesan cheese. Bake at 375F (190C) for about 30 to 40 minutes, or until tender and browned. Serve hot.

Cheese Soufflé (France)

There are many variations of this. Try them all—each one adds a different flavour and character to the dish. Serve with a light soup, like zucchini, and a well-dressed green salad.

4 tbsp	butter	60ml
2 1/2 tbsp	whole wheat flour	22ml
2 c	milk	500ml
1 tsp	mustard powder	5ml
3/4 c	grated cheese—cheddar or Swiss, or both, or other types	185ml
	salt and pepper to taste	
4	egg yolks	4
5	egg whites, whisked until stiff	5

☞ Melt the butter in a pan, add the flour and toast, stirring. Add the milk slowly, stirring to avoid lumps. Add the mustard powder and the cheese, salt and pepper to taste, and mix into a smooth sauce. Allow to thicken. Fold in the egg yolks and stir well. Fold in the egg whites and mix. If you're using a vegetable, add it now and mix well. Pour into a greased soufflé dish and bake at 400F (200C) for about 40 minutes, or until risen and browned and cooked through. Serve as is or with a sauce.

VARIATIONS ...

- Add either 1 cup (250ml) chopped spinach, 1 cup (250ml) chopped asparagus (great with Swiss cheese), 1 cup (250ml) sliced zucchini, 2 cups (500ml) sliced mushrooms sautéed with 1 tsp (5ml) dried thyme until browned, then drained, 2 cups (500ml) chopped broccoli or cauliflower or both, 1 cup (250ml) chopped green beans.

- Serve with either a lemon, tomato, mushroom or cheese sauce.

Mushrooms in Hot Honey Mustard Sauce (Asia)

This dish is spicy and delicious. It's an excellent way to serve mushrooms.

1 3/4 c	mushrooms, sliced	420ml
2 tbsp	honey	30ml
1 tbsp	Dijon mustard	15ml
1/2 tsp	mustard powder	2ml
	dash of cayenne powder	
1 tsp to 1 tbsp	water	5–15ml
	pepper and sea salt to taste	

☞ Place the mushrooms in a casserole dish and mix the remaining ingredients together. Pour the mixture over the mushrooms and bake, covered, at 350F (180C) for 20 to 25 minutes. Serve hot.

Cheese Fondue (Switzerland)

I prefer this version of cheese fondue because many people don't like the cheese used in the traditional Swiss fondue. This is more of a North Americanized version of a Swiss classic. Serve in a fondue pot at the table and let everyone dip for themselves. Light a few candles and put on some music. You'll be surprised how long dinner can really take. It becomes an event, and people actually talk to each other!

1	large garlic clove, cut in half	1
3 tbsp	flour	45ml
2 c	white wine	500ml
1 1/2 c	grated old cheddar cheese	375ml
3 1/2 c	grated mozzarella cheese	840ml
3 tbsp	grated Parmesan cheese	45ml
2 tbsp	apricot brandy, or other brandy or sherry	30ml
1 tsp	mustard powder	5ml
	pepper and salt to taste	
	pinch of nutmeg powder (optional)	
	bread cubes and veggies for dipping, such as broccoli, cauliflower, cherry tomatoes	

☞ Rub the garlic all over the surface of the fondue pot. Add the flour and toast it lightly, stirring. Add the wine slowly and heat, stirring. Slowly add the cheeses and stir to melt into a smooth sauce. Add the remaining ingredients, except the veggies and bread and heat through. When it's thick and bubbly, let everyone dip in and enjoy.

Okonomi (Asia)

This egg dish is famous in Japan and is often served in omelette houses, called Okonomi. A simple, great tasting dish. Perfect for when you have no time, or want a quick lunch.

1 tbsp	butter	15ml
2	large onions, chopped	2
1 c	fresh mung bean sprouts	250g
3	eggs, well beaten	3
2 1/2 tbsp	soy sauce	37ml
	salt and pepper to taste	
	dash of cayenne powder	
	oil for cooking	
	barbecue sauce, or honey garlic spread, or plum sauce	
	or	
1 tbsp	mayonnaise mixed with 1 tsp (5ml) lemon and 1 garlic clove, minced (optional)	15ml

☞ Sauté the onion in the butter on low heat for about 5 minutes. Beat together everything but the oil and the optional ingredients. Heat the oil in an omelette pan and cook the eggs on both sides, until golden on both sides and cooked through. Spread with one of the optional ingredients, if using, and serve hot.

Oeufs Florentine (Italy)

A delicious, yet rich, classic. Serve with something light, like a green salad and lots of steamed vegetables. Oddly enough, I first had this dish in Portugal—it was the only vegetarian option on the menu.

6	eggs	6
4 1/2 c	fresh spinach, chopped	1125ml
	salt and pepper to taste	

☞ Poach the eggs by cracking them, one by one, and dropping them carefully into a pot of gently boiling water. Let them simmer until they're done, about 3 to 5 minutes. Remove with slotted spoon. Then place them in a buttered ovenproof dish. Put the uncooked spinach on top and season with salt and pepper to taste. Make the cheese sauce.

CHEESE SAUCE ...	2 tbsp	butter	30ml
	2 tbsp	flour	30ml
	2 c	milk	500ml
	1 tsp	mustard powder	5ml
	1 c	grated cheddar cheese	250ml
	1/4 c	grated Parmesan cheese	60ml

☞ Heat the butter in a heavy saucepan and toast the flour in it, stirring. Slowly add the milk, stirring to prevent lumps. Add the mustard and the cheese and stir until thick and smooth. Pour over the spinach.

TOPPING ...	1/3 c	grated cheddar cheese	80ml
		breadcrumbs, or wheat germ	
		butter	

☞ Top with 1/3 cup (80ml) grated cheddar cheese and a thin layer of breadcrumbs or wheat germ. Dot with butter and bake at 400F (200C) until hot and browned. Serve hot.

Quiche (France)

A rich classic from France. Serve with lighter items, such as salad or steamed vegetables, for balance.

CRUST ...	1 c	grated cheddar cheese	250ml
	1 c	whole wheat flour	250ml
	1/4 tsp	salt	1ml
	1/2 tsp	mustard powder	2ml
	1/2 c	butter	125ml

☛ Mix ingredients well and press into a pie plate, or several mini tarts.

FILLING ...	1 tbsp	butter	15ml
	2	medium onions, chopped	2
	2 c	sliced mushrooms	500ml
	1	green pepper, chopped	1
		salt and pepper to taste	
	1 tsp	dried thyme	5ml
	1 c	chopped fresh spinach (optional)	250ml
	1 c	chopped fresh asparagus (optional)	

☛ Sauté the onions in the butter on low heat until tender. Add the mushrooms and green pepper and sauté for about 5 minutes. Mix together with the rest of the ingredients and half fill a 9" (23cm) diameter pie plate or mini tarts with the mixture.

SAUCE ...	2	eggs, beaten	2
	1 1/4 c	grated cheddar cheese, or Swiss if you're using asparagus	300ml
	1/2 tsp	mustard powder	2ml
		pepper to taste	
	1 c	milk	250ml

☛ Combine ingredients and pour over mixture in pie plate or mini tarts. Sprinkle with pepper and grated Parmesan cheese. Bake at 350F (180C) for 30 minutes (for tartlets) to 1 hour (for pie) or until a toothpick comes out cleanly. Cut the pie and serve in wedges, or serve the tarts as they are. Serve hot.

Spanakopita (Greece)

Delicious. I've made this dish for people at parties, for dinner guests, and for sale through a store, and everyone loves it. The traditional spanakopita is made with feta cheese, but I prefer this version. In Greece, this pie is served in peoples' homes, in restaurants, or sold from tiny street stands.

12–14	sheets phyllo pastry	12–14
	olive oil for brushing	
1 tbsp	olive oil	15ml
1	large onion, chopped	1
3 c	chopped fresh spinach, washed and dried well	750ml
2 1/2 c	grated mozzarella cheese	625ml
	pepper and salt to taste	
3–4 tsp	dried dill	15–20ml
1 tbsp	dried parsley	15ml
6	scallions, chopped	6

☞ Layer 6 or 7 sheets of phyllo pastry, folded in half and arranged in an oblong 12" x 9" (30cm x 22.5cm) baking dish, brushing each one with a little olive oil. Sauté the onion in the 1 tbsp olive oil on low heat until tender. Add the spinach and remove from heat. Add the cheese, seasonings, herbs and scallions and mix well. Pour on top of the phyllo and spread evenly. Layer another 6 or so sheets of phyllo, folded in half, on top of the filling, once again brushing each one with a little olive oil. Sprinkle the top very lightly with water and bake at 375F (190C) for about 25 to 40 minutes, or until golden. Serve hot, cut into squares, with tzatziki on the side.

Potato Latkas (Eastern Europe)

This is my husband's speciality and it was a favourite of my grandmother's. Ted would invite my grandmother and mother over every time he made it, and I would make a batch of cabbage soup and some coleslaw to go with it. Double the recipe if you have more than 4 people, because they'll eat a lot and will be disappointed if there isn't enough!

5	large potatoes, peeled and grated and soaked in cold water for 3 hours	5
2	large onions, grated	2
	salt and pepper to taste	
1 tbsp	whole wheat flour	15ml
1/8 tsp	baking powder	1/2ml
2	eggs, beaten	2
	oil for frying	
	apple sauce, sour cream, hot mustard, jam for condiments (optional)	

☞ Drain the potatoes well. Mix everything but the oil and the condiments together and form into small patties. Fry in hot oil until crisp on both sides and serve hot, with the condiments on the side, if desired. Or brush with oil and bake on a cookie sheet in the oven at 375F (190C) until browned and crisp.

Pie Filled with Green Pepper (Greece)

If you have an earthenware dish, use it for baking this pie. It looks great and tastes more authentic. Serve with a salad and perhaps a little soup.

4 tbsp	olive oil	60ml
2	medium onions, chopped	2
	or	
1 1/2 c	chopped scallions	375ml
3	green peppers, sliced	3
9 oz	mozzarella cheese, grated	260g
6 oz	feta cheese, cut into small pieces	180g
1 c	whole wheat flour	250ml
1 c	milk or soy milk	250ml
	salt and pepper to taste	
1 tbsp	dried parsley	15ml
2 1/2 tbsp	dried dill	37ml
3	eggs, beaten	3

☛ Sauté the onions in 2 tbsp (30ml) of the olive oil until they are tender. Add the green peppers and the remaining 2 tbsp (30ml) of olive oil and sauté for 10 minutes. Combine with the remaining ingredients and pour into a non-stick ovenproof dish, earthenware, or other approx. 7" (18cm) in diameter and 5"–6" (12.5–15cm) in depth. Bake at 375F (190C), covered for the first 45 minutes, then uncovered for another 30 to 45 minutes, or until golden on top and cooked through. Serve hot. You can substitute 4 sautéed chopped leeks or 4 zucchini, sliced, for the green peppers.

Cheese Curry (India)

The chewy cheese adds a great texture to this delicious, well-spiced curry. Another great addition to your next Indian feast.

2 tbsp	butter	30ml
2	large onions, chopped	2
3	cloves garlic, minced	3
19 fl oz	fresh tomatoes, cooked and chopped (see pg. 24), or use canned tomatoes and their juices, chopped	540ml
1/4 tsp	ginger powder	1ml
1 1/2 tsp	cumin powder	7ml
3 1/2 tsp	coriander powder	17ml
	dash of cayenne powder	
1	dried bay leaf	1
	salt and pepper to taste	
1 c	frozen peas	250ml
1 c	diced mozzarella cheese	250ml
	rice or Indian bread (optional)	

☛ Sauté the onions in the butter on low heat until tender. Add the garlic and sauté for a few minutes to soften. Add the tomatoes, spices, and seasonings and cook on low heat, covered and stirring occasionally, for 12 minutes. Add a little water if it starts to get dry. Add the peas and cook for 3 minutes. Add the cheese and allow it to melt. Remove the bay leaf. Serve hot, with rice or with Indian bread if desired.

Frittata (Spain)

A quick, simple dish that's open to many variations.

4	eggs, beaten	4
2 tbsp	milk or soy milk	30ml
	pepper and salt to taste	
	dash of cayenne powder	
1 tbsp	butter	15ml
1	medium onion, chopped	1

Optional Ingredients:

* 2 tbsp (30ml) soy sauce, beaten in with the eggs
* grated cheese or grated Parmesan cheese on top
* green pepper, chopped, or red or yellow pepper, cut in strips
* mushrooms, sliced
* scallions, chopped
* green beans or asparagus, chopped
* zucchini, sliced
* corn or peas
* tomatoes, chopped
* spinach
* sliced tofu dogs or tofu sausage
* bean sprouts
* cabbage
* potato, sliced
* cooked rice
* fresh dill, oregano, basil, parsley or other fresh herb

☞ Beat together eggs, milk and seasonings. Sauté the onion in the butter on low heat until tender. Pour in the eggs and allow them to set. Flip carefully and cook the other side. Serve hot. Use any of the options you like, adding the longer cooking vegetables near the beginning of the cooking time and the quick cooking ones near the end of the cooking time. You may also scramble the eggs, if desired, or if you have trouble flipping them.

Stuffed Red Cabbage (France)

A rich-tasting version of stuffed cabbage. Also good for entertaining.

2 tbsp	butter	30ml
2	medium onions, chopped	2
1	shallot, minced	1
4	cloves garlic, minced	4
2 c	sliced mushrooms	500ml
2 c	finely sliced red cabbage—before slicing the cabbage, carefully remove and save 3–5 of the outer leaves	500ml
3/4 c	peeled chestnuts puréed in a blender with 4 tbsp (60ml) red wine—if you're using fresh chestnuts, you'll need to cook them in boiling water until tender (this can take a long time depending on how fresh they are), before you can peel them; or you can use canned	185ml
2 c	cooked barley or rice	500ml
2 tsp	dried thyme	10ml
	pepper and salt to taste	
4 tbsp	red wine	60ml

SAUCE ...

1 c	red wine	250ml
	pepper and salt to taste	
1	shallot, finely chopped	1
1 c	vegetable stock	250ml

☛ Sauté the onion in the butter on low heat until tender. Add the shallots, garlic, wine and mushrooms and sauté for a few minutes, until soft. Add the sliced cabbage and sauté for about 2 minutes. Add the remaining ingredients, except the cabbage leaves, and sauté for 7 minutes. Place 3 to 5 cabbage leaves in a greased 8" x 8" (20cm x 20cm) ovenproof dish, so they form a bowl. Fill the cabbage leaf bowl with the filling. Make the sauce.

☛ Mix the sauce ingredients together and pour over the cabbage bowl. Cover and bake at 350F (180C) for about 50 minutes to an hour. Serve hot.

Gnocchi (Italy)

These are a favourite with adults and children alike, except that children seem to like them plain and adults like them with sauce.

1 c	whole wheat flour or potato flour	250ml
2 tbsp	butter	30ml
5 oz	cheddar cheese, grated	150g
2 tbsp	freshly grated Parmesan cheese	30ml
1/4 tsp	sea salt	1ml
1/4–1/2 tsp	mustard powder	1–2ml
1 tsp	garlic powder	5ml
2	eggs, beaten	2
1 c	chopped fresh spinach (optional)	250ml

☛ Mix everything together and form into small balls. You need to form a soft dough that isn't sticky. Then, using your hands, roll the dough on a floured surface into strands about the diameter of your thumb. Cut into 1" (3cm) pieces. Drop into salted, boiling water and cook about 3 to 5 minutes. Gnocchi should rise to the surface when done. Check to make sure they're cooked inside. Place in a greased casserole dish. Make a sauce, if desired.

SAUCE ...

2 tbsp	butter, melted	30ml
2	whole cloves garlic	2
6 tbsp	grated cheddar cheese	90ml
2 tbsp	grated Parmesan cheese	30ml

☛ Cook the garlic in the butter on low heat for several minutes, and take out the garlic and discard. Pour over the gnocchi and top with the cheeses. Bake at 325F (170C) for 10 minutes, or until hot and the cheese has melted. Serve hot. You may also serve with any tomato sauce, instead of the butter and garlic sauce.

Broccolied Potatoes (North America)

A filling, nutritious dish that can accompany a meal or stand alone with just a salad.

2	large potatoes	2
1 1/2 c	chopped broccoli or cauliflower, or both	375ml
1	scallion, green part only, or chives, chopped	1
	salt and pepper to taste	
1/4 c	soy milk	60ml
1 tbsp	butter	30ml
	a little freshly chopped parsley (optional)	
3/4 c	cheddar, Swiss or mozzarella cheese, grated, or a little of each	185ml
	grated Parmesan cheese (optional)	

☛ Bake the potatoes, with skins on, in foil, in the oven at 375F (190C) until they are soft, about 45 minutes. Meanwhile, steam the broccoli (or cauliflower) until soft, mash and set aside. Slice each baked potato in half, lengthwise. Remove the insides, being careful not to break the skins, and mash well. Add to the mashed broccoli along with the remaining ingredients, except the grated Parmesan, and mix well. Place back inside the skins. Sprinkle with grated Parmesan, if desired, and bake on a cookie sheet at 350F (180C) for 10 minutes. Serve hot.

Tofu Cacciatore (Italy)

Rich and garlicky. Serve with crusty bread, salad, some rice, and red wine.

1 tbsp	oil	15ml
1	medium onion, chopped	1
6	cloves garlic, minced	6
3/4 c	tofu, extra firm, cubed	185ml
2 1/2 c	tomato sauce (see pg. 24)	625ml
1 1/4 tsp	dried oregano	6ml
1/4 tsp	brown sugar	1ml
	pepper and salt to taste	
1/2 tsp	garlic powder	2ml
1	green pepper, chopped	1
1	red pepper, chopped	1
1/2 c	pineapple chunks	125ml
1	zucchini, sliced in rounds	1
1/2 tbsp	fresh basil	7ml
	cooked rice	

☛ Sauté the onion in the oil on low heat until tender. Add the garlic and the tofu and sauté for 2 minutes. Add the remaining ingredients, except the zucchini, fresh basil and rice, and cook on low heat for 15 minutes. Add the zucchini and the basil in the last 5 minutes. Serve hot, over rice.

Scalloped Potato with Kale (England)

A delicious way of eating kale that disguises its bitter flavour. Try the variations—they're all good.

1 tsp	butter or olive oil	5ml
1	medium onion, chopped	1
2	cloves garlic, minced	2
6	potatoes, peeled and thinly sliced	6
	pepper and salt to taste	
3 c	chopped fresh kale	750ml
1 tbsp	butter	15ml
2 c	milk or soy milk	500ml
4 tbsp	flour	60ml
2	eggs, beaten	2
1 1/2 c	grated Swiss cheese	375ml
1/4 c	freshly grated Parmesan cheese	60ml
	freshly grated black pepper	
1/4 tsp	cayenne powder (optional)	1ml
	fresh parsley for garnish	

☞ Sauté the onion in 1 tsp (5ml) butter, or olive oil, on low heat until tender. Add the garlic and sauté 2 minutes. In a 9" x 13" (24cm x 30cm) oblong, ovenproof dish, layer half the potatoes, pepper, salt, kale, the other half of the potatoes, onion-garlic mixture, 1 tbsp (15ml) butter dotted on top, pepper and salt. Mix together the milk, flour, eggs and cheeses and lots of pepper, and the cayenne powder, if you're using it. Pour over the vegetables in the casserole dish. Cover and bake at 375F (190C) for 45 minutes. Uncover during the last 15 minutes to brown. Eat hot, garnished with fresh parsley. You can substitute broccoli, spinach, cauliflower or other green vegetables for the kale.

Crêpes (France)

A classic. Fill with anything you like.

1 1/4 c	milk	300ml
3/4 c	whole wheat flour	185ml
2	eggs, beaten	2
1/4 tsp	salt	1ml
	dash of vanilla extract	
2 tbsp	white flour	30ml

☞ Place everything in a bowl and beat until very smooth. Lightly oil a skillet, heat to medium, and pour a very thin layer of the batter evenly in the pan. Allow it to cook on one side, until bubbles form on the top, and then gently flip it over to cook the other side—about 2 minutes on each side. Top with steamed broccoli, cauliflower, or asparagus (or whatever you wish), and fold the crêpe over the filling. Cover with cheese sauce.

CHEESE SAUCE ...

2 tbsp	butter	30ml
2 tbsp	flour	30ml
1 1/4 c	milk	300ml
	pepper to taste	
1 1/4 c	grated cheddar cheese, or Swiss if you're using asparagus	300ml
2 tbsp	freshly grated Parmesan cheese	30ml
1/4 tsp	mustard powder	1ml

☞ Melt the butter in a heavy saucepan on low heat and add the flour. Toast it lightly, stirring, and slowly add the milk, stirring to prevent lumps. Continue stirring and allow to thicken. Add the remaining ingredients and continue stirring until it's smooth and thick. Pour over the folded crêpes.

Swedish Dilled Meatless Balls (Sweden)

A vegetarian version of a Swedish classic.

1 tbsp	oil	15ml
1	large onion, chopped	1
1/4 c	breadcrumbs	60ml
1 1/2 c	texturized vegetable protein (T.V.P.)	375ml
2 tsp	dried dill	10ml
	salt and pepper to taste	
2 tsp	vegetarian Worcestershire sauce	10ml
2 tbsp	grated Parmesan cheese	30ml
1	egg, beaten	1
1 1/2 c	vegetable broth	375ml
1 tbsp	butter	15ml
3 1/2 tbsp	whole wheat flour	52ml
	salt and pepper to taste	
1 1/2 tsp	paprika powder	7ml
1 1/2 tbsp	fresh or 1 1/2 tsp (7ml) dried dill	22ml
2 c	vegetable broth	500ml
1 1/2 c	sour cream or yoghurt	375ml

☞ Sauté the onion in the oil on low heat until tender. Add the breadcrumbs, T.V.P., dill, salt and pepper to taste, Worcestershire sauce, Parmesan cheese, egg and vegetable broth. Form into small balls, about 1" (2cm) in diameter. Place them in an 8" x 8" (20cm x 20cm) casserole dish and bake at 350F (180C) for 15 to 20 minutes, being careful not to burn them on the bottom. Meanwhile, make the sauce. Heat the butter in a pot and add the flour and toast it lightly, stirring. Add the seasoning, paprika and dill, and slowly add the broth, stirring to prevent lumps. Bring to a boil and then stir in the sour cream. Heat, stirring until smooth. Pour over the meatless balls before serving.

Lemon Cabbage Rolls (Mediterranean)

A tart version of a classic that makes a nice change. Good for entertaining.

8	outer leaves of a green cabbage	8
2 tbsp	olive oil	30ml
2	medium onions, chopped	2
2	cloves garlic, minced	2
2 c	cooked brown rice	500ml
	sea salt, pepper to taste	
1 tbsp	dried parsley	15ml
1	fresh tomato, chopped (optional)	1
1 1/2 tbsp	dried oregano	22ml
2 tbsp	olive oil	30ml
1/4 c	matchstick carrots (optional)	60ml
1 tbsp	lemon juice	15ml
1/4 tsp	lemon pepper	1ml
3/4 c	crumbled feta cheese	185ml
1/4 c	slivered almonds	60ml
1 1/2 c	water, or stock	375ml
1 c	vegetable stock	250ml
1 1/2 tsp	cornstarch	7ml
3 tbsp	lemon juice	45ml

☞ Place the cabbage in boiling water for 2 to 3 minutes to help separate the outer leaves. Sauté the onions in the olive oil on low heat until tender. Add the garlic and sauté for a few minutes until soft. Mix in the rest of the ingredients, except the water, stock, cornstarch and lemon juice. Place some of the filling in each leaf. Roll into a tight packet, starting at the stem end and tucking in the ends as you roll so the filling doesn't fall out. Secure with toothpicks if necessary. Place in an 11" x 8.5" (27.5cm x 21.25cm) casserole dish and pour in the water. Cover and bake at 350F (180C) for 50 to 70 minutes, or until the cabbage is tender. Meanwhile, make the sauce.

To make the sauce, bring the stock to a low boil. Dissolve the cornstarch in 3 to 4 tbsp (45–60ml) of boiling water, and slowly add to the stock, stirring to prevent lumping. Mix well and allow to thicken. Add the lemon juice, mix well and pour over the cabbage rolls before serving.

Shepherd's Pie (England)

A delicious vegetable version that I think is better than the meat version. And it smells wonderful while it's cooking.

4	potatoes, peeled and cubed	4
1	stalk celery, diced	1
2	cloves garlic, minced	2
	pepper and salt to taste	
1 tbsp	olive oil	15ml
1/2 tsp	paprika powder	2ml
1/4 c	vegetable stock	60ml

FILLING...

1 tbsp	olive oil	15ml
1 1/2 c	chopped yellow onion	375ml
2	scallions, chopped	2
2	stalks celery with the leaves, chopped	2
4	slices whole wheat bread, chopped	4
2 1/2 tsp	dried oregano	12ml
1 tsp	dried basil	5ml
1 tsp	dried parsley	5ml
1/2 tsp	dried thyme	2ml
1/4 tsp	dried sage	1ml
	pepper to taste	
1 1/2–2 c	vegetable stock	375–500ml
1/2 tsp	paprika powder	2ml

☞ Cook the potatoes in boiling water until tender and mash them well. Add the celery, garlic, pepper and salt, olive oil, paprika and stock and mix until smooth. Place half of the mixture in a 9" (23cm) diameter pie plate and spread to form a crust. Meanwhile, make the filling. In a large skillet or frying pan, sauté the onion in the olive oil on low heat until tender. Add the scallions and cook for 2 minutes. Add the rest of the ingredients, except the stock and the paprika, and cook for 5 minutes, tossing to coat well. Add the stock and stir for 5 minutes. Put the filling on top of the potato crust and top with the rest of the potato mixture. Sprinkle with paprika and bake at 350F (180C) for 45 minutes, covered for the first 30 minutes and uncovered for the last 15, until golden. Serve hot.

Pizza (Italy)

A classic that's really not that hard to make. It tastes better than take-out and it's healthier, too. Try any vegetable combination you like and, for a more authentic flavour, use a wood-burning oven, if you have it, like they do in Italy.

1 c	whole wheat flour, or other	250ml
2 tsp	baking powder	10ml
	salt and pepper to taste	
1 tsp	dried oregano	5ml
4–5 fl oz	milk or soy milk	125–150ml

Toppings

TOMATO SAUCE ... 1 c	tomato sauce (see pg. 24): make sure it's thick (you may need to add some tomato paste to thicken it)	250ml
1 tbsp	fresh or 1 tsp dried, each, basil and thyme	15ml
1 tsp	each, dried oregano, garlic and onion powder	5ml

☛ Mix the ingredients together and spread the tomato sauce on top of the baked pizza crust. If you're using tomato sauce, sprinkle on more oregano or hot pepper flakes if desired and top with the following options:

1 c	grated cheddar cheese	250ml
1 1/2 c	grated mozzarella cheese	375ml
1/4 c	grated Parmesan cheese, or other type of cheese	60ml
	substitute with soy cheese if you prefer	

use any vegetables you like such as:
• mushrooms • sautéed onions
• red, green, yellow, and/or hot peppers
• broccoli • cauliflower • olives • zucchini
or

PESTO SAUCE ... 5–6 tbsp	olive oil	75–90ml
2 tbsp	pine nuts	30ml
2 tbsp	freshly grated Parmesan cheese	30ml
2–3 tbsp	fresh basil	30–45ml
1/2 c	fresh spinach (optional)	125ml
	red pepper, cut in strips (optional)	

☛ Process together in a blender the oil, pine nuts, cheese and basil. Spread it on the baked pizza crust. Top with the options as desired, such as sliced mushrooms, pickled artichoke hearts, eggplant, or whatever you like. Bake the pizza for about 15 to 20 minutes at 375F (190C) or until the crust is cooked and the cheese melted. Serve hot.

BARBECUE

Stuffed Peppers (North America)

Excellent, whether you do them on the barbecue or in the oven. I think stuffed peppers are quite festive, so I serve them a lot when company comes.

2	slices whole wheat bread	2
1 tbsp	dried oregano	15ml
1/2 tbsp	fresh or 1/2 tsp (2ml) dried basil	7ml
1/2 tbsp	fresh or 1/2 tsp (2ml) dried thyme	7ml
1 tbsp	fresh or 1 tsp (5ml) dried dill (optional)	15ml
1/4 tsp	salt	1ml
1/8 tsp	pepper	1/2ml
1/2 c	grated cheddar cheese (optional)	125ml
1/8 tsp	mustard powder	1/2ml
1/8 tsp	vegetarian Worcestershire sauce	1/2ml
2	green peppers, cut in half lengthwise and seeded	2
	olive oil	

☛ Tear the bread into small pieces and mix together all the ingredients except the peppers and the olive oil. Place 1/4 of the filling in each pepper and drizzle with olive oil.

Wrap in foil and either bake at 375F (190C) for 30 to 40 minutes, or barbecue for 20 to 30 minutes, or until the peppers are tender. (Hint: If baking, use dried herbs.) Serve hot.

You can also put the peppers in a casserole dish and cover with a sauce of 1 cup (250ml) fresh tomatoes, chopped, with the juice; 1 tsp (5ml) dried oregano; 1 tbsp (15ml) olive oil; 2 tbsp (30ml) lemon juice; pepper; and 1/4 cup (60ml) spaghetti sauce (see pg. 24). Bake at 375F (190C) for 30 to 40 minutes. Serve hot.

Barbecued Potatoes (North America)

Great, especially if you like onions.

6	small new potatoes, with skins on, thinly sliced	6
4	scallions, chopped	4
	olive oil	
	salt and pepper to taste	

☛ Put the potato slices on 2 layers of foil. Cover with the onions and drizzle lightly with olive oil. Add salt and pepper to taste and close the foil. Barbecue until soft. Serve hot.

Hawaiian Shish Kebab (Hawaii)

Simple and light.

1/2	pineapple, peeled and cut in chunks	1/2
1	red pepper, cut in chunks	1
1	green pepper, cut in chunks	1
1	large onion, cut in chunks	1
	mushrooms, whole	
	canned lichee nuts	
	extra firm cubed tofu squares (optional)	
1/4 c	olive oil	60ml
	salt and pepper	
1/4 c	pineapple juice	60ml
4 tbsp	bottled barbecue sauce	60ml

☞ Alternate the vegetables and fruits on skewers that have been soaked in water. Mix the remaining ingredients and brush on vegetables and fruits, barbecue, on medium, basting and turning as necessary for about 4 to 7 minutes. Do not burn, but vegetables should be cooked.

Shish Kebab (Version 1) (Asia)

Absolutely wonderful, and a favourite at barbecues. Make lots because they go fast.

	zucchini, cut into chunks	
	onion, cut into chunks	
	green and red pepper, cut into chunks	
	mushrooms	
1/2 c	soy sauce	125ml
3 tbsp	sesame oil	45ml
4 tbsp	olive oil	60ml
1/2 tsp	cayenne powder	2ml
1	garlic clove, minced	1
1 1/2 tbsp	lemon juice	22ml
2	scallions, chopped (optional)	2

☞ Soak skewers if you're using the wooden ones. Alternate the vegetables on skewers, leaving 1 1/2" (4cm) at each end for picking them up. Mix together the rest of the ingredients and brush on kebobs. Continue basting them while barbecuing. Serve hot.

Shish Kebab (Version 2) (North America)

Another barbecue favourite. These are sweet and spicy and disappear quickly, so make lots.

	pineapple	
	onions	
	green and red peppers	
	mushrooms	
1/2 c	barbecue sauce, any kind	125ml
1/4 c	pineapple juice	60ml
	pepper to taste	

☛ Cut the vegetables into 1" chunks and alternate on skewers that have been pre-soaked to keep them from burning. Mix together the barbecue sauce and pineapple juice and brush onto the kebobs. Continue basting them while barbecuing. Serve hot. Try other vegetables too.

Asian Eggplant on the Barbecue (Asia)

This one's incredible even if you don't like eggplant. It's very flavourful and people always ask for seconds and thirds. Remember this one at your next barbecue.

1	eggplant, cut into 3/4" (2cm) rounds, skin on	1
1/2 c	soy sauce	125ml
2 tbsp	sesame oil	30ml
2 tbsp	olive oil	30ml
4	scallions, chopped	4
	pinch of red pepper flakes	
2	cloves garlic, minced	2
2 tbsp	finely sliced red onion	30ml
2 tbsp	pineapple juice (optional)	30ml
2 tbsp	lemon juice	30ml
	pepper to taste	
	dash of cayenne powder	
1/4 tsp	ginger powder	1ml
	sprinkle of brown sesame seeds (optional)	
	shiitake mushrooms (optional)	
	lychee nuts (optional)	

☛ Soak the eggplant in warm, salted water for 1 hour. Drain and rinse. Mix together the remaining ingredients, except the shiitake mushrooms, and lychee nuts, and marinate the eggplant and the mushrooms (if you're using them) for 2 hours. Barbecue the eggplant on the grill, basting with the sauce as you barbecue, until cooked through. Put the shiitake mushrooms on pre-soaked skewers to barbecue, and continue to baste as you barbecue. Serve with lychee nuts on the side, if desired.

Barbecued Onions (North America)

An onion lover's delight.

4	peeled onions, cut in half, or quarters, depending on the size	4

☛ Wrap each section of onion in foil and pierce all over with a fork. Barbecue for 15 to 25 minutes or until soft. Open foil near the very end to get more flavour. Serve hot.

Barbecued Tomatoes (North America)

Simple to make and tastes incredible.

2	ripe tomatoes olive oil fresh basil, chopped salt and pepper to taste minced garlic	2

☛ Cut the tops off of the tomatoes. Using a spoon, make little slits in the flesh of the tomato, without piercing the skin, so that the oil and seasonings can find their way into the tomato. Put the tomatoes on a piece of heavy foil. Drizzle with olive oil and sprinkle with basil, salt, pepper and garlic. Wrap in the foil and barbecue until they are soft. Serve hot.

DESSERTS

Pretty Fruit in a Glass (North America)

Very attractive and great for company. And it's easy too.

2 1/2 c	grape juice, sparkling, or use purple or white, or any other type of juice, such as cranberry or raspberry	625ml
2 tbsp	lemon juice	30ml
3 tbsp	agar flakes (you can find agar in health food stores)	45ml
3–4	kinds of fruit–strawberries, raspberries, kiwi, cantaloupe, mango, peach, cut into small chunks	3–4

☛ Bring the juice to a boil and add the agar and the lemon juice, stirring. Simmer 2 minutes. Allow to cool slightly. Place the cut fruit in 3 decorative glass bowls. To prevent the bowls from breaking, place a metal spoon in the bowl while pouring in the hot liquid. Pour the juice over the fruit. When liquid has cooled, remove the spoons. Refrigerate. Serve when set. Other good combinations are:

- purple grape juice, cantaloupe, kiwi and strawberry
- cranberry juice, raspberry, mango and banana.

Greek Baked Apples (Greece)

Dinner guests always enjoy this.

4	large apples, cored, but not right to the bottom, with a little pulp removed as well–Cortlands or Macs are the best.	4
2 tbsp	water	30ml
3–4 tbsp	pounded walnuts or pecans	45–60ml
3–4 tbsp	pitted dates, chopped up	45–60ml
1 1/2 tsp	cinnamon powder	7ml
2 tbsp	brown sugar	30ml
5 tbsp	apricot brandy	75ml
2 tbsp	orange juice or apple juice (optional)	30ml

☛ Mix together all the ingredients, except the apples and water, and then stuff the apples with the mixture. Place the water, and orange juice or apple juice if you are using juice, in a baking dish and add the apples. Cover and bake at 350F (180C) for 40 to 50 minutes, adding water if it seems dry. Serve hot.

Baklava (Greece)

Another classic. I first had this on a train in Greece. It was packaged, and even still I couldn't believe how good it was. Sweet and flaky. It's rich, so try to balance the rest of the day with lighter food.

	phyllo pastry	
	butter, melted	
2 1/2 c	blanched almonds	625ml
1 1/2–2 tsp	cinnamon powder	7–10ml
1/2 c	white or brown sugar	125ml
1 c	walnuts or pistachios (optional)– if you use them omit 1 cup (250ml) of almonds	250ml
1 tsp	whole cloves (optional)	5ml

☛ In a 12" x 9" (30cm x 22.5cm) oblong cake pan, place 4 sheets of folded phyllo pastry, brushing each one with melted butter. Blend the remaining ingredients together in a food processor or blender until smooth. Spread a thin layer of the mixture on top of the phyllo. Layer 4 more sheets of phyllo, brushing each one with butter, another layer of filling, more phyllo sheets, buttered, until you have used up all the mixture. Top with another layer of phyllo. Sprinkle very lightly with water. Score the top into squares and bake at 325F (170C) for 45 to 60 minutes–it's done when the top is golden. Meanwhile, prepare the syrup.

SYRUP ...			
	2 c	white sugar	500ml
	2/3 c	honey	160ml
	3/4–1 c	water	185–250ml
	1 1/2 tsp	cinnamon powder	7ml
	1 tsp	whole cloves	5ml

☛ Bring the ingredients to a boil, stirring all the while. Do not allow to burn. Turn down the heat and maintain at a low boil for 20 to 25 minutes, stirring frequently, until it becomes slightly syrupy. Remove cloves and pour over the cooked baklava in the pan. Cut into squares. Let sit at least 2 hours before serving.

Orange Raisin Bran Muffins (North America)

A nice, fruity tasting muffin.

3/4 c	bran	185ml
1 1/4 c	whole wheat flour	300ml
3 tbsp	brown sugar	45ml
1/2 tsp	salt	2ml
1 1/2 tsp	baking powder	7ml
1	orange, peeled and chopped up in a food processor	1
1/2 c	raisins	125ml
1	egg, or egg substitute	1
	orange juice	
2 tsp	olive oil	10ml

☛ Mix all the ingredients together well. Add more orange juice if it seems a little dry. Half fill non-stick muffin tins. Bake at 375F (190C) for about 15 to 25 minutes, or until a toothpick comes out cleanly.

Chocolate Hay Stacks (North America)

Everyone who has tried these says they're the best cookies they've ever had. They're moist and chewy and filled with good things.

2 c	sugar, brown or white	500ml
1/2 c	milk/soy milk	125ml
1/2 c	cocoa powder	125ml
1 tsp	vanilla extract	5ml
1/2 c	butter	125ml
3 c	quick-cooking oatmeal	750ml
1 c	shredded coconut	250ml

☛ Bring to a boil, stirring all the while, the sugar, milk, cocoa, vanilla and butter. Turn down to a low boil for 5 minutes, and keep stirring so it doesn't burn. Remove from the heat and add the remaining ingredients. Mix well and drop from a spoon onto a cookie sheet. Refrigerate. Allow to harden and serve.

Frozen Yoghurt Dessert (North America)

A healthy, incredibly delicious treat. Great for those who can't eat refined sugars or chemical additives.

1 1/4 c	live cultured yoghurt, plain	300ml
1 1/2 c	strawberries, or other fruit, such as raspberries, blueberries, banana, kiwi, boysenberries	375ml
2 1/2–3 tbsp	soy lecithin granules	37–45ml
1 tbsp	honey (optional)	15ml

☛ Place all the ingredients in a blender or food processor and blend until well mixed. Place in a covered container and freeze. Allow to thaw in the refrigerator for a few hours before serving.

Oatmeal, Almond, Coconut, Chocolate Chip Cookies
(North America)

Everyone who has tried these says they're the best cookie they've ever had. They're moist and chewy and filled with good things.

1 1/2 c	whole wheat flour	375ml
1 1/2 c	brown sugar	375ml
1 c	vegetable shortening	250ml
1/2 c	butter	125ml
1 tsp	olive oil	5ml
3 c	quick-cooking oatmeal	750ml
1 tsp	cinnamon powder	5ml
1 tsp	salt	5ml
2 c	chocolate chips	500ml
1 c	shredded coconut	250ml
1/2 c	slivered almonds	125ml
	a drop of milk or soy milk	

☛ Mix all the ingredients together well and shape into 1" (3cm) balls. Place them 3 inches (8cm) apart on a greased cookie sheet and press down with a fork to 1/4" (1cm) thickness. Bake at 375F (190C) for 8 to 10 minutes, or until golden. Recipe can be doubled.

Date Coconut Squares (North America)

A simple, delicious treat.

1/4 c	butter	60ml
2 c	quick-cooking oatmeal	500ml
3/4 c	brown sugar	185ml
1 1/4 tsp	cinnamon powder	6ml
1/4 tsp	salt	1ml
3/4 c	shredded coconut	185ml
1 1/2 c	pitted dates	375ml
1 tbsp	brown sugar	15ml
2 tbsp	lemon juice	30ml
4 tbsp	apple juice	60ml

☛ Melt the butter and mix in the oatmeal, brown sugar, cinnamon, salt and coconut. Mix well and press 1/2 of the mixture into a greased 8" x 8" (20cm x 20cm) baking dish. Blend the remaining ingredients in a food processor, except the apple juice, and spread over the oatmeal mixture. Top with the other half of the oatmeal mixture. Pour the apple juice over top and bake at 375F (190C) for 30 minutes.

Icing (North America)

A rich, creamy icing that you can alter by adding different flavoured extracts.

3 tbsp	butter	45ml
2 1/2 c	icing sugar	625ml
	a dab of milk/soy milk	
1 tsp	vanilla extract	5ml

☛ Mix together all the ingredients and whip until fluffy. Spread on cake or muffins and allow to set before serving.

For different flavours add ...

- 3 tbsp (45ml) cocoa powder
- 1 tsp (5ml) mint extract (you can also add the cocoa for chocolate-mint flavour)
- 1 tsp (5ml) orange extract (you can add cocoa to this, too)
- 1 tsp (5ml) nut extract, with or without the chocolate

Orange Pecan Cookies (North America)

Rich and delicious.

1 c	butter	250ml
1 c	icing sugar	250ml
1 tsp	vanilla extract	5ml
1 1/2 c	whole wheat flour	375ml
1 c	crushed pecans	250ml
1	orange, peeled and chopped in a food processor—retain 1 tsp (5ml) of finely chopped peel	1
1 tsp	orange extract	5ml
1 tsp	olive oil	5ml

☛ Cream together the butter, sugar and vanilla, and then blend in the flour. Add the pecans, the orange, peel and extract and the olive oil. Mix well. Form into 1 1/2" (4cm) balls and place on a greased cookie sheet. Press down with a fork. Bake at 300F (150C) for 25 to 30 minutes. Do not brown. Makes about 14 cookies.

Raisin and Peanut Pop 'em Balls (North America)

1 1/4– 1 1/2 c	raisins	300–375ml
1/2 c	shredded coconut	125ml
1/4 c	sesame seeds (optional)	60ml
1/2 c	peanuts	125ml
1 tsp	honey (optional)	5ml
	apple juice	

☛ Put all the ingredients, except the juice, in a food processor and blend until fairly smooth. Add a little bit of juice to get the right consistency for forming it into balls. Form into balls and allow to harden.

Pop 'em Fruit and Nut Balls (Version 1) (North America)

This is a popular—and healthy—desert so you can feel good about eating it. They come in different flavours and are great for parties.

1 1/4 c	dried apricots	300ml
1/2 c	shredded coconut	125ml
1/2 c	whole almonds	125ml
1/4 c	sunflower seeds	60ml
2 tbsp	cranberry juice	30ml

☛ Put all the ingredients in a food processor, except the juice, and blend until fairly smooth. Add a little bit of juice to get the right consistency for forming it into balls. Form into small balls and allow them to harden.

Pop 'em Fruit and Nut Balls (Version 2) (North America)

Another version of this healthy snack.

1 1/4 c	pitted dates	300ml
1/2 c	raw cashews	125ml
1/2 c	shredded coconut	125ml
1/4 c	brown sesame seeds	60ml
2 tbsp	apple, or prune juice	30ml

☛ Place all the ingredients, except the juice, in a food processor and blend until fairly smooth. Add a little bit of juice to get the right consistency for forming it into balls. Form into balls and allow to harden.

Pineapple Pop 'em Balls (Caribbean)

1 c	dried pineapple	250ml
1/2 c	shredded coconut	125ml
1/4 c	sesame seeds	60ml
2 tbsp	pineapple juice	30ml

☛ Put all the ingredients, except the juice, in a food processor and blend until fairly smooth. Add a little bit of juice to get the right consistency for forming it into balls. Form into balls and allow to harden.

Mango Pop 'em Balls (India)

1 1/4 c	dried mango	300ml
1/2 c	shredded coconut	125ml
1/4 c	sesame seeds	60ml
1/4 c	cashews	60ml
2 tbsp	mango juice	30ml

☛ Put all the ingredients, except the juice, in a food processor and blend until fairly smooth. Add a little bit of juice to get the right consistency for forming it into balls. Form into balls and allow to harden.

Peanut Butter Cookies (North America)

These are the best peanut butter cookies I've ever had. They're big and they have a great texture.

1 c	vegetable shortening	250ml
2 c	brown sugar	500ml
1 tsp	vanilla extract	5ml
2	eggs, beaten	2
1 tsp	salt	5ml
1 tsp	soda dissolved in 1 tbsp boiling water	5ml
1 tsp	baking powder	5ml
2 1/2 c	whole wheat flour	625ml
1 1/4 c	natural peanut butter	300ml

☛ Mix all the ingredients together and roll into 1 1/2" to 2" (4–5cm) balls. Place on a greased cookie sheet. Press each ball flat with a fork and bake at 350F (180C) for 10 to 15 minutes or until a toothpick comes out cleanly.

Chocolate, Orange, Pecan Squares (Sabra Squares) (North America)

1	orange with peel	1
3/4 c	pitted dates	185ml
1 1/2 c	whole wheat flour	375ml
1/2 c	butter	125ml
1/3 c	cocoa	85ml
1/2 c	brown sugar	125ml
1/2 c	white sugar, or use brown	125ml
1 1/4 c	pecan halves	300ml
1 c	chocolate or carob chips	250ml

☛ Blend all the ingredients, except the pecans and chocolate chips, in a food processor until smooth. Press into a foil-lined 8" x 8" (20cm x 20cm) square pan. Cover with a layer of pecans, pressing them down. Make the following sauce:

SAUCE ...	1/2 c	butter	125ml
	1/2 c	brown sugar	125ml

☛ Bring the butter and the sugar to a boil, stirring, and then simmer 1 minute, continuing to stir. Pour over the squares. Bake at 350F (180C) for 25 to 30 minutes. Remove from oven and add a layer of chocolate chips. Bake for 2 more minutes. Allow to cool and cut into squares.

Nature's Tarts (North America)

These tarts are made almost completely from raw ingredients like seeds, nuts and fruit. They're not cooked so you get all the nutrition of raw food, like essential fatty acids. They look good and they taste good, too.

1 c	dried apricots	250ml
1/2 c	shredded coconut	125ml
1/2 c	almonds	125ml
1/4 c	sunflower seeds	60ml
2 tsp	dried cranberries	10ml
2 tsp	cranberry or raspberry juice	10ml
1	banana, peeled and sliced	1
1/2	cantaloupe, peeled and cut in chunks	1/2
1/4 c	shredded coconut	60ml
2 tbsp	agar, mixed with 1/3 cup (80ml) of water	20ml
1	kiwi, peeled and sliced	1
	strawberries, raspberries, blueberries (optional)	

☞ Place the apricots, coconut, almonds, sunflower seeds, cranberries and juice in a food processor and blend until smooth. Press into 10 small tart tins to form shells for the filling. Add a slice of banana to each tart. Blend the cantaloupe and coconut in a food processor until smooth. Boil the agar in the water for 3 minutes. Add to the cantaloupe and mix well. Pour into the lined tart shells. Top with sliced kiwi and any of the optional berries. Refrigerate for at least 2 hours to set. You can also roll the crust mixture into balls, refrigerate and eat as a snack.

Almond, Chocolate Fruit in a Glass (North America)

Rich and delicious. Looks nice, too.

1 c	whipping cream	250ml
2 tbsp	almond liqueur	30ml
1/4 tsp	almond extract	1ml
2 tbsp	icing sugar	30ml
2–3 tbsp	chocolate chips or flakes	30–45ml
1/2 c	strawberries, sliced, or other berries	125ml
1	banana, peeled and sliced	1

☞ Whip the cream, liqueur, almond extract and sugar until stiff peaks form. In two decorative glasses, put some of the whipped cream, a sprinkle of the chocolate, some strawberry slices, more whipped cream, banana slices, the rest of the whipped cream and top with a little more of the chocolate. Chill for 15 minutes before serving.

Banana Bread (North America)

I think this is the very best banana bread. It's light, moist, not too sweet, and really tastes of banana.

1 c	whole wheat flour	250ml
2 1/2 tsp	baking powder	12ml
1/4 c	butter	60ml
3 fl oz	plus 1 tbsp (15ml) honey	90ml
1/4 c	dark brown sugar	60ml
1 tbsp	maple syrup	15ml
2 tbsp	olive oil	30ml
6 tbsp	chopped walnuts	90ml
2	large bananas, peeled and mashed	2
1	egg, or egg substitute	1

☛ In a large bowl, mix together the flour and baking powder. Melt the butter in a small saucepan and add the honey and sugar. Stir until smooth and remove from the heat. Blend in the maple syrup and oil. Mix into the dry ingredients. Beat the egg and add it to the batter. Add the bananas and the walnuts and mix well. Pour the batter into a non-stick or greased 4.5" x 8.5" (11.25cm x 21.25cm) loaf pan and bake at 350F (180C) for 1 hour, or until a toothpick comes out cleanly. Serve sliced, warm or cold.

Apple Crisp (North America)

Simple and delicious, and it makes the whole house smell wonderful.

2–3 tbsp	apple juice	30–45ml
4	Granny Smith apples, or other apples, cored and sliced very thinly	4
1 tsp	cinnamon powder	5ml
2 tsp	lemon juice	10ml
1 c	quick-cooking oats	250ml
2 tsp	cinnamon powder	10ml
3 tbsp	wheat germ	45ml
1/2 c	whole wheat flour	125ml
1/2 c	brown sugar	125ml
5 tbsp	vegetable oil	75ml
1/4 tsp	salt	1ml

☛ Put the apple juice in a square 8" x 8" (20cm x 20cm) baking dish. Add the thinly sliced apples—you can leave the skins on if you like—and sprinkle with cinnamon and lemon juice. Mix together the remaining ingredients and press down, evenly, over the apples. Bake at 350F (180C) for 30 minutes. Serve hot.

Dessert Crêpes (France)

A fancy, delicious desert. Great for company or just when you want something special.

☛ Prepare recipe for Crêpes on pg. 170.

FILLING ...	1 pint	raspberries	475ml
	2 tbsp	strawberry jam	15ml

☛ Combine raspberries and jam in a saucepan and cook for 3 minutes on low-medium heat. Place some of the filling in the centre of each crepe and roll.

SAUCE ...	3/4 c	semisweet chocolate chips	185ml
	1 tsp	vanilla extract	5ml
	1 tbsp	butter	15ml
	3/4 c	icing sugar	185ml
	1/2 c	milk/soy milk	125ml
	1 tbsp	Kahlua or almond liqueur (optional)	15ml

☛ In a heavy saucepan, melt all the ingredients together slowly, stirring on low heat until thick, smooth and bubbly. Pour a little sauce over each crepe and serve. If desired, serve with chocolate shavings and almond slivers.

Chocolate, Orange, Almond, Pecan Cookies (North America)

Tasty, moist cookies for the cookie connoisseur.

1/3 c	brown sugar	85ml
1/4 c	cocoa	60ml
3	egg yolks	3
3/4 c	whole wheat flour	185ml
1/4 tsp	baking powder	1ml
1/4 c	orange juice	60ml
1 tsp	orange extract	5ml
3	egg whites	3
1/4 c	icing sugar	60ml
1 tbsp	ground almonds	15ml
1 c	finely chopped pecans	250ml

☛ With an electric beater, mix together the brown sugar, cocoa and egg yolks. Add the whole wheat flour, baking powder, orange juice and orange extract. Mix well. In a separate bowl, beat the egg whites until stiff peaks form. Fold them into the cookie mixture. Add the remaining ingredients and mix well. Drop from a tablespoon onto a greased cookie sheet, 2 inches (5cm) apart. Bake at 350F (180C) for 10 to 15 minutes until set and cooked through. Good hot or cold.

Orange Blueberry Muffins (North America)

Another moist and fruity muffin. I recommend blending the berries in. It makes them even moister. Also, use toasted oats—it gives them a nuttier taste.

3/4 c	rolled oats, toasted	185ml
3/4 c	brown sugar or sucanat	185ml
1 1/4 c	soft whole wheat flour	300ml
1 tbsp	baking powder	15ml
1/4 tsp	cinnamon powder	1ml
1/4 c	soy milk or orange juice	60ml
1/4 c	vegetable oil	60ml
1	egg, beaten	1
1/2 c	blueberries	125ml
1/2 c	orange, peeled	125ml

☞ Toast the oats in the oven on a cookie sheet at 325F (170C) for about 3 to 5 minutes, stirring frequently; do not burn. Place all the ingredients in a food processor and blend well. Pour into non-stick muffin tins, 3/4 full, and bake at 375F (190C) for 15 to 25 minutes, or until a toothpick comes out cleanly.

Fudge (North America)

This is everyone's favourite. It always disappears quickly at parties.

12 oz	semisweet chocolate chips, or white chocolate chips	350g
1	can sweetened condensed milk	1
1 1/8 c	icing sugar	280ml
1 1/4 tsp	vanilla, or almond, mint or orange extract, whichever you prefer	6ml
1/4–1/2 c	walnuts, almonds, or pecans, or coconut (optional)	60–125ml

☞ In a medium-size heavy saucepan, melt the chocolate chips and the condensed milk on low heat, stirring constantly.

Add the icing sugar and the flavour extract and mix well. Stir in the nuts and mix well. Using a wooden spoon whip until creamy and smooth. Line a square 8" x 8" (20cm x 20cm) pan with wax paper and spread the fudge evenly on it. Allow to set in the fridge for 3 hours. Remove from the paper and cut into squares.

Chocolate Almond Pudding (North America)

A low-fat alternative to regular chocolate pudding.

10 oz	firm tofu	300g
2 tbsp	honey	30ml
2 tbsp	sucanat	30ml
1 tsp	almond extract or liqueur	5ml
2 tbsp	cocoa powder	30ml

☞ Blend all the ingredients in a blender until smooth. Serve chilled in glasses with chocolate shavings and sliced almonds on top, if desired.

Tofu Cheesecake (North America)

I served this once to a very picky eater. He loved it and asked for seconds.

1 1/4 c	graham cracker crumbs	300ml
1/4 c	butter	60ml
1 tbsp	olive oil	15ml
2 tbsp	brown sugar	30ml
12 oz	extra firm tofu	350g
2 tbsp	lemon juice	30ml
6 tbsp	cocoa powder	90ml
1/2	banana (optional)	1/2
1 tsp	almond extract	5ml
1 c	brown sugar	250 ml
1/4 c	oil	60ml
2 tbsp	butter	30ml
	shaved almonds	
	chocolate shavings	
	sliced strawberries	

☛ Mix together the graham cracker crumbs, 1/4 cup (60ml) butter, 1 tbsp (15ml) oil and 2 tbsp (30ml) sugar. Press into a greased 9" (23cm) diameter pie plate or springform pan. Put the remaining ingredients, except the almonds, chocolate shavings and strawberries, in a blender and blend until smooth. Pour into the piecrust and bake at 350F (180C) for 40 to 50 minutes or until the filling is set. Allow to cool and decorate with the remaining ingredients.

Orange Date Muffins (North America)

I love these. They're moist and fruity.

1 c	pitted dates	250ml
1	large orange, peeled	1
1 tsp	finely chopped orange peel	5ml
1/2 c	orange or cranberry juice	125ml
1/4 c	olive oil	60ml
2	eggs, beaten	2
1 1/2 c	whole wheat flour	375ml
3/4 c	brown sugar or sucanat	185ml
1 tbsp	baking powder	15ml
1 tsp	baking soda	5ml
1/4 tsp	salt	1ml
2 tbsp	wheat germ	30ml

☛ In a food processor, process the dates, orange, peel, juice, and olive oil until smooth. Add the remaining ingredients and blend well. Pour into greased muffin tins, 3/4 full. Bake at 375F (190C) for 15 to 25 minutes, or until a toothpick comes out cleanly.

BEVERAGES

Almond Milk (Morocco)

This one is served a lot in Morocco. It's easy to make and healthy, too.

1 c	raw almonds, without the skins	250ml
1 1/2 c	water	375ml
1 tsp	sucanat, or honey, or maple syrup, or corn syrup	5ml
1 tsp	vanilla extract	5ml
1 tsp	almond extract	5ml
1/4 tsp	cinnamon powder	1ml

☞ Put the almonds and the water in a blender and blend until smooth. Add the sweetener, extracts and cinnamon to taste and blend.

Strain through a cheesecloth into a pitcher and pour into a glass. Sprinkle with cinnamon if desired. Serve slightly chilled. To make a thicker version, add 1/4 cup (60ml) chopped banana, dates or peaches to the blender and blend until smooth, adding more water if necessary, and don't strain.

Fruit Shakes

An excellent start to your day or a cool, refreshing snack. Try all the combinations or make up your own. They're all delicious!

2 c	freshly squeezed orange juice, or mandarin juice, or half and half	500ml
1	large banana that has been frozen, peeled	1
1	kiwi (optional)	1
1 c	berries, any kind (optional)	250ml
6	strawberries (optional)	6

☞ Put everything in a blender and blend until smooth. Serve.

Other good combinations are:

- 2 cups (500ml) pineapple juice, 1 mango (optional), 1/2 cup (125ml) of coconut milk, 1 frozen banana, peeled
- 2 cups (500ml) cranberry juice, 1 cup (250ml) raspberries, 1 frozen banana, peeled
- 2 cups (500ml) grape juice, 1 cup (250ml) cantaloupe, 1 frozen banana, peeled,
- Or leave out the juices, or use less, and blend the frozen banana with the fruits (raspberries, strawberries, etc.) for a frozen dessert that's like ice cream. You can also use frozen cantaloupe as the thickener.

No Milk Milk Shake

1 c	rice milk or soy milk, vanilla or plain	250ml
1	banana, peeled	1
1 tsp	of one of the following green powders: spirulina, barley, chlorella, alfalfa, or wheat grass (optional)	5ml
	juice of a mango or 1 cup (250ml) of berries or melon (optional)	
1 tsp	carob powder (optional)	5ml

☞ Put everything in a blender and blend until smooth. The greens will help to detoxify the body and supply valuable nutrients in an easily digestible form.

Hot Toddy (North America)

A warming, soothing drink when the weather turns cold or when you just feel like relaxing.

1 3/4 c	apple juice	430ml
1 tsp	cinnamon powder	5ml
1/4 tsp	ginger powder	1ml
1 tsp	honey	5ml
1/4 tsp	cocoa powder (optional)	1ml
	a little powdered nutmeg (optional)	
1	clove (optional)	1
	rum to desired strength (optional)	

☞ Bring all ingredients, except the rum, to a boil. Remove from heat and add the rum. Remove clove. Serve hot.

Relaxing Digestive Tea (North America)

A refreshing, relaxing tea that's good when you have a cold and also aids digestion.

- licorice (for reducing stress, clearing mucous and aiding digestion)
- Camomile (for soothing sore throats and stomach ache and aiding relaxation)
- Mint (for digestion and for refreshing a tired body)
- Anise seed (for flavour, aiding digestion, and clearing mucous)

9 fl oz	water	280ml
1 stick	licorice root, approximately 5" (12.5cm), broken up	1
1 tsp	camomile flowers, dried	5ml
1/4 tsp	fresh mint	1ml
1/2 tsp	anise seed	2ml

☞ Put the licorice root and anise in the water and bring to a boil, covered. Simmer for 30 minutes. Remove from the heat. Add the other herbs, keep covered and allow to sit for ten minutes. Strain. Drink every 2 hours or as needed. This tea is also useful against viruses.

Juices

If you have a juicer, there's nothing like fresh juice. The juices actually taste like the fruits they are made from. Delicious! These are just a few of my favourites. Try them and make up a few of your own combinations.

You can use the leftover pulp from the vegetables to make stock. Add water to cover, bring to a boil, then simmer about 20 minutes. Either strain or purée. The pulp from fruit or carrots can be added to muffins and cakes. You can also use leftover pulp as mulch in the garden.

Carrot/Apple

1 1/2	apples, cut up, including the skin, core and seeds	1 1/2	☛ Put through the juicer and serve.
3	large carrots	3	

Carrot/Celery

3	carrots	3	☛ Put through the juicer and serve.
3	stalks celery	3	

Pineapple/Banana/Coconut

1	pineapple, peeled and cut up (including the core)	1	☛ Juice the pineapple. Put everything in a blender and blend until smooth. Serve.
1	banana, peeled	1	
1 c	coconut milk, fresh or canned	250ml	
1 fl oz	rum (optional)	30ml	

**Of course, you can always juice individual fruits to make a delicious drink.
Some of my favourites are watermelon, red grapes and mango.**

Pineapple/Grape/Apple

1	apple, cut up, skin, core and seeds	1
2 c	red grapes (they're even healthier with the seeds)	500ml
1/2	pineapple, peeled and cut up (include the core—it's very healthy)	1/2

☛ Put through the juicer and serve.

Vegetable Combo

3	carrots	3
1	small beet, plus 3 leaves	1
3	spinach leaves	3
1	clove garlic or scallion (optional)	1
1	small tomato (optional)	1
2	stalks celery	2
3	sprigs of fresh parsley	3

☛ Put through the juicer and serve.

Zippy Vegetable

5	carrots	5
2	beets, plus 3 leaves	2
1	handful spinach	1
1	small tomato	1
1	clove garlic	1
1	1-inch (2cm) piece fresh ginger	1

☛ Put everything through the juicer and serve.

Index